Following Matthew

"With catchy and to the point headings for every section and chapter of the Gospel of Matthew, William Loader takes us on a fascinating tour through the first Gospel of the New Testament towards its groundbreaking end. With his special talent of making decades of research understandable for the modern reader, the author makes this ancient book relevant for today. Like his previous books on Mark, John, and Luke, this guide is a must read for every modern believer, whether inside or outside of the church, who seeks a deeper understanding of the Christian faith."

—Gerbern S. Oegema, Professor of Biblical Studies, McGill University

"This concise commentary invites us into the logic and beauty of Matthew's story of Jesus. Loader gives a fresh and vivid translation of each passage, then takes us with him on a journey following Matthew, noting religious, cultural and literary features on the way. We are helped to notice Matthew's distinctive qualities, in comparison and contrast with Mark's and Luke's Gospel accounts. With characteristic scholarly depth, and avoiding easy answers, Loader presents a pithy, wise and thought-provoking guide to following Matthew's Jesus."

—Vicky Balabanski, Professor of New Testament,
University of Divinity, Australia

"Professor Loader, an internationally known biblical scholar, helpfully renders Matthew's Gospel accessible to modern readers and interpreters by including a new translation and commentary on the text, and a suggestion for further reflection and discussion on each chapter. This approach makes the book a good basis for personal reading and group study of Matthew's Gospel."

—Dierdre Good, Professor Emerita of New Testament,
The General Theological Seminary, New York

"With his eyes fixed constantly on the central method and meaning of the Gospel of Matthew, Bill Loader skillfully leads readers through that gospel to bring out its vital insights—both old and new. This, his fourth and final commentary in the series on Gospel writings, exemplifies all the strengths of previous volumes. It is written with stunning literary verve yet in a highly accessible manner, it is attentive to the requirements of those who will preach on the text of Matthew, and it strives to be guided by the fundamental message of the evangelist. Here one finds sure-footed guidance following the text of Matthew, combined with deep reflective perspectives that enable the message of the gospel to speak afresh to new generations of readers. This is a book that will repay close and repeated study."

—Paul Foster, Professor of New Testament and Early Christianity, School of Divinity, University of Edinburgh

"A lifetime of careful, critical biblical scholarship undergirds William Loader's commentary on the Gospel of Matthew. Here that scholarship is articulated in palatable language and accompanied by a pastoral ethos to address modern concerns. In this commentary Loader seeks to shed light on the Jesus tradition as it is formed and used within an early community of Jesus's followers. A distinctive feature of this approach is Loader's willingness to identify violent and vindictive ideas within that tradition and to challenge those negative strains through the message that persists through the larger tradition of the community—God's love and forgiveness for those who need it most. This attention to the development of the Jesus tradition within an early community sets the stage to ask how modern readers might engage these claims. Loader argues that the ancient message is available to concerned readers of the present and that it is relevant for the challenges of contemporary life. His work is a part of the fulfillment of that promise."

—Edwin Broadhead, Professor of General Studies, Berea College

Following Matthew

A Commentary for People on the Road

BY
William Loader

CASCADE *Books* • Eugene, Oregon

FOLLOWING MATTHEW
A Commentary for People on the Road

Copyright © 2025 William Loader. All rights reserved. Except for brief quotations in critical publications or reviews, no part of this book may be reproduced in any manner without prior written permission from the publisher. Write: Permissions, Wipf and Stock Publishers, 199 W. 8th Ave., Suite 3, Eugene, OR 97401.

Cascade Books
An Imprint of Wipf and Stock Publishers
199 W. 8th Ave., Suite 3
Eugene, OR 97401

www.wipfandstock.com

PAPERBACK ISBN: 979-8-3852-5726-3
HARDCOVER ISBN: 979-8-3852-5727-0
EBOOK ISBN: 979-8-3852-5728-7

Cataloguing-in-Publication data:

Names: Loader, William, R. G., 1944– [author].

Title: Following Matthew : a commentary for people on the road / by William Loader.

Description: Eugene, OR: Cascade Books, 2025.

Identifiers: ISBN 979-8-3852-5726-3 (paperback) | ISBN 979-8-3852-5727-0 (hardcover) | ISBN 979-8-3852-5728-7 (ebook)

Subjects: LCSH: Bible.—Matthew—Commentaries. | Bible.—Matthew—Criticism, interpretation, etc.

Classification: BS2575.52 L63 2025 (print) | BS2575.52 (ebook)

Contents

Preface | ix
Introducing Matthew | 1

1 **The Beginning** | 3
    A Boring Genealogy? Not at All! (1:1–17)   3
    A Miraculous Conception (1:18–25)   7
    Cosmic Acclaim (2:1–23)   11
    John Points to Jesus as the Judge to Come (3:1–17)   15
    Setting Priorities (4:1–22)   21

2 **Matthew's Mini-Gospel** | 26
    Embracing Hope (4:23—5:16)   26
    What Upholding God's Law Really Means (5:17–48)   31
    Genuine Devotion (6:1–18)   39
    Setting Goals and Gaining Perspective (6:19–34)   44
    Love Matters Most (7:1–29)   48
    An Outsider's Faith (8:1–13)   53
    Tackling the Demons (8:14–34)   57
    In Collision (9:1–35)   61

3 **The Mission** | 67
    Sent to Be Agents of Jesus (9:36—11:1)   67

Wisdom Calling (11:2–30) 73
Conflict of Values (12:1–50) 80
Getting It and Not Getting It (13:1–53) 87
Stories and Symbols (13:54—14:36) 95
Questioning Assumptions (15:1–39) 101
Finding the Right Foundation (16:1–28) 107
Faith and Imagination (17:1–27) 113

4 The Community | 118
Love, Church Discipline, and Conflict Resolution (18:1–35) 118
Grow Up! (19:1–30) 124
God's Priorities (20:1–34) 130
Failure to Bear Fruit (21:1–22) 135
Get Dressed! (21:23—22:14) 142
Give to God What Is God's! (22:15–46) 148
Confronting Abuses (23:1–39) 154

5 The End | 160
Coming, Ready or Not! (24:1–51) 160
Don't Run Out of Lamp Oil! (25:1–46) 167
"Take this and eat it! This my body." (26:1–35) 173
Facing Testing Times (26:36–75) 180
Killing Subversives and Keeping the Peace (27:1–32) 186
The Cross and the Climax of History (27:33–66) 191
New and Bigger! (28:1–20) 198

Open to the World! | 204

Preface

THE CHALLENGES OF MINISTRY today mean that ministers and preachers often find they have little time to give detailed attention to the biblical passages they need to expound. This is happening at the same time as more and more people who are not preachers are wanting to have a better informed faith. As someone who has spent over half a century engaged in detailed research on the Gospels, I have seen the need and responded to the call to seek to meet that need. That means putting down the key insights which have emerged from contemporary scholarship in few but readable words, making accessible what might otherwise demand hours in a library and days of intricate engagement with the Greek text.

My response for many years has been to write online commentaries on passages set for preaching in the Revised Common Lectionary (billloader.com), something I continue to do, but it became clear to me that more is needed. For it helps greatly to see passages within the context of a Gospel as a whole and of how the Gospel is understood in contemporary scholarship. Accordingly, I have provided what I call commentaries "for people on the road." This is the third, after *Following Mark* and *Following John*, with *Following Luke* to come.

The commentary looks at sections of the Gospel in sequence in five main blocks. For each section, it provides a translation, called *Listening to Matthew*, which keeps close to the Greek text while using informal contemporary English. Comments on the passage, *Thinking About Matthew*, follow. At the end of each section there is a question to evoke discussion. The commentary, like others in the series, is designed also for use by groups wanting to explore a deeper understanding of their faith. In every case the best question to start with is: "What was new or especially interesting in what have read?"

PREFACE

Reading passages in their context is not just about seeing how they fit within a Gospel. It also about reading them within their cultural and religious world, and that means acknowledging and respecting that their world is different from ours. It is not just that we no longer believe that the earth is flat, but much more, including that we no longer understand sickness and mental illness with the framework of demonology and recognize that their social values and assumptions are in many respects different from ours. This commentary does not shy away from acknowledging such distance, while at the same time seeking to elucidate what can jump right across the two-thousand-year gap and continue to address people today.

My own contributions to research on Matthew have been related primarily to the way it depicts the Law, especially in my study *Jesus' Attitude Towards the Law: A Study of the Gospels* (Tübingen: Mohr Siebeck,1997; Grand Rapids: Eerdmans, 2002), and in *Jesus and the Fundamentalism of His Day* (Grand Rapids: Eerdmans, 2001), but I have also engaged Matthew in dealing with a wide range of issues, including, for instance, attitudes to sexuality.

These days, research is much more than an individual matter. Doing research means engaging in a network of researchers and thereby being enriched by the community of scholars who have similarly engaged and written on the text. That continues to be an enriching experience. I also want to acknowledge those who have had the patience to read earlier drafts of this book and helped me make it readable and accessible. I am especially indebted to Professors Vicky Balabanski, Edwin Broadhead, Paul Foster, Dierdre Good, and Gerbern Oegema.

William Loader

Introducing Matthew

LIKE THE OTHER THREE Gospels, Matthew's Gospel does not name its author. The name Matthew came to be attached to it at some time in the second century. Perhaps it was written in a region where the disciple Matthew had once been active. In this book we will refer to the author as Matthew for simplicity's sake. Although we have no information about the actual author, we still know a lot about what kind of person the author was.

Clearly, he had been educated to a level where he could read and write and, more than that, he knew about how to write for public performances. For that is what Matthew's Gospel is. It was written to be read aloud. An author writing for public performance needed to have the skills to keep an audience engaged and to help an audience know when a story began and ended and much else. It also meant trying to make sure you got your message across.

We see Matthew's skills in a number of ways. He was fortunate not to be the first to write about Jesus. Mark's Gospel had already come out, perhaps some fifteen or so years before Matthew, who was writing probably in the mid 80s CE. So Matthew could take Mark as his main source and rewrite it also adding material from other sources. It seems very likely that he knew one of the sources which Luke also knew when he was writing his Gospel. The Lord's Prayer, and many of the sayings of Jesus not in Mark, appear in Matthew and Luke. In Matthew they appear in a form which suggests that his version of the source had been more developed or polished than Luke's. For instance, the Lord's Prayer in Matthew had a fuller form than the one we find in Luke (Matt 6:9–13; Luke 11:2–4).

One of Matthew's creative developments was to gather Jesus' sayings, whether from the source he shared with Luke or from Mark or from elsewhere, into five main speeches. The best known is the first, the so-called Sermon on the Mount in Matt 5–7. Matthew's strong emphasis on Jesus' fulfillment of Old Testament hopes probably explains why he made a set of five speeches. It would remind his hearers of the fact that the Law of Moses comprised five books, Genesis, Exodus, Leviticus, Numbers, and Deuteronomy.

Such freedom to arrange and rearrange sayings and events in telling the story of Jesus reflects the fact that there did not appear to be a detailed CV of Jesus' ministry, aside from the fact of his birth and baptism by John the Baptist in the beginning and his trial and death in Jerusalem at the end. This is why Matthew sometimes happily changes the order of events as told in Mark, because they were all ultimately dependent on stories and sayings which had mostly circulated individually by word of mouth over some decades before being written down.

Matthew's emphasis on Jesus' fulfillment of the Old Testament is a constant theme. He portrays Jesus from the beginning as the one sent by God to teach what God's Law really means. John the Baptist had portrayed him as the one whom God had appointed to be the judge to come at the end of time. Matthew brings out that Jesus' way of interpreting the Law was to set love as its main goal.

While Matthew portrays Jesus as addressing the people of Israel, he also points to the fact that Jesus' message would also expand and reach out to all the world after his resurrection. The people for whom Matthew was writing would very likely have included not only Jews but also many others.

Matthew's portrait of Jesus has Jesus address the issues of Matthew's own time, including what leadership meant and how conflict was to be handled in congregations. In this way he helps people to gain an understanding not just of what Jesus said back in history, but also of what he believed Jesus would be saying to generations to come. It was, indeed, part of what authors were expected to do when they wrote about famous people in the past, to give an indication of what they would say to people hearing their stories in the future. The outcome of Matthew's story of Jesus is that his Gospel spoke not only to his age but has spoken to people down through the ages to our own time. It is then an invitation also for us to listen and engage.

1

The Beginning

A Boring Genealogy? Not at All! (Matthew 1:1–17)

Listening to Matthew

¹:¹ An account of the ancestry of Jesus the Messiah, the son of David, the son of Abraham.

² Abraham was the father of Isaac, and Isaac of Jacob, and Jacob of Judah and his brothers, ³ and Judah of Perez and Zerah through Tamar, and Perez of Hezron, and Hezron of Aram, ⁴ and Aram of Aminadab, and Aminadab of Nahshon, and Nahshon of Salmon, ⁵ and Salmon of Boaz through Rahab, and Boaz of Obed through Ruth, and Obed of Jesse, ⁶ and Jesse of King David.

⁷ And David was the father of Solomon through the wife of Uriah, and Solomon of Rehoboam, and Rehoboam of Abijah, and Abijah of Asaph, ⁸ and Asaph of Jehoshaphat, and Jehoshaphat of Joram, and Joram of Uzziah, ⁹ and Uzziah of Jotham, and Jotham of Ahaz, and Ahaz of Hezekiah, ¹⁰ and Hezekiah of Manasseh, and Manasseh of Amos, and Amos of Josiah, ¹¹ and Josiah of Jeconiah and his brothers around the time of the deportation to Babylon.

¹² Then after the deportation to Babylon Jeconiah became the father of Salathiel, and Salathiel of Zerubbabel, ¹³ and Zerubbabel of Abiud, and Abiud of Eliakim, and Eliakim of Azor, ¹⁴ and Azor of Zadok, and Zadok of Achim, and Achim of Eliud, ¹⁵ and Eliud of Eleazar, and Eleazar of Matthan, and Matthan of Jacob, ¹⁶ and

> Jacob of Joseph, the husband of Mary, and through her Jesus called the Messiah was born.
> ¹⁷ Accordingly, all the generations from Abraham to David were fourteen and from David to the exile in Babylon were fourteen and from the exile in Babylon to the Messiah were fourteen.

Thinking About Matthew

I wonder how many people have turned to the read the New Testament for the very first time, found themselves confronted with a list of names, and have then given up. Not so, surely, Matthew's friends and fans, who would have been used to expecting treasure in his words. Indeed, there is much treasure here that would not have been immediately apparent even for them. There are subtleties that suggest that Matthew meant people to stop and think about this genealogy, much as we are doing. He would be pleased.

Some things would have been obvious. This is about Jesus, but especially about Jesus as the Messiah, Israel's Messiah. Going back to Abraham rather than Adam, as in Luke, reflects what mattered especially to Jews and referring to him as son of David was much more than a point in the lineage. For the expectation was that the Messiah as God's agent would be a king like David, a king of David's line.

The first two words of Matthew's Gospel appear also to be suggestive. Literally they could be translated: "The Book of Genesis." Matthew's listeners would get the message. Matthew is writing new Scripture like the old, a witness to the new things God has been doing. These words allow a playful ambiguity, because they can also be translated: "account of the ancestry or origin or genealogy." The ambiguity may be deliberate.

Matthew clearly points to the significance of his genealogy when he identifies it as having three sections, each with fourteen generations. Why? His listeners would tell us immediately that 3 x 14 is the same as 6 x 7, so Jesus is the climax, the seventh set of 7. The number 7 was the number of perfection. If we then were to reply, "But why not say 6 x 7 instead of 3 x 14?" they would enlighten us further with information we cannot be expected to be aware of, namely the way Hebrew used letters to indicate digits.

Their Hebrew words comprised consonants with vowel sounds indicated by small symbols attached to the consonant that they followed. In writing David, they would write Dvd, with the vowel sound "a" attached to the first "D" and the "I" sound attached to the "v." Their alphabet has some similarity to ours, but they used consonants also to represent numbers, so the first six letters of their alphabet were also used for the numbers 1–6. When they look at the name David, Dvd, they would have seen 4 + v + 4. Their "v," also pronounced "w," was the sixth letter of their alphabet, like our "f," and sounding similar, so represented 6. Put all together in David's name they would have seen 4 + 6 + 4. That adds up to 14! So Matthew is playing with David's name when he highlights that the genealogy was made up of three lots of fourteen. Sets of three also had special value, so now we can see how the game was played, how the symbolism was applied, to highlight Jesus as the Messiah, Son of David.

There was much more in the genealogy. Almost every name had its own story, and perhaps Matthew's first hearers would have brought to mind each one. That is not, however, a particular focus. There is, however, an aspect of the genealogy that is a little unusual. Genealogies used to be traced back through men, on their assumption that men sowed the seed that kept the process going. We understand reproduction differently, for we know the seed or the egg resides in the woman and the man simply fertilizes it and that DNA passes to the child from both parents.

The unusual aspect in Matthew's genealogy is that he includes the names of women. One might wonder if this reflects an affirmation of women's roles, but Matthew is selective in choosing the names he brings. If he had been concerned just to identify women's importance, he would surely have included some of the great women of Israel's story, like Sarah and Rachel and Hannah.

Why, then, choose these women: Tamar, Rahab, Ruth, and the wife of Uriah the Hittite? There may be more than one explanation, as often in Matthew. They were all foreigners. Matthew will soon portray foreigners, namely the wise men from the east, coming to Jesus, and his Gospel will end with Jesus' instruction to the disciples to go to all peoples. It is highly likely that Matthew is already pointing to this inclusivity.

There is, however, more. These women were hailed by Jews as heroes, even though they were foreigners, and even though they might be seen as rather unorthodox or wild in their behavior. Tamar seduced Judah, her father-in-law. Rahab was a prostitute in Jericho, who helped Israel take hold in Canaan. Ruth was a virtuous model but authorized to seduce Boaz. The wife of Uriah, Bathsheba, was the woman David saw naked bathing on her rooftop and abducted and who gave birth to Solomon. All very questionable stories, but all about women playing a key role in what was seen as God's plan. It is highly likely that the story told about Mary put her in a similar category, especially as critics alleged she must have betrayed Joseph during her betrothal and that was why she fell pregnant, a claim Matthew firmly rejects.

For those steeped in Israel's traditions the message is clear. This is no boring genealogy. Far from it. It highlights God's new initiative, not just in fulfilling the promised hope for a messiah, but doing so in highly unexpected ways that put those often deemed least worthy right at the forefront of such fulfillment. Expect the unexpected!

Reflection: Why "expect the unexpected"?

A Miraculous Conception (Matthew 1:18–25)

Listening to Matthew

1:18 The origin of Jesus the Messiah was like this. It had been arranged that Mary his mother was to marry Joseph, but, before they came together, she was found to be pregnant. This was the work of the Holy Spirit. **19** Now Joseph, being a good man and unwilling to have her subject to disgrace, decided to divorce her privately. **20** While he was contemplating this action, lo and behold, an angel of the Lord appeared to him in a dream and said, "Joseph, son of David, don't be afraid to take Mary as your wife, because the child conceived in her is the work of the Holy Spirit. **21** She will give birth to a son, and you will name him Jesus, because he will save his people from their sins." **22** This all happened to fulfill what had been spoken by the Lord through the prophet: **23** "Behold a virgin will conceive and bear a son, and they will name him Emmanuel," which means "God with us." **24** So Joseph woke up from his sleep and did as the angel of the Lord told him and took her as his wife, **25** but did not have sexual intercourse with her until she gave birth to her son, and he named him Jesus.

Thinking About Matthew

Having prefaced his work with a richly allusive genealogy, Matthew turns to tell of Jesus' birth, the "origin" of Jesus the Messiah. The word "origin" is the same as in 1:1, *genesis*. If you were writing the story of famous people in the ancient world, one of the common ways of beginning was to tell stories about their birth. These were usually highly symbolic and legendary stories featuring angels, supernatural events, signs in the stars, and fantastic stories of conceptions, including sometimes sexual encounters between humans and gods. They were not stories about babies so much as stories that pointed forward to who these babies would become, often with subtle hints of their future achievements.

Like Luke, the only other Gospel writer to follow the pattern of using such birth stories, Matthew's stories are restrained. There are angels. There will be a traveling star. And there is a miraculous conception. Luke, similarly, has a miraculous conception and also angels with special announcements, but to Mary, not Joseph as in Matthew, and then to shepherds in King David's city. Already in Israel's stories we find accounts of wondrous conceptions by women previously unable to bear children, from Sarah in her nineties to Hannah, mother of Samuel. Only once do we have such an account of a miraculous conception without male sperm, as here, namely the conception of Melchizedek in the early first-century CE writing 2 Enoch.

Our story celebrates the affirmation that in Jesus people encountered God in a special way by attributing his origin to miraculous intervention. Unlike in some Greek and Roman legends, there is no suggestion that God or an angel or the Holy Spirit assumed the male role to help give birth to a hybrid, half-human, half-divine. Rather, Jesus the Messiah was fully human and God miraculously initiated his creation. It was just one of the ways that people found to explain what they encountered in Jesus. It was not surprising that, in seeking to explain how Jesus was so special, some people concluded that he must have been miraculously made.

The story itself reflects assumptions about marriage which would have needed no explanation for Matthew's first-century listeners. They included that men within the extended family will have arranged for Joseph, a man around thirty years of age, to marry Mary, one of its young teenage girls half his age. Such arrangements could be called betrothals and often would leave little room for consent on the part of the girls. They were not what we understand by getting engaged. The assumption is also that no sexual intercourse was to take place until after the wedding. There were even provisions for senior women to check whether the girl really was a virgin where there were any doubts.

Having sex during betrothal was not acceptable and would, of course, have undermined the story. Having sex with someone else, effectively premarital adultery, was seen as an abomination. Like adultery when married, it was once punishable by death, but in Matthew's time it required that the relationship cease, divorce. Hence Joseph's decision, which he knew he had to take, to divorce Mary. His virtue in the story is that he chose the kinder option of divorcing her without making a public event of it and so shaming her before all. Divorce was mandatory after adultery.

An angel of the Lord saves Joseph and Mary by intervening through a dream. People believed dreams were often vehicles of communication from the heavenly world. Not only does the angel tell Joseph that Mary's pregnancy was the work of the Holy Spirit. It also gives Joseph instructions that highlight who Jesus was to become. Mary, therefore, joins the ranks of those women mentioned in the genealogy who became sacred heroes despite their apparent or alleged misdemeanors. Through the Holy Spirit, God created the fetus in Mary's womb, an act of creation rather than procreation.

The hope for a messiah of David's line informs Matthew's opening chapter, but this leaves open the question: what will this Messiah be or do? The angel's words give us the first clue, and the name Jesus provides a first answer. Behind our anglicized form, Jesus, is Jeshua, Joshua, Hebrew: Yehoshua, variously interpreted as "God helps or saves." Matthew assumes "saves" and portrays Jesus as one who as Messiah was to save his people "from their sins." This may just mean forgiveness, but may mean much more, including liberating them from the consequences of their sins. The rest of the Gospel will show the breadth of meaning.

Matthew then refers to a passage in Isaiah in a way typical of his use of Old Testament texts as prophecy. Mounting such claims reinforces the belief that what has come in Jesus stands in continuity with God's actions in the past and brings to fulfillment what is sensed as promise for the future. In fact, Isa 7:14 is a prediction by the prophet Isaiah in the face of the alliance in the early eighth century BCE between Syria and the northern kingdom, Israel, against Judah in the south. Isaiah reassures King Ahaz of Judah that in as short a time as a young woman falls pregnant and gives birth the danger will be averted, and so the child is to be called Emmanuel, God with us, to celebrate God's deliverance. The danger was averted by the invasion of the Assyrians, who defeated the Syrians and wiped out the northern kingdom, Israel.

The Greek translation of Isa 7:14, which Matthew cites, chose to translate the Hebrew word for young woman (not a virgin) with a word in Greek that can also mean virgin, and so made it suitable for Matthew to apply it to the story of Mary's conceiving Jesus as a virgin. Matthew's use takes the statement out of context and applies it to Jesus. Despite this, we can appreciate what Matthew was seeking to emphasize, namely that Jesus will play the role of a liberator, which Matthew will go on to show. Having Jesus called Emmanuel, "God with us," celebrated what people experienced through Jesus' ministry and is echoed in what Matthew has Jesus finally promise for his disciples till the end of time (Matt 28:20).

Matthew reports Joseph's careful compliance with the angel's instructions. He marries Mary. His abstinence from sexual intercourse during her pregnancy does at one level remove any ambiguity that might call the miracle into question but also reflects a view held by some at the time that people should abstain from sexual intercourse during pregnancy.

Reflection: How important is it to read ancient stories in their cultural context? How does it help us discern what is of lasting significance and what is not?

Cosmic Acclaim (Matthew 2:1–23)

Listening to Matthew

2:1 Jesus was born in Bethlehem of Judea during the reign of King Herod, and at that time astrologers came to Jerusalem from the east, **2** saying, "Where is the one born to become king of the Jews, because we saw his star at its rising and have come to honor him?" **3** When King Herod heard this, he was troubled and all of Jerusalem along with him. **4** So he got the chief priests and the people's scribes together and asked them where the Messiah was to be born. **5** They told him, "In Bethlehem of Judea; because that is what was communicated through the prophet, **6** 'And you, Bethlehem of the land of Judah, are not the least significant among the rulers of Judah, because from you will come a leader who will be shepherd for my people Israel.'"

7 Then Herod secretly summoned the astrologers to find out from them the time when the star appeared, **8** and, sending them off to Bethlehem, said, "Go and get precise information about the child's whereabouts, and, when you find him, tell me, so that I, too, can go and honor him."

9 Having listened to the king, they set off and, lo and behold, the star that they had seen at its rising went on ahead of them leading the way until it came and stationed itself over the place where the child was. **10** Seeing the star they were absolutely thrilled. **11** When they went into the house, they saw the child with Mary his mother and knelt down before him to honor him. Then opening up their bag of valuables they presented him with gifts, gold and frankincense and myrrh. **12** Then, being warned in a dream not to return to Herod, they set off back to their own country via a different route.

13 Once they had gone, lo and behold, an angel of the Lord appeared to Joseph in a dream saying, "Get up and take the child and his mother and flee to Egypt and stay there till I tell you, because Herod is going to try to find the child to kill it." ¹⁴ So he got up and took the child and Mary his mother by night and went off to Egypt, ¹⁵ and was there until the death of Herod, so that what was spoken by the Lord through the prophet was fulfilled, which said, "Out of Egypt I have called my Son."

¹⁶ Then Herod, realizing that he had been tricked by the astrologers, was mad with rage, and initiated the killing of all the children two years of age and younger in Bethlehem and all the surrounding area, based on the information about timing he had gained from the astrologers. ¹⁷ Then the word spoken through Jeremiah the prophet came to fulfillment which said, ¹⁸ "There's a sound heard in Rama, weeping and much wailing; it's Rachel crying for her children, and she won't be comforted, because they are no longer alive."

¹⁹ After the death of Herod, lo and behold, an angel of the Lord appeared to Joseph in a dream in Egypt, ²⁰ saying, "Get up and take the child and his mother and go to the land of Israel, because those who sought the child's life are dead." ²¹ He got up and took the child and his mother and entered Israel.

²² When, however, he heard that Archelaus was ruling Judea, having succeeded his father Herod, he was afraid to go there and, being warned about it in a dream, he set off for the territory of Galilee. ²³ Arriving there, he took up residence in a town called Nazareth. That then brought to fulfillment what was spoken through the prophets, namely, "He'll be called a Nazarene."

Thinking About Matthew

Matthew offers us a wonderful story, rich in allusions. His first hearers would have found profound meaning in its detail. For us it presents itself like a work of art inviting us to stop and ponder the symbolism. If we might imagine Matthew as an artist, we could begin by observing the rich allusions in its detail.

The star is prominent. In the story of Israel's journey from Egypt there is an episode where Balak king of Moab invites his prophet Balaam to pronounce a curse on Israel. Instead, Balaam hails Israel and utters a prediction, a prophecy regarding Israel's future: "A star shall come out of Jacob, and a scepter shall rise out of Israel" (Num 24:17). In its context it refers to a ruler who would lead Israel to crushing victories over Moab and the nations around about. Later generations took up the prophecy and applied it to the hope for a messiah, sometimes taking it to refer to two people, a star and a scepter, a priestly and a royal messiah, but mostly taking it to refer to one person, the royal messiah, the Son of David.

Matthew, or a storyteller before him, could combine this well with the trend to use popular astrology to link famous people's births to signs and wonders in the heavens. It was daring to use astrology in this way, which is not otherwise promoted in the early Christian movement, but it served its purpose well to highlight Jesus' significance. The universe itself recognized him! Astral phenomena around this time, such as planet alignments or comet appearances, may have also contributed to the story. Many have attempted to match up the story to such appearances, the closest being the alignment of planets, but that would have been far from a bright star and, of course, nothing like what the story portrays of a star traveling across the sky and hovering over Bethlehem.

Adding to the rich symbolism is the fact that the astrologers would represent those who were proverbially seen as the wisest of the non-Jewish world. Their coming would foreshadow the coming to faith of gentiles through the church's mission. This wondrous star travels across the sky and settles over the place where Jesus was born, as stars can in such stories. Such artistry and fantasy celebrating who Jesus was to become!

There is, however, much more in the artist's portrait. There is King Herod, who reigned from 37 to 4 BCE. That much is history and historical in the account of Jesus' birth and finds an echo independently in Luke, who also reports the birth of Jesus and also John the Baptist during the latter years of Herod's reign (Luke 1:5). Herod was notoriously cruel, even killing members of his own family. Stories of Herod's cruelty then worked well to have him act like pharaoh of Egypt in killing baby boys (Exod 1) and so slaughtering all male infants under two in Bethlehem and surrounds. Jesus escaped. Matthew here cites Jer 31:15, the lamentation of Rachel for her children, as thus finding a terrible fulfillment in the story.

Those who knew the full story of Jesus would recognize that ultimately Pilate would succeed where Herod failed. The link with the story of Israel's sojourn in Egypt enabled the storyteller to have Jesus re-live, as it were, Israel's story. He was taken down to Egypt and then, like the children of Israel, but as God's Son, was brought back up again. Matthew cites Hos 11:1 of God's calling his Son out of Egypt, applying it to Jesus.

History returns with the reference to the rule of Archelaus, Herod's son, who succeeded him as ruler of the Judah portion of his father's larger kingdom, only to be deposed in 6 CE by the Romans for excessive cruelty and replaced by Rome's own appointees, among whom would be Pilate. Death hovers over the story. The story ends with the relocation to Galilee, to Nazareth, to avoid Archelaus's regime. Matthew alludes to Isa 11:1, which speaks of the messiah as a branch but uses a word for it which could sound like Nazarene and so reads it as such.

Running through the story is the image of Joseph, like Jacob's son of the same name, who was also a dreamer and responsible for bringing Israel to Egypt. The Joseph in our story does even more. Following instruction from an angel in a dream he also initiates Jesus' exodus from Egypt.

A wonderful story, surrounding the minimal historical data of Jesus' birth during Herod's reign and his upbringing in Nazareth, with signs in the heavens and a symbolic re-living of Israel's journeys as well as a foretaste of the success of the gentile mission, but also of Jesus' execution at the hands of the political authorities. The story is enriched by biblical citations read to foreshadow key elements of the story.

Later generations took the mention of the three gifts of gold, frankincense, and myrrh, as indicating that there were *three* wise men. They also saw the gifts as fulfilling Isaiah's prediction of such gifts (Isa 60:6) and Ps 72's prediction of those bringing such gifts as kings (Ps 72:10–11, 15); hence the carol "We Three Kings."

Reflection: This is much more than a story about a baby. What more do you see in it?

John Points to Jesus as the Judge to Come (Matthew 3:1–17)

Listening to Matthew

³:¹ In those days John the Baptist appeared in the Judean outback, preaching, ² "Turn to God, because the kingdom of heaven has come near." ³ He was the one spoken about by Isaiah the prophet when he said, "A voice calling in the outback, 'Prepare the way of the Lord; make his paths straight!'"

⁴ John had a camel-hair coat and a leather belt around his waist and his food was locusts and wild honey. ⁵ Then people started coming out to him from Jerusalem and all Judea and all the area around the Jordan. ⁶ And they were being baptized by him in the Jordan river as they confessed their sins.

⁷ When he saw many of the Pharisees and Sadducees also coming for his baptism, he challenged them saying, "You nest of snakes, who warned you to escape the impending divine anger? ⁸ Produce fruit to show you really want to change ⁹ and don't go telling yourselves, 'We've got Abraham as our father,' because I'm telling you, God can raise up children to Abraham from these stones. ¹⁰ Already the axe is lying at the base of the trees and every tree that fails to produce good fruit will be cut down and thrown into the fire. ¹¹ I baptize you with water for turning back to God, but someone's coming after me who is more powerful than me. I'm not worthy even to carry his sandals. He's going to baptize you with the Holy Spirit and with fire. ¹² His fork is in his hand, and he will clean up his threshing floor and gather the wheat into his barn and burn up the chaff with unquenchable fire."

¹³ Then Jesus came from Galilee to the Jordan to John to be baptized by him. ¹⁴ John tried to stop him, saying, "It's me who needs to be baptized by you; are you really coming to me?"

¹⁵ Jesus responded, "Let it be for now, for this way we'll be fulfilling everything God wants us to do." Then John went along with him.

¹⁶ When Jesus was baptized, immediately as he emerged from the water, lo and behold, heaven opened up and he saw the Spirit coming down like a dove and resting on him. ¹⁷ And then a voice came from heaven saying, "This is my beloved Son. I am very pleased with him."

Thinking About Matthew

Matthew's "In those days" (3:1) covers close to three decades between when Jesus was taken to Nazareth as an infant and his baptism. It is Matthew's loose connection between stories about baby Jesus and the account of Jesus' ministry which he found in the Gospel of Mark. Aside from a story told about the twelve-year-old Jesus in Luke, which is probably a symbolic tale (Luke 2:41–51), we know nothing of those intervening thirty years. Presumably Jesus had a normal childhood in his Jewish family, whose choice of their children's names after Old Testament figures (Jesus/Joshua; James/Jacob, Jude/Judah, Simon) suggests they were very traditional. He will have been educated by his family and through the local synagogue and grown up across the valley from Sepphoris, where a revolt took place after Herod the Great's death in 4 BCE and where perhaps he and his father worked on rebuilding it.

Matthew follows Mark in reporting Jesus' baptism by John. For all the artistic symbolism of the scene, there is little doubt that John the Baptist did baptize Jesus and that the two were closely connected. It is hardly likely that later followers of Jesus would have made up a story that had Jesus baptized by John, because it makes it sound like John is the more senior of the two. Matthew has indeed added to Mark's account an exchange in which John reinforces that he was not the more senior and that he thought that, really, Jesus should be baptizing him.

Historically, John's movement was one among others that looked forward to change and a return to a society where God and God's ways ruled. They hoped for God's kingdom, God's empire, to begin. Many located themselves in the wilderness or outback region on the other side of the Jordan River. In part this was safer, but it was also symbolic. Like Israel of old, they saw themselves as about to retake the land for God.

Some envisaged that as a military action, with or without help from angels. These were in that sense revolutionary movements of various kinds, including some who claimed that their leader was God's chosen Anointed One, the Messiah, who, like David, would lead them to victory.

John's movement of hope was not military, but it shared the same expectation that God's kingdom and empire would come soon. John lived a life of waiting, with scant attire and minimum sustenance. Abundance was something yet to come. Matthew's summary of John the Baptist's message makes that clear: "Turn to God, because the kingdom of heaven has come near" (3:2). Matthew summarizes Jesus' message as saying the same: "Turn to God, because the kingdom of heaven has come near" (4:17) and will later summarize the message that Jesus sends his disciples to proclaim as: "The kingdom of heaven has come near" (Matt 10:7). In that sense, as Matthew portrays it, John, Jesus, and the church share this same message. The call to "repent" was a call to turn back to God, have one's sins forgiven, and be ready for what was to come.

John was unusual because he called people not only to turn to God but also to let themselves be immersed by him in the Jordan River. Both for ritual and moral purification people usually washed or immersed themselves. This would often have been in local immersion pools or baths. Archaeology has been uncovering many from this period, and they were especially important for people wanting to prepare themselves for visiting the holy temple in Jerusalem. John's unusual practice of challenging people to let him immerse them in the Jordan River led to him being called John the Baptizer or Immerser, perhaps even as a nickname, John the Dipper.

Why did he do it? To emphasize that it is God alone who cleanses and forgives. They were to come and let themselves be immersed in God's compassion. His baptism was not like the washings and immersions that people might undertake many times, but rather a once-off return to oneness with God, ready for what was to come.

It is important to see that underlying John's message and practice was the understanding that the offer of such cleansing was for all; in that sense, a universal offer of forgiveness of sins. This then became fundamental also for Jesus' message, even though he added much more. When people reduce the Christian gospel to just forgiveness of sins, as sometimes happens, they have reached first base, as it were, with John, but they have missed what Jesus added.

Mark spoke of John's baptism as "a baptism in which people could represent their turning to God and having their sins forgiven" (Mark 1:4), literally "for the forgiveness of sins." Matthew leaves out Mark 1:4, but he adds the same phrase "for the forgiveness of sins" to Jesus' words over the cup at the last supper (Matt 26:28). Some take this to mean that Matthew does not understand John's baptism as having to do with forgiveness of sins, but this is hardly the case. Matthew describes people confessing their sins, and the reason for doing so was to have them forgiven. Forgiveness is central to both John's and Jesus' message, and people saw no problem in having it expressed in a range of ways, from John's baptism, to Jesus' declaration of forgiveness during his ministry (Matt 9:2), to seeing it made possible through his death.

Our resources for understanding John's message are very limited. Matthew had what Mark wrote, but also some sayings known also to Luke. If we piece that limited information together, we can see that John's message was dominated by the expectation that soon God would bring change. When Matthew has John and Jesus speak of "the kingdom of heaven," this is a variation of "the kingdom of God" and means: when God (that is, heaven) reigns. It is not about God reigning in heaven but about God reigning on earth.

Matthew trims the quotation with which Mark begins his account by deleting the words "Look, I am sending my messenger ahead of you, who will prepare your way" (Mark 1:2), because they come not from Isaiah, as Mark indicates, but from Malachi. It is one of a few occasions when Matthew corrects Mark. The quotation from Isaiah belongs originally to the hope that the people who had been taken into captivity in Babylonia in the early sixth century BCE would be led back by God. Hence the imagery of roadmaking to ensure a successful return. Mark, and so Matthew, reuses the text to refer now to God intervening again to bring hope and change.

Aside from these expressions of hope, John the Baptist puts emphasis on the fact that when God comes, people will be judged. He speaks of God's anger, meaning God's punishment. To escape God's punishment, people needed to turn back to God and embrace a lifestyle that was consistent with turning away from sin. Luke has John spell this out for the crowds and for tax collectors and soldiers (Luke 3:10–14). Matthew simply has John confront the religious leaders, whom he accuses of sinful behavior, and challenge them to commit themselves to change and not to rest on their laurels by claiming that as Abraham's descendants they had no need to change. His comment that God can raise up children to Abraham from stones may well go back to a wordplay: in Hebrew *ben* means child or son and *eben* means stone.

Matthew will later portray Jesus as issuing similar challenges and placing a major emphasis on behavior and not tolerating people making claims about their status. We might see the equivalent when people undergo a conversion and then see that as enough. It is like someone thinking that having had a wedding guarantees a good marriage. Matthew's portrait of Jesus puts emphasis on living lives that demonstrate the fruit of goodness and love. The imagery of behavior as fruit is a rich source for reflection. It can suggest that behavior can be the result of change within a person and not just action that follows instructions or rules. Jesus will talk about good trees producing good fruit and sick or bad trees producing bad fruit (Matt 7:15-20) and Paul speaks of the fruit of the Spirit as love (Gal 5:22).

Matthew has John do more than speak of God's judgment to come. Following Mark, he has John announce that someone greater than himself was coming. He goes beyond Mark in saying that this one to come would baptize not only with the Spirit, as in Mark, but also with fire. In other words, Matthew has John announce that this person to come, far superior to himself, would be God's agent in judgment. As in Mark, so in Matthew, this figure is identified with Jesus. Matthew has John declare that Jesus will be God's agent in the final judgment, gathering the wheat, an image of the just, into his barn, and consigning the chaff, an image of sinners, to eternal fire.

Aside from the angel's interpretation of Jesus' name as meaning he would "save his people from their sins" (Matt 1:21), these words of John the Baptist are our first introduction to how Matthew sees Jesus exercising his role as God's Messiah. As we shall see when we discuss Matt 11, it gave John's disciples the impression that this was what they should expect Jesus to go on now to do, to execute judgment. Jesus did not, however, do as John had predicted, so John sent messengers to check with Jesus if he really was the one, to which Jesus replies by pointing to his wider mission of bringing change already through his ministry (Matt 11:2-6). This was his task in the interim. His role as judge would be in the future.

In the exchange between John and Jesus, which Matthew adds to underline Jesus' superiority to John rather than the other way round, Matthew underlines that doing everything God wanted them to do, literally, "fulfilling all righteousness," is central to Jesus' mission. Matthew will return to this in the Sermon on the Mount when he has Jesus spell out what "righteousness," doing what God wants and upholding God's Law, means when applied to all. The one announced as judge to come will surely follow God's will and uphold what is right.

As in Mark, Matthew's account of Jesus' baptism is richly symbolic, typical of the narrative artistry of the time. Having allowed himself to be immersed in God's goodness and compassion through baptism in the Jordan, Jesus sees heaven opened and the Spirit coming down like a dove. The scene invites us to see the sky open up and a gentle dove fluttering down. People familiar with biblical stories might think of the wind hovering over the deep in the creation story like a bird (Gen 1:2) or the dove bringing a sign of hope to Noah after the flood (Gen 8:11).

The image of the Spirit's descent suggests a profound connection with God, traditionally pictured as above in heaven beyond the sky. Jesus will exercise his ministry through God's power, given him through the Spirit. The voice articulates that special relationship. God declares Jesus to be his beloved Son and is pleased with him. It is the language of family, a father speaking of his son. In Mark only Jesus hears the voice. Matthew changes "You are" to "This is." Everyone hears it. In Matthew's world kings could be acclaimed as God's sons, as in Ps 2:7, "You are my Son," which finds an echo here, as do the words of Isa 42:1, "Here is my servant, whom I uphold, my chosen, in whom my soul delights; I have put my spirit upon him."

Matthew's story leaves us in no doubt that Jesus is the one of whom John spoke and that Jesus is uniquely God's beloved Son. His first two chapters have celebrated his miraculous creation through Mary and his status as Messiah, Son of David, who would be Emmanuel, the one to bring God to his people and save them from their sin.

Already therefore in these first three chapters we have many clues about who Jesus is and what he will do as God's agent and Messiah, but much remains to be said. As noted above, he will do more than what John predicted. Matthew retains the emphasis on his role as God's agent in judgment and will indeed bring his account of Jesus' ministry to a close with the image of the last judgment where Jesus as Son of Man holds judgment, dividing the sheep from the goats (Matt 25:31–46). There is, however, much more in between that goes beyond John's role description of Jesus as judge to come, and Matthew will soon make that very clear.

Reflection: What message did John and Jesus share and how was that good news?

Setting Priorities (Matthew 4:1–22)

Listening to Matthew

4:1 Then Jesus was taken by the Spirit into the outback region to face an ordeal of testing at the hands of the devil. **2** After having fasted for forty days and nights, he was facing hunger. **3** So the one testing him approached him and said, "If you are the Son of God, tell these stones to turn into bread." **4** In response he said, "It is written, 'People are not to live just by bread but by every word that proceeds from the mouth of God.'"

5 Then the devil took him to the holy city and placed him on the high point of the temple **6** and said to him, "If you are the Son of God, throw yourself down from here, because it is written, 'He will instruct his angels about you and they will carry you in their hands, so you'll never dash your foot against a rock.'" **7** Jesus told him, "Again it is written, 'You shall not put the Lord your God to the test.'"

8 Again the devil took him, this time to a very high mountain and showed him all the world's kingdoms and their glory, **9** and said to him, "All this I'll give you if you bow down in submission to me." **10** Then Jesus said to him, "Off with you, Satan! For it is written, 'You shall bow in submission to the Lord your God and serve God alone.'"

11 Then the devil left him and, lo and behold, angels came and looked after him.

12 When Jesus heard that John had been arrested, he went off to Galilee. **13** Then leaving Nazareth, he went and took up residence in Capernaum by the lakeside in the territory of Zebulun and Naphtali. **14** That brought to fulfillment what had been spoken by the prophet Isaiah, saying, **15** "Land of Zebulun and Naphtali, home to the seaside way across the Jordan, Galilee of the gentiles, **16** the people sitting in darkness have seen a great light, and for those sitting in the region and shadow of death a light has dawned for them."

[17] From that time on Jesus began to proclaim his message, "Turn to God, because the kingdom of heaven has come near."

[18] As he was on his way along Lake Galilee, he saw two brothers, Simon called Peter and Andrew his brother, casting their net into the lake, for they were fishermen. [19] And he said to them, "Come, follow me and I will turn you into people who fish for people!" [20] They immediately abandoned their nets and followed him. [21] And moving on from there he saw two other brothers, James son of Zebedee and John his brother. They were in their boat with Zebedee, their father, mending their nets, and he called them. [22] They immediately left the boat and their father and followed him.

Thinking About Matthew

Just as it was not uncommon for authors writing up the stories of famous people to include accounts of their birth replete with signs and wonders, so it was also not uncommon for them to preface their accounts of their achievements with tales of testing ordeals where their heroes showed they were up to great achievements. These, too, were often highly symbolic.

Mark's account of Jesus being tested in the outback is very short and has Jesus confront the devil, the archenemy, in a setting with wild animals, which recalls Adam and Eve's confrontation and failure in the garden of Eden (Mark 1:12–13). His victory there foreshadows his victory over demonic powers through his ministry. Both Matthew and Luke know a much longer version of Jesus' ordeal that comprises three parts. It has echoes of Israel facing challenges in the wilderness and failing. By contrast, Jesus does not fail. Luke's sequence has the final temptation take place in Jerusalem. Matthew has that as the second test and makes the challenge to bow down and worship Satan the final test.

This longer account of Jesus' testing is richly imaginative, and we misread it if we do not appreciate its artistry. Like dreams, the story has surreal elements. Obviously, you cannot survive without food for forty days or, if you do, you'd be in a seriously weakened state, if not dead. And you cannot see all the kingdoms of the world from a very high mountain, even if you did believe the earth is flat, as the image assumes. The notion of Jesus finding himself on top of the temple is also surreal. Tripping to

Jerusalem and to a very high mountain while still in the Judean outback is impossible, unless we understand that it is all like a dream. But dreams can face us with reality, and that is surely happening here.

The three tests are seen as three temptations to get Jesus to deviate from his commitment to God's will for him. They begin with our having to imagine that Jesus had eaten nothing for forty days. Matthew's hearers, familiar with the biblical stories, would appreciate the symbolism of forty. Forty was a significant number. Israel spent forty years in the wilderness before they entered the land of Canaan, seen often as a story of testing and of failures. Would Jesus fail, too? The first test: stop fasting and use your powers to make stones into bread!

One might imagine that this would meet his extreme hunger and would surely not hinder his doing God's will, but that is to miss the point. The story is contrasting doing God's will with meeting one's own immediate needs. The story does not invite us to ponder whether it would have been possible for Jesus to perform such magic. The issue was whether Jesus would remain faithful to what God wants. Fasting was a way of preparing oneself for a divine commission. The story has its own way of addressing what seems an impossible requirement: it has angels come and look after Jesus, presumably also to feed him.

This first test invites further reflection, and many have found profound wisdom in its strangeness. It is not about denying the need to eat and to look after oneself. It is about what matters most. To make meeting one's own needs life's highest priority is to fail the test. The test now comes to us in appeals that we should seek instant self-gratification, not least in the constant appeals of advertising. Meeting one's own needs can also lead people in ministry into acts of exploitation and self-serving.

Matthew's second temptation has Jesus confronted with another invitation to magic, this time to jump from the top of the temple. That would certainly win him fame. If he's not the kind of Son of God who makes stones into bread, is he a Son of God who can perform miraculous stunts? The devil quotes Scripture as many will do over the years in order to justify folly. Putting God to the test would be seeing if God would really do as the Psalmist cited said (Ps 91:11–12). Jesus would not be a stunt man.

Nevertheless, stories of his miracles did indeed become the stuff of propaganda in some circles, who appealed for a following for Jesus primarily because of the miracles and often promised similar success to those who bought the appeal. John's Gospel strikingly has Jesus reject such following, such belief. Its author notes that while they believed in him, he did not believe in them (John 2:23—3:3). Paul, too, had to grapple with trends to make signs and wonders central and to promote those who could claim such powers. He confronts them with the cross and highlights love as the mark of the Spirit (1 Cor 13; Gal 5:22).

Matthew's third temptation is an appeal to Jesus to have power for himself, as a fantasy of becoming ruler of all the world. In every age there have been people who seek power over others as a way to assert and assure themselves of their worth and importance. Like the other two temptations, the offer is in any case fantasy. Jesus is secure in his knowledge of being beloved by God. That is more than enough. He has no need out of a sense of inadequacy to engage in trying to gain power over others and win glory for himself. Indeed, his way will be the way of the cross. So he returns to the center of faith: serving and loving God alone, citing Deut 6:13, "You shall bow in submission to the Lord your God and serve God alone."

Jesus' ordeal as depicted in Matt 4 will be echoed later in Matthew's account of Jesus' story. The closing verses of the Gospel have Jesus report that God has indeed given him authority over all, telling his disciples, "All authority in heaven and on earth has been given to me" (Matt 28:18), before sending them out to make disciples of all peoples. That is a very different understanding of power and authority, calling people to become learners of all that Jesus taught. We also find an echo of the ordeal when those mocking Jesus on the cross call out, "If you are the Son of God, come down from the cross!" (Matt 27:40). He was not that kind of Son of God who might magically escape suffering, but rather one who embraced love and obedience even in the face of death.

Stories of testing ordeals and of retreat into outback wilderness to reflect on priorities and goals reflect a timeless wisdom. These days we even find secular leaders of industry often doing the same with their personnel, taking them off for their "retreats," to recalibrate and revisit priorities. It is ultimately the wisdom of finding space for prayer and reflection in a world where busy-ness, even with the best of intent, can crowd out the sense of purpose and perspective essential for effective living, let alone ministry. Its ancient form, as here, was to take time out for prayer with fasting.

Matthew follows his account of Jesus' testing ordeal by returning to Mark, who briefly mentions the arrest of John the Baptist and Jesus' going to Galilee (Mark 1:14). He then adds that Jesus moved from his hometown

Nazareth to Capernaum in the territory of Zebulun and Naphtali, two of the northern tribes. He uses this detail to bring a citation from Isaiah which speaks of gentiles (Isa 9:1–2). For the mission would, indeed, reach out beyond Israel to the gentiles, to all nations, a hint already given in his account of the coming of the gentile astrologers to honor Jesus at his birth and in his inclusion of foreign women in his genealogy.

Matthew returns again to Mark's account in summarizing Jesus' message (Mark 1:15), using the same words as he had used in summarizing John's message, "Turn to God, because the kingdom of heaven has come near" (Matt 4:17; 3:2). He then goes on, as in Mark, to report Jesus' call of the first disciples. Calling them to leave their settled lives was also a statement about his mission, because he was challenging the established settled order which kept some rich and some poor.

John's proclamation of the coming of God's kingdom/empire landed him in prison and finally led to his execution. Ultimately, Jesus would similarly face execution. While John and Jesus shared the same message, there was a significance difference. Instead of remaining in the place of waiting and expectation beyond the Jordan, ready to enter the promised land, Jesus moved from there, entering the land, and began a new kind of ministry. His return to Galilee was about more than escaping danger. It represented a new claim, namely that the kingdom/empire of God would now start becoming a reality through his ministry. It was time to move out of the place of waiting into the land.

Reflection: What issues are being addressed in the temptations and how do you see them playing out in today's world?

2

Matthew's Mini-Gospel

Embracing Hope (Matthew 4:23—5:16)

Listening to Matthew

4:23 And Jesus went all around Galilee teaching in their synagogues and proclaiming the good news of the kingdom and healing every sickness and every ailment among the people. **24** And his reputation spread throughout all of Syria and people brought to him all those who were ill with various sicknesses and those suffering pain and people possessed by demons and seizures and people suffering paralysis, and he healed them. **25** And big crowds from Galilee and the Decapolis and Jerusalem and Judea and the Jordan region followed him.

5:1 Seeing the crowds Jesus climbed a hill, and while he was sitting down there his disciples joined him, **2** so he started speaking and providing them with teaching. This is what he said:

3 "Happy are those who are down and dispirited, because the kingdom of heaven is theirs.

4 "Happy are those who are mourning, because they will be comforted.

5 "Happy are those who are gentle and unassuming, because they are going to inherit the land.

⁶ "Happy are those who hunger and thirst for what is right, because they shall be satisfied.

⁷ "Happy are the compassionate, because they will be treated with compassion.

⁸ "Happy are those who are pure of mind, because they shall see God.

⁹ "Happy are the peacemakers, because they shall be called the children of God.

¹⁰ "Happy are those who are persecuted for their pursuit of what is right before God, because the kingdom of heaven is theirs.

¹¹ "Happy are you when people abuse you and persecute you and utter all kinds of slander against you because of me, ¹² be glad and happy about it, because you'll get a great reward in heaven, for that's how they persecuted the prophets before you.

¹³ "You are the salt of the earth. If salt loses its saltiness, how are you going to make it salty again? It's good for nothing but to be thrown out to be trodden on by people.

¹⁴ "You are the light of the world. No city can be hidden if it's located on a mountain. ¹⁵ And people don't light lamps and put them under a bag of grain, but rather on a lampstand so that it can produce light for everyone in the house. ¹⁶ Just so, let your light shine among people, so that they will see the good things you do and venerate your Father who is in heaven."

Thinking About Matthew

In 4:23 Matthew embarks on his grand story about Jesus with great skill. He puts a summary frame around the chapters that follow by repeating 4:23 again in almost identical words in 9:35.

> And Jesus went all around Galilee teaching in their synagogues and proclaiming the good news of the kingdom and healing every sickness and every ailment among the people. (Matt 4:23)

> And Jesus went around all the towns and villages teaching in their synagogues and proclaiming the good news of the kingdom and healing every sickness and every ailment. (Matt 9:35)

In between these two texts he arranges his material into two main sections to present a collection of Jesus' teaching (Matt 5–7) and a collection of Jesus' deeds (Matt 8:1—9:34), a kind of mini-gospel. We will discuss the collection of deeds when we come to those chapters. The collection of Jesus' teaching, widely known as the Sermon on the Mount, is the first of five collections of Jesus' teaching that Matthew brings in his Gospel: (1) Matt 5:1—7:29; (2) Matt 10:1—11:1; (3) Matt 13:1–53; (4) Matt 18:1—19:1; and (5) Matt 24:1—26:1. Matthew may well have intended that people hearing Jesus expounding the Law in these five collections would recall that the Law of Moses also comprised five parts, Genesis, Exodus, Leviticus, Numbers, and Deuteronomy. At the end of each collection, he uses the same words to make the transition to what follows, namely, "And it happened that when Jesus had finished speaking these words . . ." (Matt 7:28; 11:1; 13:53; 19:1; and 26:1).

Matthew follows the brief summary in 4:23, which is based on Mark 1:39, with a longer summary in 4:24-25, based on Mark 3:7-8. Shortly after, Mark has Jesus climb a hill, summon some of his disciples to join him (Mark 3:13) and appoint twelve of them to be his apostles or agents. Matthew describes the appointment of the twelve much later, in Matt 10:2-4. He does, however, take up the reference to Jesus climbing up the hill and having his disciples come to him and makes this the setting for Jesus' first great teaching event. Much of it has to do with expounding the Law, and this makes it highly likely that Matthew intended people to make a connection with the giving of the Law to Moses on Mount Sinai.

If we recall the way John the Baptist depicted Jesus, namely as the judge to come, then what we have before us is an image of Jesus the judge expounding the Law by which people would be judged. For Matthew, however, Jesus was much more than the judge to come. He was the bearer of good news. That good news was about the promise of the kingdom or empire of God which was to come, and which was beginning to break in through his ministry.

In compiling the collection of Jesus' sayings into this first major speech, Matthew drew primarily on the source that he shared with Luke and which Luke brings in Luke 6:20-49. That provided the basic framework into which Matthew then added more material, so that his speech now takes up three whole chapters whereas Luke's fills just half a chapter. We can see the basic outline as in Luke: the so-called Beatitudes ("Happy are . . ."); loving enemies; not judging others; bearing good fruit; and building buildings that will last. Matthew may well have known a version that had already been expanded, but he put the finishing touches to what we know as the Sermon on the Mount.

Our passage includes the opening section of the Sermon on the Mount. Luke's version, which probably reflects an earlier form, has just four statements declaring needy people to be happy or blessed because of the coming kingdom of God. The poor, the hungry, the distressed can look forward to relief, and the persecuted are promised reward (Luke 6:20–23). Matthew's version has all these but in an expanded form and adds more.

The expansion may well have occurred before Matthew, for while he now has nine beatitudes, we can see that at some stage there were eight, two lots of four, with the promise to the first and the last matching ("because the kingdom of heaven is theirs," 5:2, 10) and the fourth and eighth having "what is right before God, justice" or "righteousness" as a theme (2:6, 10).

Matthew's version has Jesus speak of those who are "down and dispirited," literally "poor in spirit," expanding the focus from poverty to people who are dispirited. It is misread when people take it to mean people who are especially humble or put themselves down. The language "poor in spirit" had been already used in Jewish tradition to describe Israel and its people facing suffering.

"Those who mourn" in Matthew's second beatitude will refer not so much to people dealing with personal grief as to those experiencing the distress which many in Israel were experiencing as a result of poverty and oppression. One of the favorite texts from Isaiah to give expression to hope and which Luke, for instance, has Jesus apply to himself speaks of his being anointed to bring good news for the poor (Isa 61:1; Luke 4:18). The Isaiah passage goes on to include comfort among the tasks: "to comfort all who mourn" (Isa 61:2). The promise to the gentle and unassuming, in Matthew's third beatitude, traditionally translated as "the meek," derives from Ps 37:11 ("The meek shall inherit the land") and is to be seen in the same broader context of hope that the land would once again be God's where God's kingdom would rule.

Matthew's version of the promise to the hungry (as in Luke 6:20) has broadened the focus to mean hungering and thirsting for what is right before God, for justice, which can mean for themselves but can also mean for others. The word which I have translated "what is right before God" also means "goodness," and traditionally, "righteousness." This can be misunderstood when people think it refers to those who try to be good, although, when we understand Matthew's view of goodness, it certainly includes being just, compassionate, and loving.

It is very evident that in the way Matthew presents these promises, they are both comfort and encouragement, comfort for the dispirited, those hungering for justice, the meek, those mourning and the persecuted, but also encouragement. The focus on encouragement helps explain the expansions that we find in Matthew in comparison with Luke, such as the implication that one may hunger for justice not just for oneself. It also helps explain the additions: the challenge to be compassionate, be pure of mind, be peacemakers, and possibly also meekness. What follows in the sermon will spell out what all this means in practice. Life in the Christian community is reflected in the promise to the persecuted, to expect for themselves what faced the prophets and what faced Jesus, if they are going to follow Jesus' teaching about compassion and love.

It is important to see that Matthew has Jesus begin not with demands and commands but with promises. Hope is based on faith in God's generosity and love. That is the good news. That also provides the assurance and security that frees people in turn to act with love and compassion toward others. Reading the Sermon on the Mount as a set of demands is to misunderstand its focus and foundation.

This becomes very evident when Matthew, using material he picked up from Mark, has Jesus go on to declare that the disciples who take this on board are salt, not to make life sour, but to preserve and protect, an essential commodity before the invention of the modern refrigerator (Matt 5:13; Mark 9:50). They are also light, and they need to let that light shine (Matt 5:14–16; Mark 4:21). Matthew will have Jesus go on to show people how to do this, how to be compassionate and caring. Again, this must not be reduced to demands and obligations. They are light. God's love has made that possible. They are to let it shine; let the love they have received flow out to others. There is no greater way to acknowledge and acclaim God than to share God's love. That, according to Matthew, is what people need to be seeing.

Reflection: What is the good news in this opening section of the Sermon on the Mount, and why does it matter for understanding what follows?

What Upholding God's Law Really Means
(Matthew 5:17–48)

Listening to Matthew

5:17 "Don't think I came to set the Law and the Prophets aside. I didn't come to set them aside but to make sure they are observed to the full. **18** Truly I tell you, until heaven and earth themselves come to an end, not a single iota or stroke of the Law is to be set aside from the Law until it's all been done. **19** What's more, anyone who breaks one of the very least of these commandments and teaches other people to do so will be called least in the kingdom of heaven, but whoever keeps them and teaches them will be called great in the kingdom of heaven. **20** I'm telling you, unless your goodness exceeds that of the scribes and Pharisees, you're never going to get into the kingdom of heaven.

21 "You've heard how it was said to people of old, 'You shall not murder; and whoever commits murder will be found guilty before the court.' **22** Well, I'm telling you that anyone who carries anger toward another is to be found guilty before the court; and whoever utters abuse against another is to be found guilty by the council; and whoever calls someone a fool is to be found guilty and sent to the fire of Gehenna.

23 "So if you're offering your gift at the altar and it occurs to you that someone has something against you, **24** hold off placing your gift before the altar and first go and get your relationship with that person sorted, and then come and offer your gift. **25** Come to terms quickly with your opponent, while you're on your way with him to a hearing, so he doesn't hand you over there to the magistrate and the magistrate to the judge and you get put into prison. **26** Truly I'm telling you, you won't get out of there until you've paid back the very last copper coin.

²⁷ "You've heard how it was said, 'You shall not commit adultery.' ²⁸ Well, I'm telling you, whoever looks at another man's wife with a view of wanting to have sex with her has already committed adultery with her in his mind. ²⁹ If your right eye gets you into trouble, pull it out and throw it away. It's better for you to lose one of your faculties than for your whole body to be thrown into Gehenna. ³⁰ "And if your right hand gets you into trouble, cut it off and throw it away. It's better to lose one of your limbs than for your whole body to go into Gehenna.

³¹ "And it was also said, 'Whoever divorces his wife, let him give her a certificate of divorce.' ³² Well, I'm telling you, anyone who divorces his wife except for sexual immorality causes her to commit adultery, and whoever marries a divorced woman commits adultery.

³³ "Again, you've heard it was said to those of old, 'You shall not commit perjury, but swear your oaths before the Lord.' ³⁴ Well, I'm telling you not to swear oaths at all, neither by heaven, because it is God's throne, ³⁵ nor by earth, because it is his footstool, nor by Jerusalem, because it is the city of the great king, ³⁶ nor are you to swear by your head, because you can't make any of your hairs white or black. ³⁷ But let what you say be simply, 'Yes, yes,' or 'No, no.' To do anything more than this is to do wrong.

³⁸ "You've heard that it was said, 'An eye for an eye and a tooth for a tooth.' ³⁹ Well, I'm telling you not to resist someone who's treating you badly, but whoever strikes you on your right cheek, offer them your other cheek as well. ⁴⁰ And if someone wants to sue you to take your tunic, let them have your coat as well. ⁴¹ And whoever forces you to go with them for a mile, go with them for two. ⁴² Give to anyone who asks you for something, and don't refuse someone wanting to borrow something from you.

⁴³ "You've heard it was said, 'You shall love your neighbor, and you shall hate your enemy.' ⁴⁴ Well, I'm telling you, love your enemies and pray for those who are persecuting you, ⁴⁵ so that you may be children of your Father in heaven, because he brings his sun up to shine on the bad and the good and sends rain on the just and the unjust. ⁴⁶ For if you love only those who love you, what reward is there in that? Don't even tax collectors do the same? ⁴⁷ And if you say hello only to your friends, what's so special about that? Don't

even gentiles do that, too? [48] So you are to be perfect as your Father in heaven is perfect."

Thinking About Matthew

The source that Matthew and Luke share had the saying about the Law's permanent validity, that not a stroke of it was to be set aside (Matt 5:18; Luke 16:17). In this, the first of the five speeches into which Matthew has gathered sayings of Jesus, this statement receives further elaboration and introduces one of the most influential passages in the New Testament.

The evidence suggests that Jesus never spoke against the Law. His disputes were all about how best to apply it. If we think of Jesus in the way John the Baptist portrays him in Matthew, namely as the judge to come, there is no way Matthew would want to suggest that Jesus watered down the Law, let alone set it aside. Matthew leaves people in no doubt. For Jesus, the Law and the Prophets, one of the standard ways of speaking of Israel's Scripture, are to be upheld.

Some have translated 5:17 using the word "fulfill" and interpreted it to mean that according to Matthew Jesus came in fulfillment of the Law and Prophets and so to replace them. This cannot be Matthew's meaning as the following context shows. Quite the opposite: the Law and the Prophets remain in force and will remain in force forever, as long as there is a heaven and an earth.

It is important to read these statements in the light of their wider context, especially the verses that follow. Again, some have read the contrast between what was said to those of old through the Law with what Jesus now says, as Jesus replacing the old. On the contrary, Matthew is having Jesus spell out how such commands are to be understood when they are taken seriously. There were also Jewish authors of the time who similarly sought to spell out what a serious understanding of the Law demands.

When Matthew has Jesus refer in 5:19 to people who might teach that parts of the Law might be set aside, he may just mean that generally. More likely he is alluding to those in the Jesus movement who were setting some laws aside. Did Matthew not agree with the general agreement to set aside the biblical Law that gentiles be circumcised if they want to join the people of God (Gen 17:10–14)? Luke, who also brings the saying about not setting a stroke of a letter aside (Luke 16:17), sees this exception as warranted only by divine intervention and an agreement among the apostles (Acts 15). Others went much further, including Mark, who has Jesus set aside food and purity laws as never really having made sense (Mark 7:15, 19), something which, we shall see, Matthew corrects when he comes to that part of Mark in Matt 13. Perhaps by saying in 5:19 that such teachers will be least in the kingdom of heaven yet will still belong there, Matthew really is reflecting disputes within the churches of his day.

Alternatively, he may be responding to criticism from fellow Jews who are alleging, as some did, that this new movement was abandoning the sacred Law. Quite the contrary, Matthew has Jesus insist in 5:20 that true followers of Jesus need to hold to a higher standard than the scribes and Pharisees whom he often depicts as so proud of their strict adherence to the Law.

When in what follows in 5:21–48 Matthew then has Jesus extrapolate from the saying about upholding the Law to the letter, we see that the focus is not on minute details and intricate observance but primarily on ethical values. In other words, Matthew, following what we know from Jesus, puts the emphasis on how to follow the Law in a way that is most in harmony with how he understands God, namely as loving and compassionate, the emphasis already clearly apparent in the Beatitudes.

Matthew has Jesus illustrate this emphasis by addressing six issues: anger, adultery, divorce, oaths, revenge, and treatment of enemies. Matthew skillfully introduces each in a similar way and has the focus of the first and the last match in the sense that they both reject hatred and affirm love. When Matthew has Jesus refer to the traditional instruction taught to the people from the beginning, he does so not to set it aside, but to spell out what it needs to mean when seen in the perspective of real caring behavior. While anger is a feeling, like other feelings, such as pain, delight, or fear, and a natural part of being human, the issue addressed here is holding onto anger, harboring anger, embracing hate. The message is clear. Don't just keep the commandment not to murder; think more deeply. Don't kill people in your thoughts and attitudes!

It is never wrong to have a feeling. The issue is what you do with it. Anger is usually a second feeling, which follows the feeling of hurt or fear. It is, therefore, in itself, like any feeling, neither good nor bad. It depends what you do with it. Some people have read this passage as declaring that the feeling of anger is itself something evil, and sometimes this is the message they have learned from those around them. Never feel anger. Never acknowledge being angry. It leads some people to deny being angry, to swallow it, to bottle it up, often with quite harmful consequences for themselves because they channel the energy of anger against themselves. Equally harmful is when bottled up anger later comes to the surface in sometimes violent and harmful outbursts out of all proportion. Usually when people acknowledge their feeling of anger they can go back and let themselves feel why, and so connect to the pain or fear that lies behind it and then deal with it. Letting feelings control us instead of controlling feelings can be disastrous for ourselves and for others. Love takes the command not to kill and tells us not even to contemplate letting anger determine what we do.

Matthew often shapes sayings of Jesus into three parts. Here, too, he has Jesus spell out instances of acting out of anger, including verbal abuse, and declares that all such behavior is to be condemned, citing as samples three different locations where that condemnation should be carried out, concluding with the ultimate penalty of being consigned to Gehenna. There are simply stylistic variations rather than indications of the relative severity of each offence. Gehenna means the valley of Hinnom, which runs down the east side of Jerusalem and where rubbish was burned. It became an image of the place where people believed God would consign the wicked, often described simply as hell. John the Baptist had used such language and it belonged also to the vocabulary of Jesus and the early church.

Matthew brings further sayings of Jesus to reinforce the teaching about not harboring anger. The first is the striking suggestion that someone about to make an offering in the temple should first go back home and deal with an unresolved conflict. The second is about sorting out a conflict over money. Both emphasize the importance of dealing with conflict in relationships and behind both is the assumption that love, not hate, is to be the way of life. The sixth issue will match this focus when it challenges people to love their enemies.

The second issue relates to how to handle sexual feelings. It is not enough just to keep the command not to commit adultery. Men—and it is men who are in mind—need to take responsibility for how they manage their sexual feelings. Like feelings of anger just addressed, sexual feelings are a natural part of being human. Directing them toward another man's wife is adulterous, whether it eventuates in action or not. Prohibiting men from lusting after other men's wives is already part of the Ten Commandments, where we read: "You shall not covet your neighbor's house; you shall not covet your neighbor's wife, or male or female slave, or ox, or donkey, or anything that belongs to your neighbor" (Exod 20:17). In a male dominated age, wives were often treated as a man's property and so adultery seen as a form of theft, quite apart from the major disruption to a household and its future which could occur when a man's wife was pregnant with another man's baby. In our day, with effective contraception, the grounds have shifted especially to the sense of hurt and betrayal experienced when intimate connections and commitments are broken.

Some translate the saying in 5:28 as indicating that any man looking at a woman and having a sexual response to her is an adulterer. Apart from this not being the way Matthew uses such language elsewhere, it leads to the conclusion that even sexual feeling in itself is something evil. This misreading had serious consequences as some parts of the church began to see sex and sexual feelings as sinful. Such thought contributed to movements that saw marriage as a compromise with evil for weak people and to be avoided and even to the belief that the human body, itself, must be evil. Some went even further and claimed that the physical world must be the creation of an evil god, not the true God, an aberration that the church in its wisdom rejected.

Seriously playful exaggeration marks some of Jesus' sayings, and this certainly applies to the advice to pluck out your eye or cut off your hand, although history shows that some took this literally or read "hand" as a reference to the male penis and so thought they should castrate themselves. In the ancient world the right side was seen as the more valuable. The point of such extreme statements, similarly to the one about leaving one's gift in the temple, is that people need to take seriously how they manage their God-given feelings and not just think about whether or not they are breaking commandments.

Divorce, the next topic, was a normal part of Jewish society. Usually, it was the man who divorced his wife. He gave her a certificate that would then free her to marry someone else. Where it was still accepted to have more than one wife, such as we see in the stories of Abraham and Jacob in Genesis, conflict in a marriage often did not end in divorce but in the man taking another wife, and there are stories of men then falling in love again with their first wife. When, under the influence of Greco-Roman culture, polygamy, having more than one wife, sometimes called polygyny, came to be seen as unacceptable, as had happened among some Jewish groups by the time of Jesus, then the alternative after conflict was divorce.

There were debates then about what could be legitimate grounds for divorce, some taking a strict line that the only ground was sexual immorality (the view of the School of Shammai according to rabbinic sources) and others allowing lesser grounds such as bad cooking (the School of Hillel). The potential for abuse of women was huge. Almost certainly, Jesus' reaction was to reject divorce altogether and insist it was never meant to be. While some might see in this a setting aside of the Law, Jewish authors of the period would rather see it as being very strict about keeping the Law and its intent, and they sometimes made similar judgments.

If divorce is not to be recognized and marriages deemed to remain intact, then, of course anyone divorcing his wife and marrying another commits adultery against his first wife, who remains his wife. Matthew focuses in this version of the prohibition on what it means for a woman. The husband, by divorcing her, forces her to the most viable option, remarriage, which therefore amounts to making her commit adultery, unless she still had the option of returning to her family or had found means, moral or otherwise, to gain financial support.

Some took Jesus' prohibition of divorce as an absolute command, but others, more in tune with Jesus' approach to interpreting the Law from the perspective of God's compassion, applied it more flexibly. Paul, for instance, having cited Jesus' prohibition in writing to the Corinthians, went on with some reluctance to acknowledge that in some circumstances such as when a non-believing partner pushed for it, it could be appropriate (1 Cor 7:10–16). Matthew's version of the prohibition, here and in 19:9, allows for an exception, namely sexual immorality, almost certainly meaning adultery. The exception may well have been assumed already from the start because it was indeed law in the empire that where adultery had taken place, a marriage must be dissolved. Later generations would seek to show appropriate flexibility, especially where there had been domestic violence but also in time when a marriage had broken down to the point where the more compassionate option for all was to dissolve it.

Another example of making the Law even stricter is the fourth issue where Jesus insists on straight and honest talk and proposes that people do away with needing to back up what they say by swearing oaths, a stance that also found echoes among some other Jewish authors of the time. To turn Jesus' statements into a fixed law prohibiting oaths, as some have demanded, misses what it is seeking to do.

The issue of how to apply Jesus' statements comes up again in the fifth issue addressed, retaliation. The point of Jesus' statements is to plead for flexibility and generosity, not vindictive revenge. To take it as instruction that people should stay in abusive relationships is to miss the point. Similarly, to take it as rejection of any restraint against abuse and aggression, such as is necessary in a community of law and order, is similarly not to understand the focus of what is being said. That focus comes to clear expression in the command to love one's enemies based on an appeal to God's goodness and generosity. Let God be your model for how to engage with people!

These are the profound perspectives which inform all six of the issues that Matthew has Jesus address. His concluding words about being perfect are more about total commitment to love than about ticking boxes to convince oneself that all commandments have been kept. Luke's version of this saying has Jesus speak of the need to be compassionate as God is compassionate (Luke 6:36). Certainly, the kind of perfection and completeness or maturity about which Jesus is speaking in Matthew has to do with such love and compassion. Matthew will have Jesus echo this perspective as he brings the Sermon on the Mount toward its conclusion when he has Jesus state: "Everything you want people to do for you, do the same for them; for this is what the Law and Prophets are about" (Matt 7:12).

Reflection: Should all commandments be given equal weight, no matter how large or small?

Genuine Devotion (Matthew 6:1–18)

Listening to Matthew

6:1 "Mind you don't make a show of doing what is right in front of people to get noticed. If you do, you won't get any reward from your Father in heaven. **2** So when you make charitable donations, don't announce it with a trumpet like the hypocrites do in the synagogues and on the streets to win people's admiration. Truly, I'm telling you, they get their reward, **3** but when you make a charitable donation, don't let your left hand know what your right hand is doing, **4** so that your generous act may remain hidden and your Father who sees what is hidden will reward you.

5 "And when you pray, you're not to be like the hypocrites who like to stand praying in the synagogues and on street corners to be seen by people. Truly, I'm telling you, they're getting their reward, **6** but you, when you pray, withdraw into your room and close the door and pray to your Father hidden from attention and your Father who sees what is hidden will reward you.

7 "And when you pray don't babble on like gentiles do, who think that they'll be heard if they use lots of words. **8** Don't be like them, because your Father knows what needs you have before you ask him.

9 "Pray like this when you pray:
Our Father in heaven, may your name be treated as holy;
10 may your kingdom come;
may your will be done, as in heaven so also on earth.
11 Give us today the bread we need for today;
12 and forgive the debts of guilt we owe,
as we also forgive the debts of guilt owed to us.
13 And don't lead us into testing times,

but save us from the evil one.
¹⁴ "For if you forgive people their wrongdoings toward you, your Father in heaven will also forgive you. ¹⁵ If you don't forgive people, your Father also won't forgive you your wrongdoings.
¹⁶ "And when you fast, don't become gloomy looking like the hypocrites, because they screw up their faces so that they can be recognized by people as fasting. Truly, I tell you, they get their reward. ¹⁷ But you, when you fast, use some hair oil on your head and wash your face, ¹⁸ so that you won't be seen by people to be fasting but by your Father in secret, and your Father who sees in secret will reward you."

Thinking About Matthew

The word I have translated by "doing what is right" in 6:1 is the same word used for goodness, justice, righteousness. Matthew portrays Jesus addressing three aspects of doing what is right the wrong way: making charitable donations (traditionally spoken of as giving alms), prayer, and fasting. Matthew sets it out neatly with matching statements linked to each. Only in the case of the second, prayer, does Matthew bring additional material, most significantly, the version of the Lord's Prayer that forms the basis of the one we commonly use.

The word for charitable donations (traditionally, "alms") is also the word for mercy or compassion, so refers to giving as an act of compassion. It was a standard expectation that people made such donations, which would then be used to help the needy, important in a society without anything like the social welfare systems that are in place in many societies today.

Matthew has Jesus say: "Don't do things to get admired!" Profiled in Matthew by John the Baptist as the judge to come, Jesus, the judge, tells people, "Don't do it!" From a broader perspective we know that Jesus did much more than that. Indeed, he was criticized for not telling sinners off but engaging with them and inviting them into a restored relationship with God. In the light of the broader perspective, we might want to say: Don't do these things to win approval and admiration. Stop yourself and ask why you are wanting to do so. What need in yourself are you wanting to address? Opening yourself to God's love and acceptance, learning to love and accept yourself, will free you from such need. You won't then spend your time and energy trying to get acceptance and love from others. Paul, in particular, helps us see that this is the best way to help change behavior, rather than giving people commands about what not to do. Don't do it, but don't stop there. Deal with why.

One way to take the advice Matthew has Jesus give is to focus narrowly on getting rewards. It is as if to say: make earning rewards from God your goal. At worst that is just transferring your goal of greed to God. Helping people not because you care but because you think it will win you a reward, even a reward from God, is not love; it can in effect just be using people and their needs for your own ends. At another level, it is not inappropriate to seek to live a life that is rewarding. Jesus does appeal to our self-interest when he points us to the way of life. Loving oneself, loving others, loving God is indeed the way to a fulfilling life, but it means a total embracing of all three that sees them not as competing but as completing a wholeness in which love generates love and in that sense is its own reward and has its origin in the heart of God. It is to live in oneness with God.

This broader perspective addresses also the sad folly of trying to win others' acceptance and admiration through making a show of prayer or of fasting. Fasting is, indeed, the opposite. It is to take time out to withdraw even from the reward of food, in order to refocus one's life on what matters.

Matthew has Jesus portray such folly as characteristic of hypocrites, people who are playing a game of "Like me!" Matthew would be badly misread if we thought he was having all fellow Jews declared as hypocrites. Some certainly would have played such games as some still do in the church, let alone in the wider community. Prayer, including praying about our needs and the needs of others, is deeply personal and not something for display. And corporate prayer also has God as its focus, not the splendor of rhetoric that can turn it into performance and turn it into a vehicle for persuasion and teaching as sometimes occurs in church services. The comments about gentiles babbling on is a generalization that does not do them justice. We, too, can all be good at babbling on.

Matthew inserts Jesus' teaching about a simple, straightforward prayer that he found in the source he shared with Luke (Luke 11:2–4), which we know as the Lord's Prayer. Luke's version is even simpler, beginning just with "Father," and not containing the reference to God's will being done on earth as in heaven, nor the reference to being saved from the evil one. Matthew's version may well have already existed in expanded form. Its balanced phrases may reflect its use already as a regular part of worship.

"Father" was a traditional way of addressing God, and it appears that it was often used by Jesus, so much so that we occasionally find the simple Aramaic word for "father," namely "abba," retained even in the Greek of the New Testament (Rom 8:15; Gal 4:6). Fathers could be aloof and authoritarian, but also caring and affectionate. The latter appears to lie behind Jesus' use and matches, for instance, his image of the father in the parable of the prodigal son. Within their social system the male parent was dominant, whereas in ours, we affirm that both mothers and fathers can be models of compassion, and it is a step backward to remain bound by male dominated imagery.

Luke's simple "Father" will likely preserve the original and "in heaven" likely reflects an elaboration from Matthew's context, who uses it frequently in rewriting Jesus' sayings, as we can see in these three blocks of sayings. The first three lines of the prayer are not really asking God to do anything but rather affirming a wish and a commitment. "Hallowed be your name" is the traditional translation of the first, which is really an expression of commitment to treating God as holy. "Name" here is not the label but simply an alternative way of speaking of the person of God. To treat God as holy or to treat anyone as holy is to respect their otherness, their identity, and let them be for us who they really are and stand in awe of that. It is indeed the secret of all good relationships. I need to let God be God for me, the God who loves me, challenges me, and invites me to partnership.

That God's kingdom may come is the longing at the heart of the movement, from John the Baptist onward. It is central to the message of Jesus and therefore to following him. In substance it means revolution, change, the placing of love at the center of community and belonging, as reflected in Jesus' image of a great feast where there is a place for all who would come. It is a hope about the future, but also for the present, namely that its reality may break into our world already through peace, justice, renewal, and love. It coheres well with Matthew's insistence that this must show itself in behavioral change that we have the addition about doing God's will here on earth.

Basic needs then come into focus in the requests that follow: enough food, forgiveness, and security. It is not as though we might think of God as pondering whether or not to feed people, like a heavenly version of a distracted human ruler who needs to have things drawn to his attention and is otherwise distracted with his own agenda. These are utterances of basic human need, however they are answered. The request for forgiveness follows, facing up to ourselves, which love makes it safe to do. It is to acknowledge failure and wrongdoing, accept forgiveness and move on, prepared to change. God is the model for forgiveness, including our forgiving others. God's love helps us face up to ourselves and, when we do, helps us then change. God does not hold back such love, nor are we to do so. Matthew reinforces this concern by adding a saying about forgiving that he found in Mark 11:25.

The final request is the basic human desire not to face hard times. Again, it is mistaken to imagine God as like a universal manager who determines when to turn on hard times and when to turn them off. Rather, this is a genuine human cry. Matthew's addition can refer to "the evil one" or just to "evil" and could even just be another way of speaking of hard times. The final words which conclude our common versions of the Lord's Prayer, "For the kingdom, the power, and the glory are yours, now and forever. Amen" are found only in later manuscripts of Matthew's Gospel and will have been added at a later stage to round off the prayer as it was used in worship.

Fasting is the last of the three topics and again emphasizes authenticity. No room for putting on a show to impress people here, either. Authenticity is the theme throughout. And while healing and change best comes when people come to terms with the need that drives inauthenticity, they do need to be challenged to desist while they do so. That can take time because strategies to compensate for a sense of inadequacy and insecurity become ingrained. There are so many examples, including of people in public life whose sad obsession with finding attention and approval helps neither them nor those around them.

It is important to take feedback seriously, whether negative or positive, and to allow ourselves to take it on board including the feelings it may evoke, of disappointment or joy. When, however, our focus shifts from our goal to the winning of positive feedback, we lose our way.

Reflection: Why do people seek to impress, and how can we help them address this pattern of behavior?

Setting Goals and Gaining Perspective (Matthew 6:19–34)

Listening to Matthew

6:19 "Don't store up treasures for yourselves here on earth where moth and rust ruin things and where burglars break in and steal things. **20** Rather, store up treasures for yourselves in heaven where there's no moths or rust to ruin things and where burglars don't break in and steal. **21** For where your treasure is, that's where your mind will be.

22 "The light of the body is the eye and if your eye is wholesome, then your whole body will have light, **23** but if your eye is not okay, then your whole body will be in the dark. And if the light that's meant to give you light is darkness, then that's really dark.

24 "No one can serve two masters, because they'll either hate the one and love the other or stick with the one and hate the other. You can't serve God and money.

25 "So that's why I'm telling you, don't get anxious about your life, what you're going to eat [or what you're going to drink] or about your body, what you're going to wear. Isn't your life more than food and your body more than clothing? **26** Look at the birds; they neither sow nor harvest nor gather produce into barns, and yet your heavenly Father feeds them. Aren't you worth more than them? **27** Which of you by worrying can make your life one bit longer? **28** And why do you worry about what you're going to wear? Learn from the lilies growing in the field, because not even Solomon in all his glory was as resplendent as one of them. **30** If God clothes the grass in the field which is alive today and tomorrow will be put into the oven for burning, how much more do you reckon he will clothe you, my friends of little faith?

31 "So don't be anxious, saying, What are we going to eat or what are we going to drink or what are we going to wear? **32** For gentiles bother about all such things. Your heavenly Father knows you need all these things. [33] But make the kingdom [of God] your top priority and his justice and you'll be supplied with all these things. [34] Don't worry about tomorrow, because tomorrow can worry about itself. Today's trouble is enough for today."

Thinking About Matthew

Setting goals is so important. A goal or life purpose has an integrating effect. We consciously or unconsciously shape our lives in the light of it. It generates its own dynamic and changes us. When, for instance, people plan to get married, they make preparations, but beyond that most of what they do will be colored or shaped by that upcoming event. Setting goals works that way.

That is part of the logic that runs through this passage. Your mind or heart will be in what you treasure and set as your highest value and goal. The warning about not setting wealth as a goal has timeless relevance. A narrow reading of the statement about treasures could pervert the saying into another invitation to greed. Go for the treasure. This would be to mistake the serious playfulness of the saying. It is not about getting treasures in heaven; it is about finding fulfillment by setting your mind on sharing in God's love, bearing it to others and taking it seriously for yourself.

The playful image of the healthy eye as opposed to the sick one is making the same point. Clear sight brings everything into focus. Lack of focus is darkness and by implication leaves our lives without vision. The saying about slaves trying to serve two masters is making the same point. Clearly, Matthew is having Jesus confront greed for wealth in particular, a plague that still powerfully afflicts our modern world.

The section about worry might just sound like a bit of stress management. The sayings will have their initial context in Jesus' sending disciples out on mission in the region around Galilee. As Matthew reports in Matt 10, Jesus sent them out with virtually nothing. The expectation was that they would be put up and supported by locals. It will have worked in their setting. It then became a pattern, especially for visiting apostles and preachers and in some ways is the ancestor of the ministerial stipend, meant not to be a wage but a living allowance.

Over time, especially as the movement spread, it was not always practicable to carry out ministry in this way. Paul, for instance, decided that in some contexts it was more appropriate for him to work part time. Those who took Jesus' words of commission as inflexible rules saw Paul as out of step with Jesus and, they alleged, as failing to trust God to supply their need. It is one of many instances where love and common sense came into conflict with fundamentalist and legalistic approaches. Paul devotes 1 Cor 9 to defending his stance.

As these verses now stand in Matthew, they can address new contexts, even those where patterns of ministry have changed. They now serve to challenge the obsession with immediate need and the way it can overwhelm or distract people from what really matters. There is a touch of generalized stereotyping in the comment about gentiles, reflected elsewhere in Matthew, like in the comment about their prayers (Matt 6:7; similarly, 18:17) and reflecting his predominantly Jewish setting. The issue addressed, however, is, in reality, universal.

The passage also challenges the debilitating effect such anxiety can have. Trust does not mean abandoning self-care, but it does mean not losing the focus on what matters most. In reality, people need to plan, develop budgets, take responsibility for addressing their needs, work for a wage, find clothes and food and drink, but these are not the main game but rather the caring that enables a person to be an effective partner of God.

The passage ends as it began with the challenge to make God and sharing God's life, God's kingdom, the vision of justice, our highest priority, and then letting all other needs be seen from that perspective. Such centeredness not only brings perspective. It also relieves anxiety and produces attitudes and behavior that cohere with the goal and so shape our lives to serve love and care for ourselves and others because that is what the goal is about.

The passage about anxiety can be used in ways that are unhelpful and unhealthy. Encouraging disciples not to be anxious in Galilee as they go out on mission because their basic needs would be met is one thing. Telling people generally they should not feel anxiety is another. Anxiety, like fear and other feelings like joy, sadness, hunger, sexual desire, etc., is a God-given part of being human and belongs to the range of sensors through which our bodies alert us to reality. We need to take our sensors seriously, so to try to suppress anxiety in ourselves or others makes little sense. Indeed, it can heighten the anxiety and lead even to feelings of anxiety where we no longer know why we are anxious or even to more serious anxiety states. Seen from the broad perspective of the gospel of love, our response to anxiety in ourselves and others needs to be to listen to it and hear what it is telling us, and that way we can address what needs to be addressed to lessen the fear that feeds it.

Sometimes, that entails dealing with fears about tomorrow and beyond, but that is something different from being anxious about tomorrow. It is about dealing with why this may be so and facing the future openly and planning, so that the fears that generate anxiety are allayed. That may be as simple as Jesus' assurance to his apostles that they would be looked after, but it may need to entail much more.

Telling someone, "Don't be anxious" when it means "Don't acknowledge and face up to reality" is the opposite of care and common sense. When we are given safe space to face reality, then we can also see the folly of obsessing about what in the end is not so important, including immediate incidentals of food and clothing. Then we can give them the attention they need, but no more, and reset our lives in the light of our ultimate priority to share God's life and love in our world.

Reflection: In what ways can readings of this passage potentially enhance human wellbeing or potentially harm it? How does the integrative effect of having goals work?

Love Matters Most (Matthew 7:1–29)

Listening to Matthew

7:1 "Don't be judgmental, so you don't get judged yourself. **2** For the judgments you use to condemn people will be used against you and the criteria you use will be used against you. **3** Why are you looking at the speck in your brother's eye and not noticing the log in your own eye? **4** Or how can you say to your brother, 'Let me be remove the speck from your eye,' when there's a log in your own eye? **5** Hypocrite, first remove the log from your own eye and then you'll see clearly to remove the speck from your brother's eye.

6 "Don't give what is holy to dogs nor throw your pearls down in front of pigs, lest they trample on them with their feet and turn and attack you.

7 "Ask and you will receive; seek and you will find; knock and the door will be opened for you. **8** For everyone who asks will get what they ask for and those seeking will find what they're looking for and those knocking will have the door opened for them. **9** Who among you if his son would ask him for bread would give him a rock, **10** or for a fish and would give him a snake? **11** If you wicked people know how to give good gifts to your children, how much more will your Father in heaven give good gifts to those who ask him for them.

12 "Everything you want people to do for you, do the same for them, for this is what the Law and the Prophets are about.

13 "Enter through the narrow gate, because the gate that leads to ruin is wide and easy to take and many go that way. **14** The gate that leads to life is narrow and not easy and those who find their way through it are few.

15 "Watch out for false prophets, who come to you dressed up like sheep, but inside are ravenous wolves. **16** You'll recognize them from their fruits. People don't gather grapes from thorn bushes, do they, or figs from thistles? [17] So every good tree produces good fruit and a sick tree produces bad fruit. [18] A good tree can't produce bad fruit nor a sick tree good fruit. [19] Every tree which fails to produce good fruit is cut down and thrown into the fire. [20] So you'll recognize them by their fruit.

[21] "Not everyone who says, 'Lord, Lord,' to me will enter the kingdom of heaven but only those who do the will of my Father in heaven. [22] Many will say to me on that day, 'Lord, Lord, haven't we prophesied in your name and cast out demons in your name and performed many wonders in your name?' [23] And then I'll make it clear to them, 'I never knew you. Get away from me you who perpetrate lawless behavior.'

[24] "All who hear my words and do them will be like a wise man who built his house on a rock; [25] and the rain came, and the rivers rose, and the wind blew and buffeted that house, and it didn't collapse because its foundations were on a rock. [26] And those who hear my words and don't do them will be like a foolish man who built his house on sand; [27] and the rain came, and the rivers rose, and the wind blew and buffeted that house, and it collapsed, and it was a huge catastrophe."

[28] Now when Jesus had finished saying these things, the crowds were amazed at his teaching; [29] because he was teaching them as a person with authority and not like their scribes.

Thinking About Matthew

The final sections of Matthew's collection of Jesus' sayings, the Sermon on the Mount, appear to be targeted toward members of faith communities of Matthew's time. Warnings against being judgmental toward others are appropriate for any community. We should probably not take the neatly balanced formulations too literally. It was surely not intended to imply that if people engage in corruption in condemning others, God would also engage in corruption!

Playful rhetoric is again in action in the saying about removing a log from one's own eye before trying to remove a speck from another's eye. Community does not work well when people are judgmental. In chapter 13 Matthew has Jesus emphasize that people should leave judging to God and not try to pull weeds out growing among the wheat; otherwise, the whole crop could be destroyed. Handling conflict is clearly an issue that Matthew sees a need to address. Already in chapter 5 he had Jesus address the handling of anger and then challenged retaliation and hatred of enemies. And in chapter 18 he sets out some rules for dealing with conflict creatively.

While the imagery makes sense in the saying about giving what is holy to dogs and throwing down pearls in front of pigs, it is not clear what Matthew sees the saying targeting. Dogs and pigs often served as images for gentiles. The issue of the holy and clean and unclean informs the image. Pigs were seen as unclean. The saying might just be advising people to be careful what they share and with whom, but it may well be a warning against having too close a contact with gentiles, especially gentiles who did not belong to the faith or rejected it, as opposed to reaching out to gentiles with the good news.

The neat playful rhetoric meets us again in the promises about receiving what you ask for, finding what you are looking for, and having doors opened for you. It is reinforced with the appeal to people to see God as like a parent wanting to respond to need in ways that are appropriate and kind. Taken out of context these sayings have sometimes fed the fantasy that greedy people could get whatever they want from God, from big, flashy cars to palatial dwellings. Rather, the sayings appear to address the need for disciples engaged in mission to trust and hope, something that would have made sense in the early contexts where people's wants were for basic food and support.

The so-called golden rule, a principle found also elsewhere among teachers of the time, states simply that people should treat others the way they want to be treated themselves. Matthew has Jesus take it up and suggest that it is really what the Law and the Prophets, Scripture, is about. That stands in contrast to other approaches to Scripture that focus on demands and commands, not on well-being. This principle follows well after the appeal to see God as like a caring parent.

The saying about gates also stands on its own without any close connection to the context but is clear in its message. It warns against what it sees as the way of the majority. It is a salutary warning against the tendencies in every age to conform to what most other people are doing. When this happens, too often the needs of minorities and those at whose expense everyone else is happy are overlooked. A faith perspective committed to love and justice for all will find itself sometimes needing to take a minority position, not for the sake of doing so, but because love is never to be watered down.

Who might the false prophets be? It seems that Matthew portrays Jesus as warning about people within his own movement, as is then explicit in the verses which follow. Matthew has Jesus warn against teachers within the church who appear acceptable but whose lives and behavior do not cohere with faith and love. We know that fairly early on there were problems with visiting preachers who exploited the rule about support being given to such visitors. Paul had to make clear that his collecting money for the poor in Judea was not about collecting money for himself, as some alleged he was doing. There were, clearly, some who engaged in such exploitation, and they may well be in view in the reference to false prophets.

The challenge to watch out for corrupt clergy and pastors becomes explicit in 7:21-23, where Matthew has Jesus declare that he will disown them, despite their calling him "Lord" and having had impressive ministries of preaching, casting out demons, and miracles in his name. We might add: TV shows! Matthew has Jesus insist that to be his follower is to embrace a commitment to love, as expounded in the Sermon on the Mount. All the rest is just religion, however spectacular and popular, and not the way of Jesus.

Paul challenged such distortions of faith when he wrote his famous chapter on love as the sign of the Spirit in 1 Cor 13. Without it, miracles, speaking in tongues, and other claims to spiritual power are nothing when love is not present. John's Gospel similarly addresses the problem of people seeing miracles as the basis for faith, declaring that even when people believed in Jesus because of them, he did not believe in them (2:23-25). He then went on to have Jesus tell Nicodemus, who acclaimed Jesus as a teacher from God because of his miracles, that he was completely missing the point and needed to be reborn (John 3:1-3).

Matthew then reaches the end of the sermon outline which was in the source which he and Luke shared, namely with the image of building soundly. Jesus' teaching on love as expounded in all that went before is the secure foundation, both for individuals and for faith communities.

At the conclusion of the speech, Matthew uses the same formulation to be found also after the other four speeches which he has compiled, namely with the words, "Now when Jesus had finished saying these things . . ." In this first instance in 7:29 he picks up a verse he found in Mark, in the introduction to what was Mark's first episode in Jesus' public life about Jesus' teaching in the synagogue, and which Matthew otherwise passes over. Mark wrote: "And they were amazed at his teaching because he was teaching them as one who had authority and not like the scribes" (Mark 1:22). It fit well as a response to the Sermon on the Mount. Matthew's revision reads "their scribes" because for Matthew there were also scribes within his faith communities, as indicated in Matt 13:52.

The effect of the way Matthew concludes Jesus' speech is to bring it as a challenge to the people of his time and people since, in particular to members of the community of faith, including leaders in the church. It becomes a major trend in Matthew to shape and reshape Jesus' words so that they address believers of Matthew's own time (and so address believers of all time). In particular, Matthew puts the focus on living out the faith in daily life. This reaches a climax in the closing speech of Jesus' public ministry in Matthew where we have an image of judgment day (Matt 25:31–46). Judgment is based on whether people have demonstrated love toward those in need in their community. This is not about earning credit by doing good works. It is about demonstrating an ongoing commitment to be partners with God in love.

Reflection: In what ways does Matthew's Sermon on the Mount have Jesus address issues of Matthew's day—and our own day?

An Outsider's Faith (Matthew 8:1–13)

Listening to Matthew

⁸:¹ When Jesus came down from the hill, many crowds followed him. ² And, lo and behold, a leper approached him and, kneeling down in front of him, said, "Sir, if you're happy to do so, you can heal me." ³ So Jesus stretched out his hand and touched him, saying, "I am happy to do so. Be healed!" and straightaway his leprosy left him. ⁴ Then Jesus said to him, "Don't tell anyone, but go and show yourself to the priest, and make the offering which Moses laid down, as evidence for them."

⁵ When he entered Capernaum, a centurion approached him wanting help ⁶ and asked him, "Sir, a slave of mine is laid low at my place, paralyzed, and suffering terribly." ⁷ And Jesus said, "Am I to come and heal him?" ⁸ In response the centurion said, "Sir, I'm not worthy that you come under my roof, but just say the word, and my servant will be healed. ⁹ You see, I'm a person with authority, having soldiers under me, and I give the command to one, 'Go!' and he goes and to another, 'Come!' and he comes and to my slave, 'Do this!' and he does it." ¹⁰ When Jesus heard this, he was amazed and said to those following him, "Truly I tell you, I haven't found such faith like this in anyone in Israel. ¹¹ I tell you, many will come from east and west and take their place at table with Abraham and Isaac and Jacob in the kingdom of heaven, ¹² and the kingdom's own children will be thrown out into darkness and there'll be weeping and grinding of teeth." ¹³ Then Jesus said to the centurion, "Go, let it turn out for you just as you believed it would." And his servant was healed at that very hour.

FOLLOWING MATTHEW

Thinking About Matthew

Matthew created a framework in which to bring his first depiction of Jesus' teaching and activity. He did so by repeating almost word for word the summary of Jesus' ministry in 4:23 and 9:35. Having brought his major collection of Jesus' teaching in chapters 5–7, the so-called Sermon on the Mount, Matthew then brings a collection of anecdotes about Jesus' activity. To appreciate them we need to enter Matthew's world, which is one where mental illness was understood as demon possession, weather as driven also by demons, and healings as achieved by acts of power, by word, or by touch.

For his opening episode Matthew chooses the story he found in Mark 1:40–45, Jesus' healing of a leper by uttering the words, "Be healed." Mark's story reflects some sensitivity about the way lepers should behave. Their leprosy, different from leprosy as it is understood today, was a contagious skin disease, and biblical law therefore required that lepers keep their distance, much as in the days of the Covid pandemic people were asked to keep distance. Some manuscripts of Mark even have Jesus backing off in anger from the leper's inappropriate approach, perhaps original, and Jesus then healing him but dealing with him sternly. Matthew drops those details and simply has Jesus utter the word of healing and send the man off to the health authorities to be certified as no longer being a leper. Jesus is here following what is laid down in the Law. One of the roles of a priest was to act as such a health authority. Getting the man to make the required offering associated with his regaining normal status was a way of making sure the priest knew that he had indeed been a leper. Matthew includes Mark's detail that Jesus told him not to talk about it because crowds were causing a problem and bringing the kind of attention which Jesus preferred to avoid. Fame is not everything. Fame for what?

Matthew's second anecdote is one he found in the source he shared with Luke, who brings it in Luke 7:1–10. It, too, needs to be read with an awareness of norms and expectations of the time. The centurion was a soldier in Rome's militia, a gentile, but not otherwise identified, and holding a rank which traditionally meant he would have command of one hundred men. He had a very sick slave. The word used here for "slave" happens also to be the word used for "child." This may explain how it is that John's Gospel seems to know a different version of the anecdote where the officer (not identified as a gentile) asks for help for his son (John 4:46–52).

Luke adds that the centurion valued the slave highly. Based on this, some, wanting to find support in the Bible for accepting homosexuality, have read into the story that the slave was in fact a slave boy for whom the centurion had sexual affection. Such sexual exploitation did and does occur. Nothing in the text, however, suggests this. It would have caused outrage then and would imply an acceptance of pederasty. Accepting and affirming sexual diversity is not helped by such quasi-fundamentalist maneuvers. It needs only an informed love, which also accepts that there are many assumptions of the ancient world which we rightly no longer share, beginning with belief in a flat earth.

I have translated Jesus' response to the centurion's request as a question. Our ancient manuscripts did not use punctuation. Jesus may have said he would go, as most translate the sentence, or he may have said, "Am I to go?" as I have translated it. The latter would reflect a very natural response of a Jew of the time, to avoid entering houses of gentiles. In any case, this is what underlies the centurion's reply when he declares himself unworthy to have Jesus do so. The healing therefore takes place at a distance.

It is noteworthy that the other instance of Jesus' healing a gentile, the Syrophoenician's daughter, also occurred at a distance (Mark 7:24-30; Matt 15:21-28). There was no absolute rule that Jews should not enter gentile homes or share meals with them, but generally it was to be avoided and certainly they were not do so on a regular basis. It was one of the things they needed to sort out once the mission spread out into the gentile world. Paul tells how the issue created tensions between himself and the more conservative Peter (Gal 2:11-14); and Luke in Acts 10 reports how God changed Peter's attitude in a vision which resulted in his overcoming his reluctance to go to the centurion Cornelius's house.

People of Matthew's time would understand the relevance of the centurion's comment about being in a position of authority to command others, because they would have understood Jesus' acts of healing as also commanding, namely commanding evil spirits which caused sickness and paralysis to stop doing so. Such stories strain credibility in our world, but they serve to convey the message that Jesus, and ultimately God, wants people to be made well and wants all to be partners in such love and care. They would not ask questions such as why, if Jesus could perform such healings at a distance, did he not extend that power to all who needed healing everywhere and commission his followers to do the same. Such was not their understanding of Jesus' ministry.

Matthew inserts into the story a saying found elsewhere in Luke about people from other nations far and wide coming to share the great feast of togetherness in the kingdom of God (Luke 13:28–29), one of Jesus' favorite images of hope, which we also enact in Holy Communion as a foretaste of that vision. This is another instance of Matthew hinting at the gentile mission to come, such as he was doing already by including foreign women in his genealogy and in having the world's wisest come and offer Jesus gifts.

Reflection: Why do you think Matthew cited the centurion as exemplary and how does it relate to the challenge then and now to be inclusive?

Tackling the Demons (Matthew 8:14–34)

Listening to Matthew

⁸:¹⁴ Then Jesus entered Peter's house and saw his mother-in-law laid low with a fever; ¹⁵ and he touched her hand, and the fever left her, and she got up and started playing host to him.

¹⁶ That evening they brought to him many who were possessed with demons, and he expelled the spirits with a word of command and healed everyone who was sick. ¹⁷ In this way the saying spoken by Isaiah the prophet found fulfillment, "He took away our illnesses and bore our diseases."

¹⁸ Seeing the crowd around him, Jesus commanded that they (he and his disciples) set off for the other side. ¹⁹ And one scribe approached him and said, "Teacher, I'll follow you wherever you go." ²⁰ And Jesus responded to him, "Foxes have holes and birds have nests, but the Son of Man has nowhere to lay his head." ²¹ Another of his disciples said to him, "Master, let me first go off and bury my father." ²² But Jesus said to him, "Follow me and let the dead bury their own dead."

²³ Then he got into the boat and his disciples followed him. ²⁴ Now there was a big storm on the lake, so much so that waves were breaking over the boat, all while he himself was asleep. ²⁵ So they came and woke him up and said, "Master, save us, we're going to die." ²⁶ He said to them, "Why are you scared, you weak-faithed lot?" Then he got up, told the wind and sea to stop, and there was a great calm. ²⁷ The people with him were amazed and said, "Who is this that the winds and the sea do what he tells them?"

²⁸ When they reached the other side, they entered the territory of the Gadarenes and two men possessed by demons came out of the cemetery to meet him. They were so very violent that no one

could travel along that way. ²⁹ And, lo and behold, they shouted out, "What business have you with us, Son of God? Have you come to torment us before the due time?"

³⁰ Now there was a large herd of pigs feeding some distance away from them ³¹ and the demons pleaded with him, "If you're going to expel us, send us into the herd of pigs." ³² So Jesus told them, "Go!" And they went and entered the pigs and, lo and behold, the whole herd then rushed off down the steep slope into the lake and drowned in the water. ³³ Those looking after them ran for their lives and, going off into the city, told people about all this and what had happened to those men who had been demon possessed. ³⁴ Then the whole city turned out to meet Jesus and, when they saw him, begged him to leave their territory.

Thinking About Matthew

When Matthew takes up Mark's story of Jesus' healing Peter's mother-in-law (Mark 1:29–31), he trims it to its bare essentials, having Jesus heal her of her fever by touching her hand. Gone is the reference to Andrew and also James and John and their asking him to help. Matthew has also changed the reference to her then playing host to them (all) to have it refer only to Jesus. Luke's version helps us see how people would have understood Jesus' act. He has Jesus rebuke the fever, that is, rebuke the fever spirit, such was their understanding, a very different pathology from ours.

Matthew follows Mark in reporting Jesus' healing activities that evening. Mark says he healed "many." Matthew changes this to "all," a tendency with which we might be familiar in telling our stories. Healings occur through the expulsion of what were believed to be evil spirits.

Such power over unclean spirits also underlies the story of the storm on the lake, which Matthew picks up from later in Mark (Mark 4:35–41). I have had personal experience of being on Lake Galilee when suddenly winds came up, presumably sea breezes coming in from the Mediterranean. Behind such forces are spirits according to their meteorology and so Jesus tells them to stop, and they do. The imagery has inspired symbolic reflection on the calm which faith can bring amid the storms of life, and perhaps Matthew is already turning the story in that direction when he uses the word for following as a disciple to portray the disciples joining Jesus in the boat.

Indeed, immediately before the story is a passage about being a disciple, which Matthew shares with Luke (Luke 9:57–62). It uses typically shocking language to challenge people to take being a disciple seriously. Of course, Jesus had a place to sleep at night, but the point of the saying about having no place is to highlight the vulnerability of becoming a disciple by highlighting Jesus' vulnerability. Son of Man, a title used for God's agent at the climax of history, also simply means a human and so is playfully set in contrast here to animals and birds.

Family loyalty was paramount, especially on a death. Whether the man's father had died or he meant he should wait until he does, the shocking reversal of norms in the next encounter belongs to Jesus' subversive actions of calling people to abandon the family social systems which in part conspired to keep some people poor.

Social and cultural norms are also significant for understanding Matthew's next story, which in Mark also follows the scene on the lake (Mark 5:1–20). Once again, Matthew has reworked it, bringing out its symbolic significance. This is the first of two occasions when Matthew's storytelling takes Mark's central figure and doubles it. So, instead of one demon possessed man as in Mark, we have two. Later he does the same with the story of blind Bartimaeus, which he turns into the healing of two blind men. This playful artistry also reflects the assumption at the time that two witnesses count much more than one and was, indeed, a principle in legal cases (Deut 17:6).

Another of Matthew's changes was to relocate the event from Gerasa, about sixty km from Lake Galilee (5:1–20), to the territory of Gadara, which reaches to the lake. As Mark's story developed, someone had not noticed that Gerasa was a rather long way for the pigs to have to run and get drowned in the Galilean lake!

Matthew's story still reflects issues which would strike any observant Jew. Jesus faced contamination: this was gentile territory; cemeteries are places deemed unclean, which does not mean evil, but are places which would render it necessary for a person to undergo ritual purification. Pigs were also unclean, and the deep was viewed as the home of evil spirits. Thus the scene is set for the encounter in Matthew with two men possessed by demons.

Matthew mentions only briefly their uncontrollable ferocity before having them confront Jesus with words which show that, as inhabitants of the spirit world, they know who he is: the Son of God. Mark had told of such an encounter already in the first anecdote he brings of Jesus' ministry where he is confronted with such a man in the synagogue who addresses him similarly (Mark 1:21–28) and mentions that the demons in other such people also recognized Jesus (Mark 1:34). Matthew omits these stories and concentrates the focus on this one encounter. It is as though he uses the scene to foreshadow what was to come at the climax of history when Jesus as God's agent, the Son of Man and Son of God, would confront evil and do away with it. Accordingly, Matthew has the evil spirits in the two men add: "Have you come to torment us before the due time?" (Matt 8:29). "Before the due time" alludes to Jesus' future role, according to Matthew, to be the judge to come.

Matthew omits Mark's account of the conversation in which Jesus asks after the name of the demons and they answer "Legion," suggestive of Rome's soldiers being a source of evil, and also omits Jesus' telling the healed man to go back home and bear witness to what had happened. Instead, Matthew simply reports the demons' demise as they return to the deep and then the hostility of the locals who want Jesus to go away.

This is another instance of our having to engage our imagination to enter a very different world from our own. What they saw as demon possession we understand with empathy as mental illness. They saw life as a battle between evil spirits and the good and resolution as victory over the devil and his angels in the interim and then finally in the end. There is a vast chasm between their understandings and ours, yet there is important common ground. They envisaged the fulfillment of the vision "Your kingdom come" as something primarily in the spirit world and its control of what happens on earth, but ultimately also as hope and healing, restoration and reconciliation for people. We embrace the same vision, however differently we explain it, and also see God's reign breaking into our reality when people are lifted out of poverty, restored to health and partnership with God, and liberated from the forces that dehumanize and destroy people. We do not personalize such forces, but we call them out as greed, abuse, violence, discrimination, and systemic oppression. They are indeed "legion," "many," but in a different sense.

Reflection: Close and far away: what do you see as the abiding relevance of such stories, and what do you see as needing to be respected as belonging to a different world?

In Collision (Matthew 9:1–35)

Listening to Matthew

⁹:¹ Then getting into the boat he crossed over and came to his own town, ² and, lo and behold, people were bringing him a paralyzed man lying on a stretcher and, when Jesus saw their faith, he told the paralyzed man, "Cheer up, my child, your sins are forgiven." ³ Then some scribes commented to each other, "This guy is blaspheming." ⁴ When Jesus noticed their concerns, he said, "Why do such wicked thoughts cross your minds? ⁵ What is easier, to say 'Your sins are forgiven' or to say, 'Get up and walk'? ⁶ But so you can know that the Son of Man has authority to forgive sins on earth"—then he said to the paralyzed man—"Get up, take your stretcher and go home." ⁷ He got up and went home. ⁸ When the crowds saw this, they were filled with awe and glorified God who had given such authority to human beings.

⁹ As Jesus was moving on from there, he saw a man sitting at the customs post, called Matthew, and said to him, "Follow me!" And he got up and followed him. ¹⁰ And then it happened that he was having a meal at his place when, lo and behold, many toll collectors and sinners came and joined Jesus and the disciples at the meal. ¹¹ Seeing this, the Pharisees started saying to his disciples, "Why is your teacher eating with toll collectors and sinners?" ¹² When Jesus heard them, he said, "The well don't need a doctor; the sick do. ¹³ Go and learn what this means, 'I want compassion not sacrifice'; because I didn't come to summon the righteous, but sinners."

¹⁴ Then John's disciples came to him and asked, "Why do we and the Pharisees fast, but your disciples don't?" ¹⁵ Jesus told them, "The bridegroom's men can't be mournful as long as the bridegroom is with them. But the days will come when the bridegroom will be

taken away from them and then they'll fast. ¹⁶ No one sews a piece of unshrunk cloth onto an old garment; otherwise, the patch will pull away from the garment and the tear will become worse. ¹⁷ And no one puts new wine into old wineskins; otherwise, the wineskins will burst and the wine will pour out and wineskins will be lost; but they put new wine into new wineskins and both are preserved."

¹⁸ While he was telling them this, one of the leaders came and knelt before him, saying, "My daughter has died just now, but please come and lay your hand on her and she will come back to life." ¹⁹ Jesus got up and followed him along with his disciples.

²⁰ Then, lo and behold, a woman who'd had a hemorrhage for twelve years came up behind him and touched the fringe of his garment. ²¹ For she had been telling herself, "If only I can touch his garment, I'll be cured." ²² Jesus turned round and saw her and said, "Cheer up, my daughter; your faith has cured you." And the woman was cured from that very hour.

²³ So Jesus came to the leader's house and saw the flute players and the upset crowd ²⁴ and started saying, "Go away. The girl hasn't died. She's just sleeping." And they laughed at him. ²⁵ When the crowd had gone, he went inside and took her by the hand, and she got up. ²⁶ His reputation for doing this spread through the whole land.

²⁷ As he was moving on from there, two blind men followed him and called out to him, "Have pity on us, Son of David." ²⁸ When he got home, the blind men approached him, and Jesus asked them, "Do you believe I can do this?" They answered him, "Yes, sir." ²⁹ Then he touched their eyes and said, "May it happen for you according to your faith." ³⁰ And their eyes were opened and Jesus told them sternly, "Mind, you don't let anyone know." ³¹ But they went off and spread his fame in that whole region.

³² As they were leaving, people brought a man possessed of a demon that rendered him unable to speak. ³³ Once the demon was expelled, the man could talk again. And the crowds were amazed saying, "There's never been anything like this in Israel." ³⁴ But the Pharisees said, "He's expelling demons with the aid of the chief of the demons." ³⁵ And Jesus went around all the towns and villages teaching in their synagogues and proclaiming the good news of the kingdom and healing every sickness and every ailment.

MATTHEW'S MINI-GOSPEL

Thinking About Matthew

Matthew continues his collection of Jesus' deeds by going back to Mark 2, to retell its stories. He had just told of the story of the Gadarene demoniacs which he had adapted from Mark 5:1–20. Changing the order of events was not a problem because Matthew would have known that Mark had to create an order of events from the many anecdotes which came his way and put them together as he found fit. So Matthew does the same, with the same freedom and creativity.

The story of Jesus' healing the paralyzed man by telling him that God forgave his sins came at the beginning of Mark 2. It had the drama of the man's friends lowering him down from the roof. Matthew leaves out that dramatic detail and keeps the story simple but still with its main point, namely that Jesus as Son of Man, as God's agent, had the authority to declare God's forgiveness. John the Baptist had exercised that authority, too, and Matthew's addition at the end of Mark's story, that the crowd glorified God who "had given such authority to human beings," may hint that this is also an authority which would be exercised by those who would proclaim the gospel far and wide.

First-century medicine in the Jewish world did sometimes link paralysis to guilt. It could lead to people blaming those who were sick or had disabilities on the assumption that it was all their own fault. According to John's Gospel, Jesus' disciples were attributing a man's blindness to sin and wondering whether it was his sin or his parents' sin. Jesus rejected the theory (John 9:2–3). Today we might sometimes see a connection between guilt and paralysis, but we know that paralysis has many causes and blaming people for being paralyzed seems highly inappropriate. At most, we might reflect that for some people their obsession with guilt will indeed block their growth and limit their ability to find fulfillment, let alone engage positively and helpfully toward others.

Mark shows no interest in explaining what they might have seen as the link between the man's guilt and his paralysis, nor does Matthew. It simply is so. The focus is on Jesus' liberating act of love. It is also, however, on the critics who appear to imagine that in claiming an authority independent of God, Jesus was claiming to be a God or to be God. That would, indeed, be blasphemy, one of the charges brought against Jesus at his Jewish trial. Mark, and Matthew following him, make it quite clear that such an assumption is false. Jesus, like John before him, was acting on God's authority. His declaration, if filled out, would read "Your sins are forgiven by God." What was easier: to tell a lame person to walk or tell them that their sins were forgiven? Obviously, the latter in practical terms, but for those worried about offending their God, obviously the former. Jesus' understanding of God's priorities was very different.

Matthew then moves on to the call of the disciple who had been working as a customs official at a checkpoint on the border between Antipas's and Philip's territory, between Capernaum and Bethsaida. Mark named him Levi, but Matthew names him Matthew, perhaps one of the reasons why people in the following century would identify the author of this Gospel as Matthew.

Matthew then follows Mark in bringing the exchange between Jesus and his critics over sharing a meal with people like Matthew. Linking customs officials and sinners reflects an assumption that in exercising their official duties of charging tax on imported goods, they overcharged. Jesus' willingness to have such people share a meal with him was a major source of controversy, as reflected in a number of anecdotes and sayings.

The criticism is based on a value system which saw remaining ritually and morally pure as the highest priority and God's primary concern. Jesus clearly did not share that view, but rather saw his engagement with such people in love and openness as reflecting what he believed was God's primary concern, namely, seeking to restore people to wholeness. Here he uses the medical image of being a doctor. His mission is to help make people well. It is not that Jesus rejected the laws about ritual and moral purity. It was rather that he saw the outreach of love and compassion as having more weight, being more important. It reflects his understanding of what matters most to God.

Not only Jesus, but also Paul, and then also many others would find themselves caught up in conflicts about how to interpret the Law and more generally the Bible. For some, detailed adherence equally to every commandment is what God demands, who will condemn any attempt to do otherwise, whereas others saw love and compassion as God's priority, leading sometimes to the setting aside of some commandments as situations required it or even permanently if new, informed understanding required it.

Matthew reinforces Jesus' response by adding a reference to Hos 6:6, "I want compassion, not sacrifice," and adds it into his source again in Matt 12:7. Its meaning in Hosea and also in Matthew is not to oppose sacrifice and the sacrificial system, but to underline what matters most. Matthew knows that this setting of priorities was expressed both in the prophets and in the psalms. The problem of putting emphasis in the wrong place was not new.

Following Mark, Matthew goes on to the question of fasting, which would inevitably have arisen, and brings the response, central to their image of Jesus, that they were not in the period of waiting for the kingdom of God, but were already experiencing it as beginning to break in. Even then, in the interim before its final fulfillment and Jesus' return, as they expected it, there would be a place for waiting, praying and fasting, alongside finding hopes being fulfilled.

The sayings that follow this section about new patches on old garments and new wine and new wineskins address issues of continuity and discontinuity. The main focus is that something new was happening and how it related to what went before. This is not a rejection, let alone a replacement of Israel's faith, but it does point to a new way of expressing that faith which is different from what had become dominant at the time, as expressed by Jesus' critics. Matthew's citation of Hos 6:6 shows that this newness is at the time a recovery of what was always God's priority, lost by the way Jesus' critics treated biblical tradition.

Matthew now jumps ahead to where he had left off in retelling Mark 5. There, what he had rewritten as the Gadarene healings comes before the story of the synagogue ruler's daughter and the woman with the hemorrhage (Mark 5:21–43). Matthew again trims the story, describes the daughter's father simply as a leader, omits his name and the link with the synagogue, and has the father announce she was already dead, unlike Mark who said she was at the point of dying. Now the father approaches Jesus while he is at home. He also trims the story of the woman who touches Jesus, omitting Mark's information about the extent of her previous efforts at getting help and Jesus' reaction to being touched. Instead, Matthew simply tells us that Jesus heals her and then moves on to a much simpler rendering of Jesus' raising the girl back to life.

Matthew concludes his collection of Jesus' deeds with the healing of two blind man and healing of a man described as possessed by a demon which prevented him from being able to speak. Matthew appears to have adapted Mark's story of the healing of blind Bartimaeus (Mark 10:46–52), to bring it here even though he also brings it where Mark had it, at the end of Jesus' ministry (Matt 20:29–34). As with the adaptation of the healing of the possessed man at Gerasa, Matthew doubles the figure, so that the stories now speak of two blind men. They address Jesus as Bartimaeus had done, calling out to him as "Son of David." That was a title used of the Messiah to come of David's line, but, taken more literally, it would recall Solomon, believed to have passed on the secrets of healing, so very appropriate here. The exchange between Jesus and two is based on Mark's account of the exchange between Jesus and Bartimaeus.

The exorcism of the man who could not speak results in the accusation from the Pharisees that Jesus was in league with the chief of demons. The same accusation is repeated in 12:22–24, where another man unable to speak but also blind is healed and again Jesus is hailed as "Son of David." Matthew may well have doubled this story, too. This story in 9:32–34 brings to a conclusion the collection of Jesus' deeds in which he shows miraculous powers understood within the world of his time as indicating that he could stand up to and defeat the forces of evil and affliction. It also points forward to the discussion in Matt 12 of the accusation that Jesus was in league with demonic powers.

Finally in 9:35 Matthew returns to the statement with which he began his account of Jesus' words and deeds in chapters 5–9, namely 4:23, "And Jesus went all around Galilee teaching in their synagogues and proclaiming the good news of the kingdom and healing every sickness and every ailment among the people," echoed in 9:35, "And Jesus went around all the towns and villages teaching in their synagogues and proclaiming the good news of the kingdom and healing every sickness and every ailment." These two summaries form the bookends of what we might then describe as Matthew's mini-gospel.

Reflection: What values do you see colliding in these passages?

3

The Mission

Sent to Be Agents of Jesus (Matthew 9:36—11:1)

Listening to Matthew

⁹:³⁶ When Jesus saw the crowds, he was filled with compassion toward them, because they were troubled and helpless "like sheep without a shepherd." ³⁷ Then he told his disciples, "The harvest is great, but the workers are few on the ground. ³⁸ Pray therefore to the Lord of the harvest that he may send workers for his harvest."
¹⁰:¹ Then, calling his twelve disciples together, he gave them authority over unclean spirits to be able to expel them and to heal every sickness and every ailment. ² These are the names of the twelve apostles: first, Simon called Peter and Andrew his brother, and James, son of Zebedee, and John, his brother, ³ Philip and Bartholomew, Thomas and Matthew the toll collector, James, son of Alphaeus, and Thaddeus, ⁴ Simon the Canaanite, and Judas, the one who betrayed him.
⁵ He sent these twelve with the instructions, "Don't go off to places where gentiles live and don't enter Samaritan towns, ⁶ but go rather to the lost sheep of the house of Israel. ⁷ And as you go, preach, saying, 'The kingdom of heaven has come near.' ⁸ Heal the sick, raise the dead, cure the lepers, expel demons. You've benefited at no charge; give at no charge. ⁹ Don't acquire gold and silver and copper to carry in your belts, ¹⁰ nor a bag for your travels, nor two

tunics, nor sandals, nor a staff, because a worker deserves to be fed. [11] "And whatever town or village you enter, find out who's worthy to have you and stay there until you leave. [12] When you enter someone's household, greet them, [13] and if the household is worthy, wish them well, but if they're not worthy, let your well wishes bounce back to you. [14] And whoever does not welcome you and listen to what you have to say, when you leave that household or town, shake the dust off your feet. [15] Truly I tell you, on the day of judgment it will be more tolerable for the land of Sodom and Gomorrah than for that town.

[16] "Look, I'm sending you out as sheep in the midst of wolves. So be as wise as snakes and as innocent as doves. [17] Beware of what people will do, because they will arrest you and bring you to trial before their councils and flog you in their synagogues. [18] And you'll be hauled up before governors and kings because of me as a testimony to them and to the gentiles. [19] When they arrest you and put you on trial, don't worry about how you should respond, because you'll be given what to say at that moment, [20] because it's not you speaking, but the Spirit of your Father speaking in you.

[21] "Brother will hand over brother to death and fathers, their children, and children will rise up against their parents and kill them. [22] And you will be hated by everyone because of me, but whoever puts up with it to the end will be saved.

[23] "When they persecute you in one town, escape to another. Truly I'm telling you, you won't have finished going through Israel's towns before the Son of Man returns.

[24] "A disciple is not superior to a teacher nor slaves to their master. [25] It's enough for a disciple to be like the teacher and a slave like the master. If they called the householder Beelzebul, how much more will they abuse the members of his household.

[26] "Don't be afraid of them, because there's nothing concealed that will not be uncovered and hidden that won't be made known. [27] What I tell you in darkness, declare in the light, and what is whispered into your ear, proclaim on the rooftops. [28] And don't be afraid of those who can kill your body but can't kill your soul. Rather, fear the one who can bring both body and soul to destruction in Gehenna. [29] Aren't two sparrows sold for a copper coin? And yet not one of them falls to the ground without your Father knowing. [30] But as for

you, even the hairs of your head are all counted. [31] So don't be afraid. You're worth more than many sparrows.

[32] "Everyone who confesses allegiance to me before people I will confess allegiance to them before my Father in heaven. [33] And whoever denies their allegiance to me before people, I'll also deny my allegiance to them before my Father in heaven.

[34] "Don't think I came to bring peace to the earth. I didn't come to bring peace but a sword. [35] I have come to pit 'a man against his father and a daughter against her mother and a daughter-in-law against her mother-in-law, [36] and a man's own household will become his enemy.' [37] Whoever loves father or mother more than me is not worthy of belonging to me and whoever loves son or daughter more than me is not worthy of belonging to me. [38] And those who don't take up their cross and follow me will not be worthy of belonging to me. [39] Those who find their life will lose it, and those who lose their life for my sake will find it.

[40] "Whoever welcomes you welcomes me, and whoever welcomes me welcomes the one who sent me. [41] Anyone welcoming a prophet in the name of a prophet gets a prophet's reward, and whoever welcomes a just person in the name of a just person receives a just person's reward. [42] And whoever gives one of these little ones a drink of cold water in the name of a disciple, truly I tell you, will by no means lose out on getting their reward."

[11:1] Now when Jesus had finished giving these instructions to the twelve disciples, he set off from there, teaching and preaching in their towns.

Thinking About Matthew

Matthew brought a collection of Jesus' sayings and deeds in Matt 4:23—9:35. Now he brings a collection of Jesus instructions to those who would follow in his path. It is Matthew's second of the five major speeches he composed to bring together the teachings of Jesus.

As in the earlier chapters we can mostly trace his sources. The list of the twelve disciples comes from Mark. Mark had Jesus go up a hill to appoint the twelve disciples (Mark 3:13–19). Matthew instead has him deliver the so-called Sermon on the Mount on the hillside, so now Matthew finally gives us the list of names. Mark has Jesus send them out as his agents (the literal meaning of "apostles") in Mark 6. That now forms the basis for our passage, but Matthew also knew another version of that sending in the source he shared with Luke. Whereas Luke decided therefore to have two sendings, of the twelve and of seventy, in Luke 9 and 10, Matthew combines both sources and brings the result here. The result is our passage, which not only tells about what Jesus told the twelve to do, but also more broadly what all who follow Jesus should do, including us.

I have commenced our passage with the closing verses of chapter 9 because these form the introduction where Jesus points to the need for others beside himself to be engaged in saying and doing what he had been doing. People of Matthew's time would be fully aware that the number Jesus chose, namely twelve, was highly symbolic and matched the number of the tribes of Israel. Jesus was, after all, speaking of the renewal and restoration of Israel, so that he and his group symbolically represent that hope. They are all male, reflecting the assumptions about leadership of the period, but, as we know, women also came to play important roles in the movement.

Peter is the first on the list. Matthew and his sources identify Peter as the first disciple to be called, along with his brother. Many Easter traditions identify Peter as also the first to see the risen Jesus (Mark 16:8; Luke 24:34; 1 Cor 15:5), although both Matthew and John's Gospel mention a prior encounter with Mary Magdalene; in Matthew's case, that Mary and another Mary. Matthew also brings a version of Jesus' giving Simon, as he was called, the name Peter (Aramaic: Cephas), which means a rock, and has Jesus make him the foundation member of the church (Matt 16:18). John's version has Simon given the name at his initial calling (John 1:42). We know just a little of James and John, and of Thomas, and more about Judas. Of the others, aside from Matthew himself, we know next to nothing. Imagination filled the gaps even then, accounting for the differences in the stories about callings.

Matthew's version of Jesus' instruction, drawn from Mark 6 and the source behind Luke 10, begins with some unique features which Matthew adds. They are told to go only to "the lost sheep of the house of Israel," matching what Matthew later has Jesus describe as his own commission (Matt 15:24). They are not to go to the gentiles nor to the Samaritans. That will come only after Jesus rises from the dead when Matthew has Jesus declare that from then on he was given authority over all peoples and so all peoples were to hear his teaching (Matt 28:18–20). Encounters with gentiles during Jesus' ministry were an exception and incidental. Paul echoes this sequence when he talks about the good news as coming first to Jews and only then to gentiles, whom he calls "Greeks" (Rom 1:16).

After this distinctive beginning Matthew brings mission instructions which other sources indicate applied to all commissioned to be Jesus' agents and carry on his work. In drawing on both Mark's account and the one he shared with Luke, Matthew opts for the stricter version reflected in the source he shared with Luke. Mark's version allows sandals, a staff, and a tunic. Matthew's and Luke's does not. If we think of the setting in Galilee, the instructions assume that these agents of Jesus will do as he did. They will travel and be put up by locals who would feed them and house them. That probably worked well with the relatively short distances between towns in Galilee. It would not work well once the movement found itself in the vast expanses of the Roman Empire, but still the principle generally applied that upkeep was the responsibility of locals, the origins of the notion of a stipend meant as a living allowance, so normally at the same level however long you serve and whatever your qualifications and seniority.

They were to go out and do what Jesus did. As in the summaries of Jesus' activity, that meant in their world preaching, healing, and exorcisms. In our world two thousand years later with very different understandings of pathology, nevertheless the principle of doing what Jesus did remains a helpful guide, especially for those in leadership. Proclaiming a vision of hope which entails good news for the poor, restoring people to a sound relation with God, themselves, and others, as a mission of love, remains the mandate.

Much of what follows in Matt 10 deals with how to handle rejection. He has brought the material together partly from Mark 13 and partly from the source he shares with Luke. Accepting rejection and pulling back where you are not wanted remains good advice, though we may not want to embrace the acts of judgment signified by shaking off dust at people, which could lead us away from the mandate of love. Matthew will be writing after a good half a century of experience of rejection, and this is reflected in how he shapes Jesus' words, as he often does, to have them address the people of his time. Some of them will indeed have been flogged and others hauled before civic authorities.

Matthew has already mentioned the charge against Jesus that he was in league with Beelzebul the chief of demonic powers (Matt 9:34). The twelve but also others could expect similar abuse. Citing Mic 7:6 about divisions within households, Matthew may well be alluding to painful conflicts that some had faced or were facing. A controversial strategy of Jesus was to challenge some to leave family and join him on the road, taking the risk that they would survive through local support. It was a protest against the tight family and social systems that kept some people rich and others poor, systems which still live on in our world. The commitment to love and justice must outweigh the powerful demands of family loyalty, as much still today as then. Some embraced that commitment by becoming itinerant. Others remained at home but embraced love and justice, the good news of the kingdom, where they were, as we can do, too.

The success of such an endeavor depends very much on support. That meant support for those called to be prophets and those advocating justice, but also all who embrace the vision. While "little ones" could refer to children, it more likely refers as elsewhere to everyday members of the movement committed to its message of love (Matt 18:6, 10, 14; 25:40, 45).

In the ancient world, without our modern means of communication, agents (sent ones, apostles) were essential and were needed to be able to act on behalf of the sender. Welcoming the person sent equated to welcoming the sender. It became one of the most valuable ways of depicting the task of those who were sent and the implications of how people responded to them. In that sense Matthew has been informing us about what it means to be church as a community which takes risks and cares, what it means to be agents of God in the world.

Matthew concludes this second major speech of Jesus as he does the other four speeches, beginning with the words, "Now when Jesus had finished . . ." (Matt 7:28; 13:53; 19:1; and 26:1). We are ready to move on, and he depicts Jesus as doing just that.

Reflection: Agents of Jesus in their world and in ours: what are the similarities and differences?

Wisdom Calling (Matthew 11:2–30)

Listening to Matthew

11:2 When John in prison heard about the activities of the Messiah, he sent his disciples **3** to ask, "Are you the one to come or should we be expecting someone else?" **4** In response Jesus told them, "Go and tell John what you're hearing and seeing: **5** blind people are recovering their sight and lame people are walking, lepers are being cured and deaf people are hearing, and dead people are being raised back to life and the poor are being given good news; **6** and happy are those who don't take offense at me."

7 And as they went on their way, Jesus started telling the crowds about John, saying, "What did you go to the outback to see? A reed being blown by the wind? **8** But really, what did you go out to see? A person dressed in fine attire? But those wearing fine attire are to be found in the households of kings. **9** But really, what did you go out to see? A prophet? Yes, and I tell you, more than just a prophet. **10** This was the one written about in the Scriptures, 'Look, I am sending my messenger ahead of you, who will prepare the way before you.' **11** Truly I tell you, among those born of women no one is greater than John the Baptist, though the one who is least in the kingdom of heaven is greater than he is. **12** From the days of John the Baptist until now the kingdom of God has been coming under assault and violent people have tried to take it by force. **13** For all the Prophets and the Law made their statements up till the time of John; **14** and, if you're willing to accept it, he is Elijah who has been expected to come. **15** Whoever has ears, listen!

16 "What can I compare this generation to? It's like kids playing in the marketplace, calling out to others, saying, **17** 'We played the flute for you and you didn't dance, and we played a dirge for you and you didn't mourn.' ¹⁸ For John came neither eating nor drinking and they say, 'He's got a demon,' ¹⁹ and the Son of Man came eating and drinking and they say, 'Look, he's a glutton and a drunkard, a friend of tax collectors and sinners'. But wisdom will be vindicated by her achievements."

²⁰ Then he started to denounce the towns in which most of his miracles occurred because they had not turned to God: ²¹ "Woe betide you, Chorazin, and woe betide you, Bethsaida, because had the miracles which took place in you taken place in Tyre and Sidon, they would have long since turned to God in sackcloth and ashes. ²² Only I tell you, it will be more tolerable for Tyre and Sidon on the day of judgment than for you. ²³ And as for you, Capernaum, you're not really going to elevate yourself to the sky, are you? You're going to end up down in Hades, because had the miracles which happened in you happened in Sodom, it would still be here today. ²⁴ Only I tell you, it will be more tolerable for the land of Sodom on the day of judgment than for you."

²⁵ At that moment, Jesus responded to God saying, "I acknowledge before you, Father, Lord of heaven and earth, that you have hidden these things from the wise and knowledgeable and have revealed them to infants. ²⁶ Yes, Father, because that was what gave you pleasure. ²⁷ Everything has been given me by my Father, and no one recognizes who the Son is except the Father and no one recognizes who the Father is except the Son and those to whom the Son wants to reveal him.

²⁸ "Come to me all who are wearied and weighed down with burdens and I will bring you relief. ²⁹ Take on my yoke and learn from me, because I am gentle and not bossy, and 'you'll find relief for your souls' ³⁰ because my yoke is kindly and what I ask you to carry is not heavy."

Thinking About Matthew

Matthew has brought us his mini-gospel (Matt 4:23—9:35), presenting Jesus' words and deeds, and then his second major collection of Jesus' sayings, focused on mission (Matt 9:36—11:1). He now returns to where Jesus' ministry began with John the Baptist and to a problem. The problem is that John announced that Jesus would come as God's agent to execute judgment, with a harvesting fork and an axe and fire, but Jesus had done no such thing.

The problem was probably felt very early and may well reflect issues which went right back to the beginning. Jesus was like John and not like John. He is the one who John predicted would come, but he wasn't the way John described him. The source which Matthew and Luke shared brings us a story about John taking the initiative to sort out the problem.

Jesus' response to John's disciples which they are to relay to him points to his activities which were bringing significant change for people and assumes John should understand. Those familiar with Israel's traditions would have been familiar with the hopes that such changes for good would happen. In Isaiah we read: "On that day the deaf shall hear the words of a scroll, and out of their gloom and darkness the eyes of the blind shall see. The meek shall obtain fresh joy in the Lord, and the neediest people shall exult in the Holy One of Israel. For the tyrant shall be no more" (Isa 29:18–20). And a little later we read: "Then the eyes of the blind shall be opened, and the ears of the deaf unstopped; then the lame shall leap like a deer, and the tongue of the speechless sing for joy" (Isa 35:5–6).

Whereas Matthew and his source portray John the Baptist as seeing himself on the brink of God's intervention which would bring judgment to punish the wicked and reward the good, Jesus brings a modification to John's message. The hope that God's kingdom would come and, with it, judgment and reward, still a major emphasis in Matthew, is not the full story. Instead, in the interim, between now and then the change and transformation can already begin. The difference between the two is reflected in the fact that John is pictured as in the waiting area, on the other side of the Jordan, ready to take the land, whereas Jesus crosses the Jordan, enters the land, and shows fulfillment already happening.

We know far too little about the historical John the Baptist to be able to assess how much this matched history, but it is certainly the difference which the Gospels presuppose. That difference then became central to Christian faith as the early expectation of the impending climax of history subsided. The focus then moved to engagement in making the vision of hope and change a life agenda in the present and ultimately to expressing and understanding it in the light of new understandings of the nature of human need over two thousand years.

Jesus' praise of John the Baptist also goes back to early times and doubtless reflects the view of Jesus, himself. The caveat in 11:11 that the least significant person in the kingdom of heaven is still greater than John may seem like a retreat from such praise in the interests of the new movement, but may be no more than a claim that the people of the new era, the kingdom, are of a higher order of being. Matthew has Jesus cite Mal 3:1, which Mark had used in combination with a citation from Isaiah and attributed wrongly also to Isaiah (Mark 1:2). He brings it here instead with the same minor modification as in Mark to have it read as addressed to Jesus, reading "your way" instead of "my way," which originally referred to God.

Thus, John is portrayed as preparing the way for Jesus. The image of God's kingdom being under assault (Matt 11:12) reflects the understanding that God's reign and power are challenged by the devil's power. Change means liberating people from the powers that oppress them. Matthew depicts John's role as standing in continuity with Scripture's hope, the Law and the Prophets, and suggests he fulfills the role that the Scriptures had attributed to Elijah. The story of Elijah tells how instead of dying he was transported into heaven and as a result people believed he would one day return. Matthew, but already Mark, then identifies John with Elijah (Mark 9:12–13), an identification not, however, shared by the Gospel of John, which has John declare, when asked about it, that he was not Elijah (John 1:21).

Matthew then turns to the responses to John and Jesus, drawing on his source shared with Luke, which uses the imagery of children at play. It again highlights their difference: John's stance was one of waiting and fasting; Jesus' stance was one of reaching out to people deemed beyond the pale, like tax collectors and sinners, and sharing in their feasts. In Jesus' concluding comment he identifies himself with Wisdom.

Many in Matthew's time would recognize the connection with the figure of Wisdom as a woman in Proverbs, portrayed as God's companion and as acting on God's behalf (Prov 8:22–31). Some, later, portrayed the Law as Wisdom's voice, and portrayed Wisdom as sending prophets and even as active in creation. Here, Jesus sees himself as embodying the spirit of Wisdom by doing her deeds.

This identification becomes a major feature in John's Gospel which explicitly identifies Jesus with Wisdom, spoken of as the Word. It portrays Jesus as the Word made flesh and so takes up the many images used of Wisdom and the Law in Jewish tradition and applies them to Jesus. The author therefore has Jesus declare in the famous "I am" statements that he was the light, life, and bread, attributes associated with the Law as Wisdom.

At this point Matthew brings a series of confrontations of the people of Chorazin, Bethsaida, and Capernaum, which were also in the source shared with Luke, who brings them elsewhere (Luke 10:12–15). Matthew has typically gathered them into this collection. They are generalizations and we should probably not ask: does he mean every man, woman, and child in those towns? Threats of judgment belonged to the tradition and were designed to challenge complacency, but were a feature shared with John the Baptist.

Matthew moves to the conclusion of Jesus' reflections to bring two statements of central significance for his understanding of Jesus. In the first he brings a prayer on the part of Jesus, which Luke also knew (Luke 10:21). In it he uses language at home in discussions about Wisdom. Those who respond to Jesus' message are described as infants and contrasted with the wise. Wisdom, knowledge, expertise, is no guarantee that you have grasped what is really important in life.

This first statement in 12:25–26 continues in 12:27 but changes from being a prayer to being a declaration. The claim that all things had been handed over to him by his Father sounds extraordinary. At one level, it can be understood as what one should expect as a father hands over his inheritance to his son, all of it. At another level, it is a statement of authorization of Jesus as God's agent who would on God's behalf conduct the judgment to come. It finds an echo in Jesus' final words to his disciples after his resurrection according to Matthew where he declares that all authority in heaven and on earth had been handed over to him (Matt 28:18).

If we ask what significance Matthew wants us to see in this, we have to look at the context. In Matt 28 what follows is the commissioning of the disciples to go and teach what Jesus had taught them. Here in Matt 11 it is closely linked to the exclusive claim to know who God is. This, too, needs explanation and is clearly related to the statement that no one knows who the Son is except the Father. At one level, people did know who Jesus was as much as they would know anyone from their world. The meaning is, however, at a different level and is speaking about the unique role being given to Jesus as the Son.

The exclusive claims continue with the assertion that no one knows who God is unless the Son reveals who God is. This could be an attempt to deny all prior knowledge of God before Jesus, but this is highly unlikely. When, however, we take into account that Matthew is having Jesus speak as the bearer of God's Wisdom, then this becomes true. Only God's Wisdom reveals who God is, and this was always so and will always be so. Jesus speaks with the voice of Wisdom.

This receives confirmation when we turn to the second statement, because it echoes what Wisdom was depicted as declaring in the Jewish wisdom book Ben Sira, where the author has God's Wisdom declare:

> Draw near to me, you who are uneducated, and lodge in the house of instruction. Why do you say you are lacking in these things, and why do you endure such great thirst? I opened my mouth and said, "Acquire wisdom for yourselves without money. Put your neck under her yoke, and let your souls receive instruction; it is to be found close by." (Sir 51:23–26)

Jesus had already identified himself with Wisdom just a few verses earlier in the statement: "Wisdom will be vindicated by her achievements" (Matt 11:19). Luke's version reads: "Wisdom will be vindicated by her children" (Luke 7:35). Especially in Ben Sira, but also elsewhere, Wisdom speaks God's will and so speaks God's word, God's Law. Matthew is having Jesus again speak with the voice of Wisdom, inviting people to take on Wisdom's yoke assuring them that it will not crush people. Matthew will later confront fellow Jewish teachers for doing so when they impose heavy burdens on people in the way they interpret the Law (Matt 23:4). Jesus' exposition of the Law, as already laid out in the Sermon on the Mount, does not impose an unbearable burden on people but one that is light and loving and relieves people of such impositions.

This second closing statement has become a much-loved expression of God's generosity, the invitation to learn God's way as taught by Jesus and find rest and fulfillment in doing so. Deeds of liberation are a mark of Jesus' priorities according to Matthew, but that extends also to liberating people from what can be the burdensome impositions of religion.

Matthew has Jesus channel the voice of Wisdom also in chapter 23, where Wisdom's words about being like a hen seeking to gather its chicks will refer to Israel's history from ancient times (Matt 23:37) and just before it Matthew has Jesus speak words about sending prophets (Matt 23:34–35), which in Luke's version are cited as said directly by Wisdom, herself (Luke 11:49). The implication of this intimate connection between Jesus and Wisdom is that Matthew is saying that what we encounter in the stories and sayings of Jesus which he brings is more than the words of

Jesus. It is ultimately an encounter with God and with what makes sense of the universe. True rest and peace are found in oneness with God's Wisdom, not in burdensome religious rules and regulations.

Reflection: What is Wisdom's call according to Matthew?

Conflict of Values (Matthew 12:1–50)

Listening to Matthew

12:1 At that time Jesus went on his way through the wheatfields on the Sabbath. His disciples were hungry, so they started plucking heads of wheat to eat. **2** The Pharisees saw them and said to him, "Look, your disciples are doing what is forbidden to do on the Sabbath." **3** He said to them, "Haven't you read about what David did when he was hungry along with those who were with him, **4** how he entered the house of God and ate the loaves of bread set aside as an offering, which was not permitted for him and his companions to eat but allowed only for the priests? **5** Or haven't you read in the Law that on the Sabbath priests in the temple can break the Sabbath and are not considered guilty? **6** I tell you, something greater than the temple is here. **7** If you knew what this means, 'I want compassion, not sacrifice,' you wouldn't have condemned the innocent. **8** For the Son of Man is lord of the Sabbath."

9 And moving on from there he entered their synagogue, **10** and, lo and behold, there was a man with a shriveled-up hand. And they asked him, "Is it allowed to heal on the Sabbath?" Their aim was to be able to accuse him. **11** He said to them, "Who among you if he had a single sheep that had fallen into a ditch on the Sabbath wouldn't get hold of it and lift it out? **12** Isn't a human being worth more than a sheep? So, it is okay to do good on the Sabbath." **13** Then he said to the man, "Stretch out your hand." And he stretched it out and it was restored to be the same as his other hand. **14** But the Pharisees left and plotted together against him, how they could destroy him.

15 Jesus sensed what they were up to and so left the area, and many crowds followed him and he healed them all **16** and ordered them not to blab about him. **17** This was to fulfill what was said by the prophet Isaiah, namely, ¹⁸ "Look, this is my servant whom I've chosen, my beloved one in whom my soul delights. I shall put my Spirit upon him and he will declare judgment to the gentiles. ¹⁹ He won't be contentious nor go around shouting nor will anyone hear his voice out on the streets. ²⁰ He won't even break a bruised reed and won't put out a smoldering wick until the time when he brings judgment to its triumph. ²¹ And the gentiles are going to put their hope in his name."

²² Then a person possessed by a demon was brought to him, blind and unable to speak, and he healed him with the result that the mute man could speak and could see. ²³ The crowds were all astonished and said, "Could this be the Son of David?" ²⁴ But the Pharisees hearing this response said, "No, he's not expelling demons without the assistance of Beelzebul the chief of the demons." ²⁵ Knowing what they were thinking, he said to them, "Every kingdom divided against itself becomes a wasteland and every city divided against itself fails to survive. ²⁶ And if Satan expels Satan, he'd be divided against himself. How then would his kingdom survive? ²⁷ And if I'm supposed to be expelling demons with the aid of Beelzebul, who are your exorcists in league with when they expel demons? So they will turn out to be your judges. ²⁸ But if I expel demons with the aid of the Spirit of God then the kingdom of God has arrived for you. ²⁹ Or how can anyone enter a strong man's house to steal his goods without first tying the strong man up? And then he can burgle his house. ³⁰ If you're not with me, you're against me, and those not joining me in gathering are scatterers.

³¹ "For this reason I'm telling you, all kinds of sin and blasphemy will be forgiven people, but blasphemy against the Spirit will never be. ³² And anyone uttering slander against the Son of Man will be forgiven, but whoever slanders the Holy Spirit will never be forgiven, neither in this age nor in the age to come.

³³ "Either get the tree good and healthy and it will produce good fruit or let it get into poor shape and it will produce poor fruit, because you'll know the state of the tree from its fruit. ³⁴ You nest of snakes, how can you who are wicked talk about what is good? For what people say results from what dominates their thinking. ³⁵ Good people produce what is good from the goodness they treasure, and bad people produce what is bad from the evil they treasure. ³⁶ I'm telling you, every thoughtless utterance which people speak

will be brought to account concerning them on the day of judgment. ³⁷ You'll be justified on the basis of what you've said and be condemned also on the basis of what you've said."

³⁸ Then some of the scribes and Pharisees responded to him and said, "Teacher, we want to see a sign from you." ³⁹ He answered, "A wicked adulterous generation is looking for a sign and no sign will be given to it except the sign of the prophet Jonah. ⁴⁰ For as 'Jonah was in the sea monster's stomach for three days and three nights,' so also the Son of Man will be in the heart of the earth for three days and three nights. ⁴¹ The men of Nineveh will rise up against this generation on the day of judgment and condemn it, because they turned to God in response to Jonah's message and look, something greater than Jonah is here. ⁴² The queen of the south will rise up on the day of judgment against this generation and condemn it, because she came from the ends of the earth to listen to Solomon's wisdom and look, something greater than Solomon is here.

⁴³ When an unclean spirit leaves someone, it wanders around dry places looking for a place to rest and when it doesn't find one, ⁴⁴ then it says, 'I'll return to the house I left'; and returning, it finds it empty and swept and tidied up. ⁴⁵ Then it goes and brings seven more spirits with it more wicked than itself and they enter and make themselves at home there, and the last state of the person is worse than the first. That's the way it will be with this wicked generation."

⁴⁶ While he was still speaking to the crowd, lo and behold, his mother and brothers were standing outside wanting to speak with him. ⁴⁷ [Someone told him, "Look, your mother and brothers are standing outside want to speak with you."] ⁴⁸ In response he said to the one who was telling him, "Who is my mother and who are my brothers?" ⁴⁹ And pointing to his disciples he said, "Look, my mother and my brothers! ⁵⁰ Whoever does the will of my Father in heaven is my brother and sister and mother."

Thinking About Matthew

Matthew was last following Mark 2 back in Matt 9. Now he returns to pick up two stories from Mark 2 about Jesus facing criticism because of his treatment of the Sabbath (Mark 2:23–28; 3:1–6). They follow well after the way Matt 11 ended, where Matthew portrayed Jesus as the one whose teaching of the Law did not impose unreasonable burdens. The first episode is about Jesus' disciples picking ears of wheat and chewing them on the Sabbath while walking across a field of wheat and the Pharisees raising this with Jesus as a breach of the commandment not to work on the Sabbath.

Matthew follows Mark's story closely but also tweaks it with some minor changes. The first is that he portrays the disciples as hungry. Mark did not say they were hungry but were simply picking some heads of wheat as they went along. Mark has Jesus meet the objection by recalling what David did for his men when they were hungry. By depicting Jesus' disciples as hungry, the reference to David in Matthew is a better fit.

Another minor change is a correction. Mark's story has Jesus refer to David's initiative happening when Abiathar was high priest, but both Matthew and Luke recognize that this was an error (1 Sam 21:1-7). Abiathar was not high priest at that time, so both delete reference to him. Matthew then adds a second biblical reference in Jesus' response, having him point out that priests in the temple had to work on the Sabbath. The effect is to reinforce the claim that Jesus' approach to Sabbath law had precedent, quite apart from the issue of responding to hunger. The final comment of this addition by Matthew appeals also to Jesus' status and what he was doing as something more important than the Sabbath. It fits well with Matthew's conclusion that the Son of Man was lord of the Sabbath, especially when we understand that for Matthew the Son of Man is after all to be the judge at the last judgment.

Between the two appeals to Scripture, to David and to priests, and Matthew's appeal to Jesus' status as judge to come, the Son of Man, Matthew has Jesus cite Hos 6:6, "I want compassion, not sacrifice," just as he had added it back in 9:13 in response to criticism that he engaged in a meal with toll collectors and sinners. Matthew has Jesus appeal not just to Jesus' authority, but also to the value of compassion that provides the key to the way he expounds God's will and so interprets the Law. Neither Matthew nor Luke picks up what Mark brings as Jesus' comment: "The Sabbath was made for people; not people for the Sabbath" (Mark 2:27), probably because they saw it as potentially misleading if read as meaning the Sabbath was not important.

Matthew continues with Mark's stories as he brings the next scene of Jesus' healing the man with the shriveled hand in the synagogue. Mark has Jesus respond with a quip, typical of Jesus' responses in anecdotes going back to his time: "Is it lawful on the Sabbath to do good or do harm, to save life or to kill?" (Mark 3:4), a contentious response. Matthew simplifies it to a statement that it is lawful to do good on the Sabbath, but only after inserting into Jesus' reply a common sense argument that surely you'd rescue an animal on the Sabbath, then why not a human being? Matthew drops Mark's reference to Jesus being angry, as he often omits references to strong feelings, but retains Mark's closing comment about his critics going off to plot his downfall.

As in the previous scene, Matthew reinforces the principle that compassionate response to human need mattered most. He clearly would also not have agreed with the suggestion, had it been made, that Jesus should have postponed the healing to the following day to avoid doing work on the Sabbath. The implication is that his critics were extreme, and indeed, they seem to be so when we look at the range of interpretations of Sabbath law likely to have existed at the time.

Matthew has already made it very clear in the Sermon on the Mount that keeping the Law is a priority, but operates with an understanding of God for whom compassion for human need matters most, not with an image of God as like an obsessive man more concerned with ensuring his laws are kept to the very last detail than with love and flexibility.

In following the next section in Mark, Matthew has reduced Mark's summary of Jesus' activity over six verses (Mark 3:7-12) down to a simple statement that he healed everyone and told them to refrain from reporting it widely (Matt 12:15-16). He then adds the observation that this fulfilled the prediction about God's servant made in Isa 42:1-4, which spoke of the servant engaging modestly and not in self-promotion. The passage was important for much more. It recalled and will have inspired the account of Jesus' baptism where Jesus was hailed by God as God's beloved and was given the Spirit. It also recalls how Matthew has John the Baptist speak of Jesus' role, namely as the one who would be God's agent in judgment. There is even more: the allusion to gentiles, who would one day also turn to God when Jesus would be proclaimed through the world.

Matthew remains with Mark's sequence in having Jesus address the charge that in performing exorcisms he was in league with Beelzebul, the chief of demons. Matthew had already alluded to this charge back in 10:25 and even earlier in 9:34 without the name Beelzebul. That earlier occasion finds an echo here where Matthew again reports Jesus' healing someone who was not able to speak, but in this instance was also blind, and it recalls the scene which immediately precedes it in Matt 9, namely of the healing of two blind men and people then wondering if this was the Son of David. There as here, Son of David will include an allusion to Solomon who, as legend had it, knew secrets about how to bring healing and deal with demons.

We enter a world where illness, physical and mental, and disability are attributed to demons and where Jesus is portrayed as having the ability to expel such demons. Our understanding of physical and mental illness and disability is quite different, which also means we have similar difficulty with the notion of Jesus as practicing exorcism. Whatever he did and within whatever frame of reference, at most we can identify the intent to liberate people from the forces which oppressed them in whatever way. We can identify our own "demons," more in terms of viruses and destructive and self-destructive dynamics. The kingdom of God, God's reign of love, breaks into reality when such liberation is achieved, and the fruit of the Spirit, love, as Paul tells us, is the key (1 Cor 13; Gal 5:22).

In this section about Beelzebul, Matthew draws not only on Mark but also on the source he shares with Luke and typically brings sayings together to enhance the range and impact of Jesus' speech. The key issue is to recognize where God's Spirit is bringing liberation and not block it. Even slandering (blaspheming against) Jesus himself does not count as much as slandering or denying love when you see it, the work of the Spirit.

Matthew adds to the collection some sayings that recall John the Baptist's teaching and also the teaching given in the Sermon on the Mount, namely the reference to trees and fruit. It is a psychological insight which puts the focus not just on behavior but also on what generates it, one's state of being. That is not irrelevant to understanding what it means to keep the Law. The Law of love is best fulfilled not by trying to keep rules and commandments, but by opening oneself to love, being freed from preoccupation with whether one is valued, learning self-acceptance and love, and so being free to love others.

In citing the examples of Jonah and of the queen of Sheba listening to Solomon, Matthew returns to the kind of confrontation and threats he had Jesus bring back in 10:15 and 11:20-24. It brings him back also to demonology and the image of a demon having been expelled but then returning with even worse fiends, as a warning to the hearers.

Finally, Matthew returns to how Mark ends his third chapter, namely with reference to Jesus' family. Mark has them even contemplate that Jesus may have been mad or at least to worry that others thought so and so go to fetch him (Mark 3:21). Neither Matthew nor Luke, who have idealized Jesus' parents, would have found that something they would want to report and so omit it and retain simply Jesus' response on hearing that they were wanting to talk to him. It is still confronting but matches the insistence Matthew has Jesus bring, namely that one's prior commitment needed to be to God and love, not to the family and social systems of the day that held people captive. Jesus was on about liberating people also from such systems, a challenge in every age.

Some have wondered about there being no reference to Joseph, Jesus' father. The most likely explanation is that he would have died, assuming like most men he had married around the age of thirty and that Jesus was now thirty and most men did not make it to sixty.

Reflection: What values are in conflict in this passage and how might we see them in conflict in our own age?

Getting It and Not Getting It (Matthew 13:1–53)

Listening to Matthew

^{13:1} That day Jesus left the house and was sitting on the lakeshore. ² And many crowds flocked to him, and as a result he got into a boat to sit there while the crowd were all standing on the shore.

³ And he talked a lot using parables and said, "Once a wheat farmer went out to sow seed. ⁴ And, as he was sowing, some seeds fell along the path and birds came and ate them up; ⁵ and others fell on stony ground where there wasn't much soil, and they sprang up straightaway because of the shallow soil, ⁶ but when the sun came up they were scorched and without adequate roots they shriveled up; ⁷ and others fell where there had been thornbushes, and the thornbushes sprang up and choked them; ⁸ but others fell on good soil and started to produce, some a hundredfold, some, sixty, and some, thirtyfold. ⁹ Anyone with ears, let them hear this!"

¹⁰ Then his disciples approached him asking him, "Why are you talking in parables?" ¹¹ In response he said, "You've been given the privilege of knowing the secrets of the kingdom of heaven, but they haven't. ¹² For whoever has been given that privilege will be given much more, but whoever hasn't, even what they've got will be taken from them. ¹³ That's why I speak to them in parables because 'when they look, they don't see and when they listen, they don't hear or understand,' ¹⁴ and so Isaiah's prophecy is coming true which said, 'You've got ears but you won't understand, and you look and see but you won't really see. ¹⁵ For this people's minds are dumb, and they can't really hear with their ears, and their eyes are closed, lest they see with their eyes and hear with their ears and understand with their minds and turn to me so that I can heal them.' ¹⁶ Happy are your eyes because they see and your ears because they hear. ¹⁷ For I tell

you, many prophets and upright folk have longed to see what you see and didn't see it, and to hear what you are hearing and didn't hear it.

[18] "So listen to the meaning of the parable of the sower. [19] As for all who hear the message of the kingdom and don't understand it, the evil one comes and snatches away what was sown in their mind. This is the seed sown along the path. [20] And the seed sown on stony ground—they're the ones who hear the message and immediately welcome it happily, [21] but don't have any root and so last only for a little while, and when they face affliction or persecution because of the message, they immediately fall away. [22] And the seed sown where thorns grow—they're the ones who hear the message, but the world's priorities and the deceitfulness of greed for wealth choke the message and they don't go on to produce anything. [23] And the seed falling into good soil—they're the ones who hear the message and understand it, and they go on to produce, some a hundredfold, some, sixty, and some, thirtyfold."

[24] And he presented them with another parable, saying, "The kingdom of heaven is like a man who sowed good seed in his field [25] and while people were asleep, his enemy came and sowed weeds among his wheat and then off he went. [26] When the plants came up and started to produce, the weeds also appeared. [27] So the householder's slave approached him and said, 'Master, didn't you sow good seed in your field? Where, then, did the weeds come from?' [28] He replied to them, 'An enemy has done this.' The slaves then asked him, 'Do you want us to go and pull all the weeds out?' [29] He said, 'No, so you don't end up pulling out the wheat in the process of pulling out the weeds. [30] Leave them both to grow until the harvest. Then at harvest time I'll tell those doing the harvesting, "Collect the weeds first and tie them up in bundles to burn them and then bring the wheat into my barn."'"

[31] He presented them with another parable saying, "The kingdom of heaven is like a mustard seed which someone took and sowed in his field. [32] Smaller than all other seeds, when it grows, however, it becomes larger than other plants and turns into a tree, such that birds can come and nest in its branches." [33] He told them yet another parable: "The kingdom of heaven is like yeast, which a woman took and hid in three measures of flour until it made the whole loaf rise."

[34] Jesus talked to the crowds about all these things in parables and didn't address them without using parables, [35] so that the

prophet's prediction came true which says, "I shall open my mouth to speak parables, I shall expound what has been hidden since the world began."

⁣³⁶ Then leaving the crowd, he returned home, and his disciples approached him with the request, "Explain for us the parable of the weeds in the field." ³⁷ He responded: "The sower sowing good seed is the Son of Man. ³⁸ The field is the world. The good seed are the children of the kingdom; and the weeds are the children of the evil one. ³⁹ The enemy sowing them is the devil, and the harvest is the end of the world, and those doing the harvesting are the angels. ⁴⁰ As the weeds are gathered to be burned, so it will be at the end of the world. ⁴¹ The Son of Man will send his angels out and they will gather out of his kingdom all that's offensive sin and those who have engaged in lawlessness, ⁴² and they will throw them into the fiery furnace and there will be weeping and grinding of teeth. ⁴³ Then the good folk will shine like the sun in the kingdom of their Father. Anyone with ears, let them hear this!

⁴⁴ "The kingdom of heaven is like a treasure hidden in a field which someone finds and then hides and so happily goes off and sells all he has and buys that field.

⁴⁵ "And again the kingdom of heaven is like a merchant who was on the lookout for valuable pearls, ⁴⁶ and who, having found a precious pearl, went off and sold all he had and bought it.

⁴⁷ "And again, the kingdom of heaven is like a net thrown into the sea and which caught all kinds of fish. ⁴⁸ When it was full and brought up onto the shore, people sat down and sorted out the good fish into containers and threw the bad ones away. ⁴⁹ That's how it will be at the end of the world. The angels will go out and sort out the wicked from among the good folk ⁵⁰ and throw them into the fiery furnace and there will be weeping and grinding of teeth.

⁵¹ "Do you understand all this?" They replied, "Yes." ⁵² Then he said to them, "This is why every scribe trained for the kingdom of heaven is like a householder who brings both new and old out of his treasure chest."

⁵³ Now when Jesus had finished telling these parables, he set off from there.

FOLLOWING MATTHEW

Thinking About Matthew

This is the famous chapter of parables in Matthew. As usual, he has picked up the collection of parables which Mark brought in Mark 4 but has supplemented them to create now the third major address given by Jesus after the Sermon on the Mount (Matt 5–7) and the address about mission (Matt 10).

Parables are stories or images which stretch the mind and imagination to lead people to new insights. They are often very simple. Sometimes, as people say, "the penny drops," and people get the point, and sometimes they don't. We often use words and phrases to say more than they mean on the surface. To say someone is "a tower of strength," for instance, is not a claim that someone is a tower, but is strong, the way a tower can be. That is how parables work.

There is little doubt that Jesus told parables and there is also little doubt that they were told and retold, often with further reflection and sometimes in such a way that they serve to bring new insights or are used to illustrate new emphases. We can see this happening as Matthew and Luke, for instance, retell parables they found in Mark, often adding interpretations or modifying the parables, and we can be confident that the same went on before Mark's time.

Matthew follows Mark in starting his collection of Jesus' parables with the parable of the wheat farmer. Wheat was grown around the Galilee region, so Jesus was picking up something from everyday life to address his audience, many of whom may well have been farmers. Jesus points to what they all knew happened when they sowed a field of wheat. You lose some. That's just how it goes, whether it's from birds eating the seed or its landing where there wasn't much soil or where the seed would not be able to compete with thistles and such like. But you don't give up, because the miracle of growth occurs, and heads of wheat will come and produce a harvest. They were all familiar with that, though some might have smiled at the optimism of thinking a seed of wheat might reproduce itself a hundredfold. Mark had made that the climax: thirty, sixty, one hundred! Matthew reverses the order (one hundred, sixty, thirty), probably because he is already reading it the way the interpretation will explain it, where the focus is less on the dramatic outcome and more on the diverse responses in the interim.

What's the point? Why rehearse what they all knew, unless it somehow connected with what Jesus was on about? And, yes, it did, because he had used harvest to speak of the hope of God's kingdom coming and, yes, not everyone listened and took his message on board. But there would be a harvest, even if it didn't look like it. "Oh, I see what he means," some would have said, while others would have wondered: "Why say all this?" It was Jesus' way of saying: "The kingdom of God really is at hand, trust me!"

The parable laid the door wide open for it to be played with further. We can see signs that this happened once faith communities got underway and so people added an account of how they thought Jesus might apply it to their situation (Matt 13:18-23; Mark 4:13-20). It is not a very neat fit, because, if the seed is really the message in the original parable, the seed becomes a symbol of people and their responses in the interpretation. It all made sense, however, and could help with understanding success and lack of success as the church engaged in mission. Yes, some responded but didn't last long, and others had little depth and others got waylaid by worries about making money and others couldn't cope when people in the church faced persecution, but some were faithful and bore fruit. The interpretation both comforts those who had to cope with seeing failure among their members and also challenges everyone not to let it happen to themselves.

In between the original parable and the interpretation Mark or his source inserts a conversation between Jesus and his disciples (Mark 4:10-12), which Matthew repeats, expands, and modifies (Matt 13:10-17). The disciples were privileged because they had already got the message, understood it. It sounds initially, especially in Mark, like parables were being told so that others would not get the message. For Mark has Jesus say that parables were "so that" people may not understand, quoting Isaiah, as if telling parables was not about communication but blocking communication and stopping people from responding. This is surely not the case, and Matthew edits Mark so that instead of "so that" he has Jesus say "because" when introducing the citation from Isa 6:9-10. Most are missing the point *because* they are not listening properly.

Putting things in the form of parables did mean that some would get the point and some would not. They listen but they're not getting it. This, too, is in some ways a comfort for those who found mission sometimes a failure. It could, however, easily then morph into blame. Despite these disparaging and confronting words, however, the assumption is that some will respond. Once they do, they'll get the point and, along with that, will begin to understand so much more. Matthew has Jesus add that what they will grasp is what the prophets and upright have longed for over the centuries, namely the time when God's kingdom would be established.

The focus on the church's situation may well account for Matthew adding at this point the parable about weeds growing up in the field of wheat (Matt 13:24–30). What do you do when you think some people in the church are not the real thing? Perhaps Jesus was applying it originally to judgmentalism in the world of his time. Don't get judgmental and start weeding them out. Leave God to be the judge. This recalls his teaching in the Sermon on the Mount, "Don't be judgmental, so you don't get judged yourself" (Matt 7:1).

This parable, too, has a detailed interpretation which explains it along the lines of what Matthew envisaged would happen at the end of history (Matt 13:36–43). Jesus would come as Son of Man, Matthew's term for Jesus when he exercises his role as judge which John the Baptist had already identified. The Son of Man would send out angels to collect the weeds, the unbelievers, and confine them to the fires of hell, and then gather the believers who would shine like the sun in God's kingdom. Already the book of Daniel had described the resurrection in this way: "Those who are wise shall shine like the brightness of the sky, and those who lead many to righteousness, like the stars for ever and ever" (Dan 12:3). Paul speaks in similar terms of Jesus returning to gather his own (1 Thess 4:16–17; similarly, Mark 13:27) and of believers being raised to life: "In a moment, in the twinkling of an eye, at the last trumpet. For the trumpet will sound, and the dead will be raised imperishable, and we will be changed" (1 Cor 15:52).

In between the weeds parable and its interpretation, Matthew returns to Mark and brings the parable of the mustard seed, which he also knew from the source he shared with Luke (Luke 13:20–21). What seems insignificant will become great, a similar message to the parable of the wheat farmer. Matthew's other source goes beyond Mark, who calls it a shrub, to call it a tree, an exaggeration, but it made the point. Birds were sometimes used as an image of gentiles. Reference to birds benefiting from its shade or branches may allude to the future when gentiles would come to be with Israel, but that is uncertain. The message of the parable of the yeast is similar. Again, Matthew cites Scripture from Ps 78:2 to underline that what was hidden in the parables was a message which went to the heart of faith and tradition.

Matthew next turns to imagery which illustrates the kind of total commitment which the message of the kingdom of God invites, like someone finding a treasure or someone finding a precious pearl and selling all to get hold of it. Stories of Jesus calling some to leave families and jobs to join him on the way mirror this commitment.

Matthew then has Jesus bring another parable about judgment day, this time using a fishing image. Sorting fish from a net to keep the ones you want and discarding the rest is Matthew's image of what will happen on the day of judgment. It is typical of the five speeches of Jesus that Matthew has created by bringing related material together that he has them end with the threat of judgment. It fitted the way he has Jesus introduced by John the Baptist as God's agent in executing judgment.

People imagined the future. Hope filled the gap of actual knowledge about the future with imagination. The same was true for what people thought might happen to the wicked. Some of the images are terrifying and cruel and go way beyond what in civilized times we would tolerate. In our justice systems, regard for fellow human beings, even for those who have committed the worst of crimes, never means consigning people to ongoing, excruciating pain. Gospel values have contributed to a commitment never to write people off. This, then, jars with images of God doing what vengeful people would perpetrate and would therefore like to see happen.

At most, we can read such texts with the sense that they are imagination and that they are very human ways of asserting that, in the end, surely people will need to face up to who they are and what they have done, whatever that might look like. The alternative is to promote a religion based on fear, which assumes that God's love is only temporary. Such belief then all too often becomes the justification for people seeing vengeance and violence as modeled by their image of God and therefore as acceptable if they feel they are in the right.

Accountability matters also because love matters, and Matthew also allows us to see that Jesus affirmed love for enemies and an invitation to all to embrace that relationship of love.

Matthew has Jesus conclude this third speech with what many find surprising. He has Jesus speak of scribes in his own movement, "scribes trained for the kingdom of heaven." This reflects the strongly Jewish character of Matthew's world and the faith of both Matthew and Jesus. To some extent this is also underscored by what follows when Matthew has Jesus speak of such scribes bringing out treasures that are both old and new, an image for affirming that faith draws on both Israel's ancient traditions and on the new developments within it which Jesus and others like Matthew bring.

Matthew concludes the account of Jesus' third main speech as he does the others, namely with the words about Jesus having finished, "Now when Jesus had finished telling these parables, he set off from there." We are ready for something new.

Reflection: What was it that made parables engaging yet also meant that only some got the point? Why not just make plain statements which everyone can understand?

Stories and Symbols (Matthew 13:54—14:36)

Listening to Matthew

13:54 Then Jesus came to his home territory and was teaching the people in their synagogue. The outcome was that they were amazed and said, "Where did he get this wisdom from and this power to perform miracles? **55** Isn't this the builder's son and isn't his mother's name Mary and aren't his brothers, James and Joses and Simon and Judas? **56** And aren't his sisters also all here with us? Where did he get all this from?" **57** And they took offense at him. But Jesus responded to them, "A prophet isn't without honor except in his own homeland and household." **58** And he couldn't do many miracles there because of their unbelief.

14:1 At that time Herod the tetrarch heard reports about Jesus **2** and said to his slaves, "This'll be John the Baptist; he's been raised from the dead and that's why these powers are at work in him." **3** For Herod had arrested John, bound him, and put him in prison because of the matter of Herodias, his brother Philip's wife. **4** John had been telling him, "It's against the Law for you to have her." **5** He had been wanting to kill John but feared the crowd's response because they held him to be a prophet. **6** Then at Herod's birthday party Herodias's daughter put on a dance for them and she wowed Herod, **7** so much so that he swore an oath that he would give her whatever she wanted. **8** At the suggestion of her mother she then said, "Bring me here the head of John the Baptist on a platter." **9** The king was upset, but because of his oath and what the guests might think, he commanded that it be done. **10** He sent and had John decapitated in the prison, and **11** his head was brought on a platter and given to the girl and she took it to her mother. **12** Then his disciples took his corpse and buried it and went and told Jesus.

¹³ When Jesus heard about this, he set off from there by boat for an isolated place to be on his own, but when the crowds got wind of it, they followed him on foot from the towns. ¹⁴ Then when he disembarked he saw a big crowd and had pity on them and healed the sick people among them.

¹⁵ When evening came, his disciples approached him saying, "We're in an isolated spot here and it's already very late. Send the crowds off, so they can go into the villages and buy themselves some food." ¹⁶ But Jesus told them, "They don't need to go. You give them something to eat." ¹⁷ They said to him. "We've got nothing here except five loaves and a couple of fish." ¹⁸ He said to them, "Bring them here to me," ¹⁹ and ordered the crowds to sit down on the grass. Then taking the five loaves and the couple of fish, he looked up to heaven and gave thanks and broke them in pieces and gave the bread to the disciples, and the disciples then gave them to the crowds. ²⁰ They all ate and had enough to eat, and they picked up what was left over of the pieces of bread, and it filled twelve baskets. ²¹ There were around 5,000 men who ate, not to mention women and children.

²² Then immediately he made his disciples get into the boat and sail off over to the other side of the lake while he sent the crowds on their way. ²³ Having sent them away, he went off alone up a hill to pray. When evening came, he was there all on his own. ²⁴ Now the boat, having already sailed quite some way from land, was being buffeted by the waves, because they were sailing into the wind. ²⁵ At the fourth watch of the night Jesus came to them walking on the lake. ²⁶ When the disciples saw him walking on the lake, they were terrified thinking that they had seen a ghost and cried out in fear. ²⁷ Then immediately Jesus spoke to them saying, "Cheer up! It's me. Don't be scared!" ²⁸ Then Peter said in response, "Lord, if it's you, command that I come over to you on the water." ²⁹ He said, "Come on!" So, getting out of the boat, Peter started walking on the water and came to Jesus. ³⁰ But when he saw how strong the wind was, he became scared and started to sink, and so cried out, "Lord, rescue me!" ³¹ Immediately Jesus reached out his hand and lifted him up and told him, "My weak-faithed friend, why did you doubt?" ³² When they got into the boat, the wind subsided. ³³ Those in the boat bowed in awe before Jesus and said, "You truly are the Son of God!"

³⁴ When they got to the other side, they reached land at Gennesaret. ³⁵ When the men of that place recognized him, they sent

word to the whole of that region and people brought to him everyone who was sick, [36] and they asked him just to be allowed to touch the fringe of his coat and as many as did so were healed.

Thinking About Matthew

Having produced his third speech of Jesus in Matt 13, based mainly on Mark 4's collection of parables, Matthew skips over to Mark 6. He had already recounted the stories of Mark 5. Matthew therefore takes up the account of Jesus visiting his own townsfolk in the synagogue at Nazareth (Mark 6:1–6). It was a model of what was to come, also for his followers, namely an initial welcome followed by rejection. The scene was so important that Luke relocated it to make it the opening scene of Jesus' ministry (Luke 4:14–30).

The hometown hero comes home. They are so proud of him. That might have been the response. Instead, the locals, while initially admiring his wisdom, needed to put him in his place. "He's just the boy from down the road," we might have heard them say. He shouldn't be "up himself." He should know his place. After all, he's one of us and we know his mum and brothers and sisters. His dad was probably already dead because most men did not make it to sixty, which is how old Joseph would have to have been at this stage, given that most men married around thirty and Jesus was now thirty.

This encounter echoes the situations where Jesus called people to follow him, literally therefore leaving behind their families. Families played a vital role in their society and were part of a stable system which kept society in order, and that meant, of course, ensuring the rich remained rich and the poor remained poor. It was expected that people bowed to family pressure. By contrast, whether you joined Jesus on the road or stayed where you were, to embrace Jesus' message meant committing oneself to the vision and agenda of God's reign, not to the family and social agenda of the time. That challenge faces followers of Jesus in every age. Whether you're a prophet or just a person committed to change and good news for the poor, you won't find easy acceptance where no one wants such change.

In Mark an account of Jesus sending out his disciples follows, but Matthew had already incorporated it in his second major speech which he composed for Jesus in Matt 10. He therefore goes on to what comes next in Mark, namely the account of John the Baptist's execution, an extreme example of the rejection just reflected, but this time by the state authority. As in Mark, Matthew introduces the account with mention of Herod's hearing about Jesus and fearing it may be in some way John the Baptist coming back from the dead to haunt him, as it were. Mark calls Herod a king; but while Matthew, too, will refer to Herod as a king once (Matt 14:9), he mainly uses the more correct title, "tetrarch," the governor of a region. This Herod was Herod Antipas, entrusted with ruling the Galilee and Perea region of his father, Herod the Great's kingdom, when he died in 4 BCE.

We know more about Herod Antipas from the historian Josephus, who tells us that he had an affair with Herodias, his niece and wife of his stepbrother, Herod Philip. As a result she and Philip divorced, and Antipas also divorced his wife, daughter of King Aretas of Damascus, and so Antipas married Herodias, who had a daughter named Salome. Following Mark, Matthew suggests that Antipas was annoyed by John the Baptist's critique, which is expressed as an objection not to the divorces, but to his marrying the divorced wife of his stepbrother in contravention of a very strict reading of Lev 18:16 (Matt 14:4). Most cultures these days would not see a marriage between such divorcees as illegal. Josephus, however, tells us that there was a much broader issue than the criticism of the marriage. For John's preaching about hope for God's kingdom necessarily implied criticism of the injustices of Antipas's rule.

Matthew's trimmed down account has Salome dance and wow Antipas. The legendary story in Mark has him offer to give her up to half of his kingdom, echoing the story of Esther (Esth 5:3, 5; 7:2). Matthew drops that allusion but retains the image of the besotted (and perhaps half-drunk) monarch offering to do things for her. It is in some ways a standard scene of male stupidity. In Mark it is clear that the respectable women are not in the same room as the men, who were being entertained by this dancing girl, and it is left to our imagination what kind of dancing this was and how exploitive and predatory the response to it was. The outcome was Antipas's allegedly reluctant connivance in John's gruesome execution. What a party! What callous abuse of power! Matthew assumes we know that an equally gruesome death would await Jesus who also proclaimed an alternative vision for his world, and ours.

Matthew follows Mark's sequence in telling the story of Jesus feeding the five thousand. Mark tells the story in a way that underlines the fact that these were fellow Israelites that Jesus was feeding. Some of that symbolism is still there in Matthew such as using the number five (five thousand and five loaves), which recalled the five books of the Law, and using twelve, which recalled the twelve tribes. However, Matthew omits other elements such as Jesus seeing the crowd as like sheep without a shepherd, an image used of Israel in Num 27:17 which he had already used in 9:36, and having them sit in groups of fifty and one hundred, like Israel in the wilderness (Exod 18:25; Num 31:14). The result is that Matthew's story focuses primarily on the miraculous feeding, not on the symbolism of these being fellow Jews. Similarly, when he comes to tell of the feeding of the four thousand, portrayed in Mark symbolically as gentiles, Matthew has them depicted as Jews in Jewish territory, not gentiles.

Jesus' gesture of looking to heaven and giving thanks may have had some recall his last meal with his disciples, which formed the basis of their celebration of Holy Communion, an association exploited by the author of John's Gospel. For others the image of a feast would evoke the vision of the great feast which Jesus used as an image of hope. The focus in Matthew on the miracle itself is reflected in his emphasizing that the reference to five thousand men implied that there were women and children, too, making it an even greater achievement.

While the story is still rich in symbolism, almost certainly Matthew would have believed it actually happened and Jesus achieved this on the basis of his supernatural powers and would not have doubted it as many would in today's world. They would not have entertained thoughts such as why, if Jesus had such abilities, he did not use them more widely in his world where there was so much poverty, and why the Spirit which enabled him to do so did not enable his followers to do the same. Such stories had a symbolic function, even for those who took them literally, and to ask such questions demands too much for what they are.

We meet a similar set of questions in the story which follows, which has Jesus walking on water. Of course, the ability to do so would be an enormous help when facing tragedies at sea, but the story is a one-off, not meant to be generalized or treated as a model for what might be possible for others. In Matthew's instance we see how such stories could be developed for symbolic effect. Matthew does this by having the one he will depict as the church's foundation, Peter, also authorized to walk, but then failing. We miss the point if we take Matthew to mean that Peter and others could be walking on water if only they had enough faith. The enhanced symbolism declares that Jesus can deal with the dangers they believed dwelt in the deep, the abode of demons, and that this is indeed an ability that Jesus shares with his disciples. We might put it differently in a world where demonology is not our language of prognosis and say that radical love and acceptance can liberate people from their deepest fears and guilt.

Matthew's other significant elaboration of the story is the detail where the disciples acclaim Jesus Son of God. Acclaiming Jesus the Messiah for the first time came later according to Mark, when Jesus conversed with his disciples at Caesarea Philippi and Peter declared it (Mark 8:29). Matthew reshapes that story and so has them already acclaim him here. As Messiah and Son of God, Jesus is God's agent to deal with human fears of being overwhelmed by life's storms and to bring people peace.

Matthew continues with Mark as he then tells of healing in Gennesaret and how people believed that they could be healed just by touching the fringe of Jesus' coat. The woman with the hemorrhage had done so in the earlier story in Matt 9:21. Here the same quasi-magical power is assumed, reflecting assumptions of the time. Acts even mentions people bringing handkerchiefs and aprons that had been in contact with Paul's skin to the sick, which had healing power and could expel demons (Acts 19:12), a world very different from our own.

Reflection: What do you see as of abiding relevance in these stories and what do you see as not so?

Questioning Assumptions (Matthew 15:1–39)

Listening to Matthew

15:1 Then Pharisees and scribes from Jerusalem approached Jesus saying, **2** "Why do your disciples not follow the tradition of the elders, because they're not washing their hands before they eat their food?" **3** In response he said to them, "Why because of your commitment to your tradition do you not keep God's commandment? **4** For God says, 'Honor your father and your mother,' and 'Whoever slanders their father or mother let them face the death penalty,' **5** but you say, 'Whoever says to his father or mother, "This is a dedicated gift which you've got no right to get from me,"' **6** doesn't need to honor his father or mother and so you seek to invalidate God's word by sticking with your tradition. **7** Hypocrites, well did Isaiah prophesy about you when he said, **8** 'This people honors me with their lips but their heart is far from me. **9** They worship me in vain, and for their teaching they teach the commandments which people want.'"

10 Then summoning the crowd he told them, "Listen and understand this: **11** It's not what enters the mouth which makes people unclean but what comes out of their mouth. That makes people unclean."

12 Then his disciples approached him and said, "Do you realize that the Pharisees were deeply offended when they heard your response?" **13** He answered, "Every plant which my heavenly Father did not plant will be uprooted. **14** Let them be. They are blind guides. When a blind person leads another blind person, they'll both end up falling into the ditch."

15 Peter said in response, "Explain this parable to us." **16** He said, "Do you still fail to understand? **17** Don't you know that everything that goes into your mouth ends up in your stomach and then exits into the toilet? ¹⁸ Things that come out of the mouth, that in fact come from people's minds, they are what make people unclean. ¹⁹ You see, it's from people's minds that evil thoughts emerge, like murder, adultery, sexual immorality, stealing, telling lies, slander. ²⁰ These are what make people unclean; it's not eating with unwashed hands that makes a person unclean."

²¹ And going on from there Jesus went to the region around Tyre and Sidon. ²² And, lo and behold, a Canaanite woman who hailed from that territory started calling out to him, "Have pity on me, sir, Son of David, because my daughter is severely demon possessed." ²³ He didn't respond to her. Then his disciples said to him, "Send her away. She keeps following us and shouting." ²⁴ In response he said, "I was sent only to the lost sheep of the house of Israel." ²⁵ But she came and bowed down before him and said, "Sir, help me!" ²⁶ He answered, "It's not right to take the children's bread and throw it to the dogs." ²⁷ She said, "Yes, sir, but the dogs do get to eat some of the crumbs that fall from their masters' table." ²⁸ Then Jesus answered, "Dear woman, you've got great faith. May what you're wanting to happen, happen!" And her daughter was healed at that very hour.

²⁹ Then Jesus set off from there and came to Lake Galilee, got into a boat and sat down in it there. ³⁰ And many crowds came to him bringing with them people who were lame, blind, unable to walk or speak, and many others, and they laid them at his feet, and he healed them. ³¹ When then the crowd saw the mute people speaking, and those unable to walk now walking, and the lame also walking freely and the blind seeing, they were amazed and glorified the God of Israel.

³² Jesus then summoned his disciples and said, "I am filled with compassion for the crowd because they've been with me already for three days and they don't have anything to eat, and I don't want to send them away hungry, in case they collapse on the way." ³³ His disciples then said to him, "Where are we going to get enough bread out here in the outback to be able to give them enough food?" ³⁴ Jesus said to them, "How many loaves do you have?" They said, "Seven and a few fish." ³⁵ Then he instructed the crowd to sit down on the ground ³⁶ and taking the seven loaves of bread and the fish, he gave thanks and broke them up into pieces and distributed them to the disciples, and the disciples distributed them to the crowds. ³⁷ They all ate and had enough to eat. They picked up what was leftover

of the pieces of bread, and it filled seven baskets. [38] Those who ate numbered 4,000 men, not to mention women and children. [39] Then, sending the crowds away, he got into the boat and sailed to the region around Magadan.

Thinking About Matthew

As Matthew continues with Mark, he makes some significant changes. The first is in his recounting of Mark's story of Jesus' disciples being criticized for not following the established practice of purifying their hands before eating. Mark will have been aware that this would need some explanation for many listening to his Gospel who were not Jews, so gives it (Mark 7:3-4). Matthew assumes his predominantly Jewish listeners needed no such explanation, so leaves that out.

The issue was not hygiene—always sound advice to wash your hands before you eat! It was ritual impurity and the possibility that if by chance your hands had become ritually unclean, such as if you had touched something dead or deemed unclean like blood, then to avoid contaminating your food with your uncleanness, you should wash them ritually clean up to the wrist and then eat. Such concern with ritual purity was widespread and accounts also for the large number of ritual baths which archaeologists have uncovered from the time. There was no biblical command requiring washing hands, but it made sense to be careful and so became at least oral law as passed down by the community elders.

Matthew, as usual, trims the account somewhat but brings at least the accusation on the lips of Jesus that his critics were guilty of using their tradition of rules to circumvent some biblical commandments such as love and respect for parents. Withholding benefit from one's parents on the basis that what you had to give you had assigned to be a gift to God was apparently used as a swindle by greedy people who did not want to assist their parents. It was an abuse, and most would have seen it so.

Jesus' real answer comes in what he explains to the crowd. Here is where he makes some key changes to Mark. Mark reports Jesus saying, "Nothing entering a person from outside them can render a person ritually unclean, but it's what comes out of people that makes them dirty" (Mark 7:15). It has a slight touch of toilet humor. Mark goes on to observe that "In this way he was declaring all foods clean as such" (Mark 7:19). That is a radical claim because it in effect sets aside biblical laws about clean and unclean food and calls into question the whole concept of cleanness and uncleanness.

Matthew, on the other hand, like Luke, has asserted that Jesus set no part of the Law aside (Matt 5:18; Luke 16:17). So his version has Jesus declare: "It's not what enters the mouth which makes people unclean but what comes out of their mouth. That makes people unclean" (Matt 15:11). The playful toilet humor about what really stinks has gone from the saying, although he retains the explanation that mentions how food enters the stomach and then exits into the toilet. Gone, too, is Mark's observation of what he thought Jesus was doing, namely setting biblical law about uncleanness aside, declaring that all foods are clean. For Matthew probably understood the saying to mean, "Not so much what enters a person's mouth . . ." in much the same way as he would have understood "I want compassion, not sacrifice," which he twice cites, not as rejecting sacrifice, but as prioritizing compassion. It was an inclusive rather than an exclusive contrast, and it is likely also to have been Jesus' original meaning when he expressed it in words similar to Mark's version.

Matthew's observation of its meaning comes in his final statement where what he sees Jesus rejecting is only the non-biblical oral tradition, not part of the biblical law as in Mark. Thus Matthew has Jesus conclude: "It's not eating with unwashed hands that makes a person unclean" (Matt 15:20). Aside from that, Matthew retains Mark's report of Jesus putting the emphasis on the uncleanness that emerges from people's minds and attitudes. It fits what Matthew had portrayed as Jesus' teaching in the Sermon on the Mount, about hateful and adulterous attitudes in expounding what really mattered in keeping the Law.

Matthew then follows Mark in telling the story of Jesus' encounter with a gentile woman asking help for her daughter, whom she describes as possessed by a demon. It was part of Mark's composition of these chapters to symbolize the gospel going equally to Jews, represented by the feeding of the five thousand, and to gentiles, represented by the feeding of four thousand gentiles, and depicting the setting aside of biblical laws of clean and unclean foods as making this possible and having the story of the gentile woman illustrating how the boundary was already crossed by Jesus.

Sharing meals with gentiles was a controversial matter, and Paul records his frustration that the conservative behavior of Peter and Barnabas created a barrier to fellowship between Jewish and gentile believers. Mark has Jesus declare such conservatism inappropriate. Matthew does not follow Mark in this. For he has turned the feeding of the four thousand into a feeding of Jews, locating it in Jewish territory, and, as we have noted, reduces Jesus' meaning about uncleanness to setting aside the extra oral law provision of purifying hands before meals.

While not going along with Mark's broader theme in these chapters, Matthew does bring the story of this encounter between Jesus and a gentile woman, described by Matthew as a Canaanite. He makes additions. One is that he has Jesus declare that he was sent only to Israel, echoing the instruction he had Jesus give to his disciples not to go to gentiles (Matt 10:5). Matthew knows that after Easter the gate would be opened to gentiles, but it was not opened yet. Responding to this gentile woman, like his responding to the gentile centurion in 8:5–13, was an exception. Notably on both occasions Jesus does not enter a gentile house, performing the healing from a distance. Both, however, also exhibit exceptional faith which Jesus praises, and both shame his fellow Jews who fail to exhibit such faith. This is also part of Matthew's theme of depicting the most unlikely people seeing the light and the pious failing to do so.

The story itself is daring. It portrays Jesus as voicing a prejudice that others will have shared, which depicted gentiles as unworthy, as dogs. It makes no sense of the story to suggest he means lovely little puppy dogs. It is disparaging. Did Jesus really utter such a comment or was it depicted like this to highlight the contrast, namely that Jesus was willing to cross the boundary that he would have been brought up with? The purpose of the story, as told in the context where the gentile mission was well underway, was to celebrate openness to gentiles, and perhaps its first storytellers were not sensitive to the negative side.

In a sense Mark softens it by having Jesus say, "Let the children be fed first" (Mark 7:27), the word "first" already pointing forward to the broadening. Matthew omits this but also by implication softens it by speaking of his specific mission as being only to Israel. Elsewhere, Matthew is quite happy to portray Jesus as speaking disparagingly of gentiles, such as in the way they pray or the way they pursue wealth (Matt 6:7, 32). His Gospel is, however, pointing forward ultimately to a scenario where gentiles would also be equally loved and cherished, even if it is not directly expressed.

Matthew continues with Mark but again trimming detail and making changes. For Mark goes on to tell of the healing of a man who was deaf and also unable to speak and Jesus' healing actions, using his hands and his spit and touching his tongue. Matthew omits that particular healing, perhaps a little off-put by its depiction of the healing process, and instead has Jesus return specifically to Jewish territory on the west side of the lake and there perform all kinds of healings.

He then, like Mark, brings the account of the feeding of the four thousand. It retains the elements that served Mark's theme of affirming that the Gospel comes to both Jew and gentile, such as especially the play with numbers. The four in four thousand evoked the four corners of the earth or the four winds, suggestive of the whole world, and seven (loaves and baskets) was seen as the number of completeness or perfection. But Matthew has relocated the event to Jewish territory, the west side of the lake, so it is no longer a feeding of four thousand gentiles.

While Matthew, too, embraced openness to gentiles, he portrays it as something that happened only after Jesus was raised from the dead and depicts the risen Jesus as setting it into action (Matt 28:18–20). This was, indeed, the sequence historically. Luke in Acts even depicts the decision to embark on a mission to gentiles as something that took some time. He, too, related it to setting food laws aside, but as something instructed by God in a vision to Peter in Acts 10. That is why he will have chosen not to reproduce the large block of Mark's Gospel, from Mark 6:34—8:26. The apostles' witness to Jesus reached out into the empire as he had Jesus predict (Acts 1:8), but only gradually did it become a witnessing also directly to gentiles. That then entailed a process, sometimes controversial, of working out on what basis gentiles could be counted among God's children, reflected in Acts 15. And Paul, too, reflected the historical sequence when he wrote to the Romans about the good news as being "the power of God for salvation for all who believe, first for the Jew and then for the Greek" (Rom 1:16).

Reflection: What assumptions do these passages address and why did they prove to be so controversial? Do you see equivalent tensions in your faith world?

Finding the Right Foundation (Matthew 16:1–28)

Listening to Matthew

16:1 Some Pharisees and Sadducees approached Jesus to test him out and asked him to show them a sign from heaven. **2** He responded by saying to them, "In the evenings you'll say the weather's going to be fine because the sky is red. **3** And in the morning you'll say today's going to be stormy because the sky is red and threatening. So you know how to read the weather from what the sky looks like, but you can't read the signs of the times. **4** A wicked and adulterous generation wants a sign, but no sign will be given it except the sign of Jonah." Then he left them and went away.

5 When the disciples crossed to the other shore, they had forgotten to take bread. **6** Then Jesus said to them, "Watch and be wary of the Pharisees' and Sadducees' yeast!" **7** They started discussing among themselves whether what he said was because they had no bread. **8** Becoming aware of this, Jesus said, "Why are you having this discussion about having no bread, you weak-faithed lot? **9** Do you still not understand or remember about the five loaves feeding the 5000 and how many baskets of leftovers you picked up? **10** And the seven loaves which fed the 4000 and how many baskets of leftovers you picked up? **11** How come you don't understand that I wasn't speaking to you about bread? Be wary of the Pharisees' and Sadducees' yeast!" **12** Then they realized that he was not telling them to be wary of the yeast in bread but to be wary of the Pharisees' and Sadducees' teaching.

13 When Jesus came to the region of Caesarea Philippi, he asked his disciples, "Who are people saying the Son of Man is?" **14** They replied, "Some say John the Baptist; others, Elijah, and still others, Jeremiah or one of the prophets." **15** He said to them, "And what about you, who do you say I am?" ¹⁶ Simon Peter answered, "You are the Messiah, the Son of the living God." ¹⁷ In response Jesus said to him, "Happy are you, Simon bar Jonah, because flesh and blood did not reveal this to you but my Father in heaven. ¹⁸ And I tell you, you are Peter and on this rock I will build my church and the gates of Hades will not hold out against it. ¹⁹ I shall give you the keys of the kingdom of heaven and whatever you bind on earth will be bound in heaven and whatever you loosen on earth will be loosened in heaven." ²⁰ Then he instructed his disciples to tell no one that he was the Messiah.

²¹ From that time Jesus started to show his disciples that he had to go to Jerusalem and suffer greatly there at the hands of the elders and chief priests and scribes and be put to death and be raised again on the third day. ²² Then, taking him aside, Peter started to contradict him, saying, "Far from it, Lord! No way is this going to happen to you!" ²³ Turning round, he said to Peter, "Off with you, Satan! You're wanting to block my path, because your priorities are not God's but those of human beings."

²⁴ Then Jesus said to his disciples, "If anyone wants to come after me, let them deny themselves and take up their cross and follow me. ²⁵ For whoever wants to save their life will lose it and whoever loses their life for my sake will find it. ²⁶ What benefit is there for anyone if they gain the whole world but lose their life? Or what are people going to give in exchange for their life? ²⁷ For the Son of Man is going to come in the glory of his Father with his angels and then he will reward each person according to how they lived. ²⁸ I'm telling you truly, there are some standing here who won't taste death before they see the Son of Man coming in his kingdom."

Thinking About Matthew

Matthew continues to bring his revised version of Mark's stories. Mark mentions Pharisees wanting a sign from Jesus, and Matthew adds "and Sadducees." By his time in the 80s CE the Sadducees would have been seen as belonging to the past but nevertheless as the ones who had held power in the temple establishment. That may account for Matthew's adding them here. Mark has Jesus refuse to give any sign, but Matthew and Luke's additional source has Jesus refer to the sign of Jonah who, as the story goes, was three days in the monster fish (Matt 12:38–39; Luke 11:29). People will have made the link with Jonah because of the Easter story of Jesus being raised after three days.

The exchange about bread that follows in Matt 16:5–12 plays with bread or yeast as an image for teachings, a not uncommon ploy. It is not altogether clear how Jesus' warning about the Pharisees' and Sadducees' teaching relates to the two feeding miracles to which Jesus points, unless Matthew means us to see them as symbolizing Jesus' teaching. This is likely. In Mark's version this is more clearly the case, for he has Jesus ask the disciples how many baskets of loaves were gathered on each occasion, twelve and seven, and challenges them to see what this symbolized, namely the gospel coming to both Jew and gentiles (Mark 8:19–21). He had Jesus confront the disciples, using imagery from Isa 6:9 of seeing but not really seeing and listening but not really hearing (Mark 8:17–18), something Matthew omits. Matthew, as we have seen, does not take up Mark's depiction of the feedings in this way, but does see them as symbolic of teaching and so pits Jesus' teaching against that of the rival Jewish groups of the Pharisees and Sadducees.

Matthew then chooses not to take up Mark's account of the healing of the blind man at Bethsaida (Mark 8:22–26), perhaps realizing that Mark was employing it symbolically in contrast to the disciples' blindness. Instead, he moves straight to Jesus' conversation with his disciples in the north of the Galilee region, near Caesarea Philippi. In Mark the episode is a turning point, for here for the first time the disciples, represented by Peter, acclaim Jesus as Messiah (Mark 8:27–29). In Matthew it is not the first time they acclaim him as Messiah. They had acclaimed him Son of God, the equivalent, already when they encountered him walking on the lake (Matt 14:33). Matthew even has Jesus ask the question about his identity by already including his identity in his question. Thus, instead of asking, "Who do people say I am?" (Mark 8:27), Jesus in Matthew asks, "Who are people saying the Son of Man is?" clearly referring to himself as Son of Man and therefore Messiah as Matthew understands it.

Peter's response as spokesperson for the disciples declares: "You are the Messiah, the Son of the living God." In Mark it was simply: "You are the Messiah." "Son of God" was one of the titles given a king when he was enthroned, as Ps 2:7 illustrates, where the king reports: "I will tell of the decree of the Lord: he said to me, 'You are my son; today I have begotten you.'" "Son of God" was therefore also a title of the anointed king, the Messiah, and over time came to mean much more.

The focus of the passage falls not so much on this acclamation, because it had been made before, but on Peter's special role. This fits Matthew's earlier emphasis on Peter's significance, for instance, when he has Jesus invite Peter to join him walking on the lake (Matt 14:28–29). The words spoken about Peter in 16:17–19 are Matthew's unique addition to what he found in Mark and they recall traditions found elsewhere about Peter's status. It is interesting, for instance, that when Paul speaks of his own authorization to be an apostle to the gentiles, he used similar language: "For I want you to know, brothers and sisters, that the gospel that was proclaimed by me is not of human origin; for I did not receive it from a human source, nor was I taught it, but I received it through a revelation of Jesus Christ" (Gal 1:11–12).

There is some diversity among the traditions about Peter and his leadership. Three separate traditions identify him as the first to see the risen Jesus (Mark 16:7; Luke 24:34; 1 Cor 15:5) and so in that sense he was the foundation of the church, though traditions also appeared later which had women see him first. Luke has Peter called in the context of a fishing miracle (Luke 5:1–11), but John's Gospel has that occur with the risen Jesus, who then appoints Peter shepherd of the sheep (John 21:4–8, 15–19). Legendary stories inevitably grew up about leaders, but Peter's leadership at least since Easter and possibly before that must lie at their base.

The name Peter means "rock," as does its equivalent in Aramaic, Cephas, and so this makes it possible to speak of Peter as the foundation stone, the beginning of what would become the church. Not even the powers associated with death and Hades would be able to hold out against the impact of what the church would become or threaten it. We are moving in the world of demonology that saw demonic forces as the powers from which people needed to be released and saw the church as constituted to bring such liberation.

The passage continues with references to binding and releasing. This is not about binding and releasing people, but more likely is using the language of applying the Law, about imposing and exempting laws, in other words, about the authority to teach, in contrast to the teachings of the Pharisees and Sadducees. In chapter 18 Matthew portrays Jesus giving the same authority in almost identical words to local congregations when faced with issues of discipline: "Truly I tell you, whatever you bind on earth will be bound in heaven and whatever you loosen on earth will be loosened in heaven" (Matt 18:18).

Such claims, whether made of Peter or of local congregations, reflect the life of the church and so probably derive from that context where people sought to imagine what Jesus would say as they faced new situations. History makes us wary of reading them uncritically, not least because they have also been used to do harm and must be read in the light of human fallibility. Heaven does not rubberstamp church authorities.

That fallibility comes to the fore as Matthew returns to Mark. Keeping silent about Jesus' identity as Messiah made historical sense when it would normally be read as a claim to want to overthrow Rome. That could get you crucified, and we know that this was what happened. Matthew follows Mark in portraying Peter as countering Jesus' indication that he would go to Jerusalem, suffer, and die, and then be raised. For being a messiah normally meant not failure but success. Peter had the title right but the idea of Jesus' messiahship very wrong. In a dramatic reversal, from being the very model of true faith Peter becomes the opposite, someone standing in Jesus' way, acting not for God and God's priorities but Satan's. This is even more potent in Matthew because the words "Off with you, Satan!" were the very words which Matthew has Jesus use in his encounter with Satan in the outback during his time of testing (Matt 4:10).

Mark's composition at this point flows across to chapter 10, presenting over three chapters three occasions where Jesus intimates his fate only to find disciples thinking in quite opposite terms, continuing blindly (Mark 8:31–33; 9:30–34; 10:32–45). Matthew fills the following chapters with much more, with the result that the contrast is not so dramatic, but the exposure of competing values remains. We see it as Matthew goes on to bring Mark's sayings that challenge people to think about what it really means to have life (Matt 16:24–26; Mark 8:34–37).

Some read the sayings about self-denial as encouragement to embrace a humility which can easily lead to lack of self-love. That is not what they are about. Jesus' sayings are best understood not as appealing to people not to love themselves, but rather the opposite. For, in fact, he is appealing to their self-interest with the claim that embracing love for God and others and oneself is the way to find life. Creating a false self which seeks to manipulate others to gain their affection is usually driven by a lack of self-love—that kind of self love is not the way to life. Allowing oneself to embrace love from God liberates people from such demons and frees them to be bearers of love to others, including when it proves costly, as the allusion to the cross reflects. The challenge is not to be fanatics for the cause, as if that is implied in "for my sake," but to be committed to love and the way of Jesus.

John the Baptist emphasized that Jesus would be the judge to come and so Matthew often alludes to that role when giving Jesus that judge's title, the Son of Man. Throughout his Gospel, Matthew reiterates that what God wants is not people appealing to their status, whether as genuinely born Jews or as converts, but people who share God's life and love in the world. Judgment will be on the basis of what people actually do, as Matthew puts it, "then he will reward each person according to how they lived" (Matt 16:27).

Like Mark before him, Matthew is still able to believe that Jesus would come again during the lifetime of some of that generation (Matt 16:28), which we know did not happen, but hope imagines what love might mean. Often what remains is the love as the imaginations crumble. Love is the substance of faith, however we imagine that the hope it generates in us might look like.

Reflection: Why was Peter right and wrong, and why does it matter?

Faith and Imagination (Matthew 17:1–27)

Listening to Matthew

17:1 Then six days later Jesus took Peter and James and John, his brother, along with him, and brought them up a high mountain on their own. **2** And his appearance changed in front of them and his face shone like the sun and his clothes became gleaming white. **3** Then, lo and behold, Moses appeared to them and Elijah, and they were conversing with him. **4** In response Peter said to Jesus, "Lord, it's great that we're here. If you like, I'll put up three tents here, one for you, one for Moses, and one for Elijah." **5** While he was saying this suddenly a bright cloud overshadowed them and a voice spoke from out of the cloud saying, "This is my beloved Son. I am very pleased with him. Listen to him!" **6** When the disciples heard this they fell with their faces to the ground and were very scared. **7** Then Jesus came and touched them and said, "Get up and don't be scared!" **8** When they looked up, they saw no one, but just Jesus himself on his own.

9 As they were coming down from the mountain Jesus gave them instructions saying, "Tell no one about this vision, until the Son of Man has been raised from the dead!" **10** The disciples then asked him, "Why do the scribes say that first Elijah must come?" **11** He replied, "Elijah is coming and will restore everything, **12** and I tell you, Elijah has already come and people didn't recognize him but did what they liked to him. And similarly, the Son of Man is going to suffer at their hands." **13** Then the disciples understood that he was speaking to them about John the Baptist.

14 When they got back to the crowd, a man approached him and knelt before him with the request, **15** "Sir, have pity on me because of my boy, because he's been moonstruck and suffers badly. For often he'll fall into the fire and often into water. [16] And I brought him to your disciples, and they couldn't heal him." [17] In response Jesus declared, "What a faithless and perverse generation! Just how long do I have to hang around putting up with you? Bring him here!" [18] Then Jesus addressed a rebuke to him and out came the demon from him and the boy was healed from that very moment.

[19] Then the disciples came to Jesus when he was on his own and asked, "Why couldn't we expel it?" [20] He told them, "It's because you're weak-faithed. Truly I tell you, if you had faith as small as a mustard seed, you would say to this mountain, 'Move from here to there!' and it would move, and nothing would be impossible for you."

[22] When they came together in Galilee, Jesus said to them, "The Son of Man is going to be handed over to the hands of men [23] and they will kill him and on the third day he will be raised"; and they became distraught.

[24] When they arrived at Capernaum, those collecting the tax of two drachmas approached Peter and said, "Does your teacher not pay the tax?" [25] He said, "Yes, he does." Then anticipating Peter, who had entered the house, Jesus said, "What do you reckon, Simon? Who do the kings of this world get their indirect or direct taxes from? From their own children or from others?" [26] When he replied, "From others," Jesus said, "That means their children are exempt. [27] But so we don't cause offense, go and throw a hooked fishing line into the lake and bring me the first fish you catch and then when you open its mouth you'll find a stater. Take it and give it to them to cover for both of us."

Thinking About Matthew

Matthew follows Mark in taking us next to the highly symbolic scene best known as the transfiguration. Already the fact that it places the event on a mountain reflects the symbolism of mountains as places where one might encounter the holy. Heaven is above, and the same word is used for heaven as for the sky. In their universe, where earth is below and heaven is above, it made sense. Immediately before this account in Mark, and so also in Matthew, Jesus had spoken of the climax of history.

The transfiguration scene is like a film trailer. Matthew even has Jesus call it a vision (Matt 17:9). It presents us with a vision of how history will be in the end. One of the ways in which Jews spoke of the climax of history was to say that Elijah would come (Mal 4:5). He was believed to be still alive since, as the story goes, he was transported up into heaven in a chariot (2 Kgs 2:11). Some also believed that Moses, too, had not died but had ascended to heaven and so many expected him, too, to return. Some connected this hope with the prophetic promise in Deuteronomy that a prophet like Moses would arise (Deut 18:15). These expectations have already been mentioned in the previous chapter where Jesus asked his disciples who people thought he might be (Matt 16:14).

Symbolism is probably also to be seen in the unusual reference to this event taking place after six days, probably a deliberate echo of Moses going up Mount Sinai and after six days receiving the Law (Exod 24:15). This may well have prompted Matthew to add that Jesus' face shone, as had Moses' face on Mount Sinai (Exod 34:29–30). "Transfiguration" is the traditional term used for what in effect is a metamorphosis, a change of Jesus' appearance.

Generally, it was believed that when people would rise from the dead their bodies would be of a different nature, often described as shining and bright. Paul imagines how he thought it would be when Jesus would return during his lifetime and speaks of a transformation of physical bodies to become spiritual bodies: "In a moment, in the twinkling of an eye, at the last trumpet. For the trumpet will sound, and the dead will be raised imperishable, and we will be changed" (1 Cor 15:52). Thus, Jesus appears here in his spiritual resurrection body. Angels, too, were often depicted as appearing wearing shining clothes. Thus the angel who would remove the rock sealing Jesus' tomb had an appearance "like lightning and his clothes as white as snow" (Matt 28:3).

Moses and Elijah are there, as many expected would be the case when the Messiah would come. While Mark reflects the greater emphasis on Elijah and so lists him first and Moses as with him, Matthew changes the order to put Moses first, perhaps because he was thinking of the sequence in the Scriptures where the Law of Moses comes first and then the Prophets, here represented by Elijah. Neither Matthew nor Mark tells us the topic of conversation in which the three were involved, although Luke suggests it was about Jesus' impending fate in Jerusalem (Luke 9:31).

Matthew follows Mark's account of Peter's enthusiastic response of wanting to create a place for all three to stay on the mountain, another instance of portraying Peter's fallibility or his missing the point. Many will smile at his setting a precedent for all those for whom the energy of faith is directed toward buildings and their maintenance.

The voice from the cloud, like the voice from the cloud at Jesus' baptism in Matthew (Matt 3:17), repeats the declaration that Jesus is God's beloved Son and God's approval of him, adding as in Mark, "Listen to him!" In both Mark and Matthew this reminds the disciples, and all disciples since, to listen to the instruction that will follow in the rest of their Gospels, particularly because they are predominantly about what it means to live in a faith community.

The scene ends with Jesus' calling the stunned disciples to get up and telling them not to mention the vision till after Easter. That may well also reflect the likelihood that the scene itself was part of the artistry of faith after Easter as the church reflected on who Jesus was.

Matthew follows Mark also in having Jesus address the issue of Elijah, the key figure expected to come. That hope finds an echo in the story of Jesus' death where some misheard his final cry as calling for Elijah to come (Matt 27:46-47; Mark 15:34-35). One of the ways of dealing with the complex issue of John's status and Jesus' status was to place John within the overall expectation of Jesus as the Messiah by identifying him with Elijah. Earlier, Matthew reports that Herod Antipas pondered whether Jesus was John coming back (Matt 14:1-2). There was the belief that such figures could return in a different guise.

While the first three Gospels embrace the identification of John with Elijah, the author of the fourth Gospel firmly contradicts it (John 1:21). Inevitably there were differences as people tried to make sense of the relationship between key figures and especially between Jesus and John the Baptist. These differences, too, will reflect concerns of the church after Easter as it needed to grapple with its identity and differentiate itself from other Jewish groups and expectations.

Back down the mountain, Matthew has Jesus confronted with his disciples' failure to expel a demon. In their world of demonology, they described what we understand as epilepsy as caused by demons and saw the moon as having a key role, hence my literal translation, "moonstruck." Lunatic has in it the word for the moon in Latin, *luna*. Perhaps the crisis reflects failures during the time of the early church.

Matthew follows Mark in having Jesus rather bluntly tell them all off and declare his impatience with people and in particular with the faith of the disciples. He then trims Mark's detail about what the demon then did to the boy and about Jesus' conversation with the father, whose faith he affirms (Mark 9:26-27). Instead, he reports the successful exorcism and revises Jesus' comments to his disciples from telling them that such exorcism needed much prayer and fasting to assuring them instead that with enough faith they could move mountains, a saying typical of Jesus' use of exaggeration to make a point. Older translations include a verse 21, but most now see this as a later addition inserted from Mark 9:29.

Matthew follows Mark in having Jesus go on to repeat his prediction about what was to happen to him in Jerusalem from which he would then be raised from the dead. This leaves them distraught. "Son of Man" into the hands of "men" is probably a deliberate play on "man," "men," as already in Mark. Mark has this prediction of lowly suffering immediately followed by a deliberately sharp contrast in values, namely, the depiction of the disciples arguing about who among them was to be the greatest (Mark 9:33-34).

Before Matthew brings his version of that scene, Matthew inserts a rather fanciful scene about tax. The two drachmas were the tax males were expected to pay for the upkeep of the temple (Exod 30:13) and, after it was destroyed, the Romans continued to collect it for support of the temple to Jupiter in Rome. It must have been an issue in Matthew's time. If children of kings need pay no tax, then children of God's kingdom should pay no temple tax, but to avoid trouble the advice is: pay! There follows the fanciful story of catching a fish with a shekel, a stater, in its mouth, which made payment possible. The message in Matthew's age is clear: listen to Jesus! Pay the tax and avoid getting into trouble! The amounts adds up: two drachma are the equivalent of two denarii, two days' wages, and add up to half a shekel. The stater or shekel in the fish's mouth therefore meets the tax requirement for Jesus and Peter.

Reflection: In what ways are faith and imagination reflected in these passages, and what might moving mountains mean?

4

The Community

Love, Church Discipline, and Conflict Resolution (Matthew 18:1–35)

Listening to Matthew

18:1 At that time the disciples came to Jesus and said, "Who is the greatest in the kingdom of heaven?" **2** He then summoned a child, and had it stand among them **3** and said, "Truly I tell you, unless you turn and become like children you won't enter the kingdom of heaven. **4** Whoever therefore humbles themselves like this child, that'll be who is the greatest in the kingdom of heaven. **5** And whoever welcomes one such child in my name welcomes me.

6 "And whoever makes one of these little ones who believe in me stumble into sin, it would better for them to have a millstone hung around their neck and be thrown into the depths of the sea. **7** Woe betide this world because of stumbling blocks! There'll inevitably be such stumbling blocks, but woe betide the person who sets them up. **8** If your hand or your foot causes you to engage in abusive behavior, cut it off and throw it away. It's better for you to enter life disabled or lame than to be thrown into eternal fire with both hands and both feet. **9** And if your eye has you engaging in abusive behavior, pull it out and throw it away; it's better for you to enter life with one eye than to be thrown into the fire of Gehenna with two eyes.

¹⁰ "Mind that you don't despise one of these little ones, because I'm telling you, their angels in heaven are constantly looking upon the face of my Father in heaven.

¹² "What do you reckon? If a man has a hundred sheep and one of them gets lost, wouldn't he leave the ninety-nine on the hillside and go and try to find the one that's lost? ¹³ And then if it happens that he finds it, I tell you, he'll be filled with more happiness over that one than over all the ninety-nine who didn't get lost. ¹⁴ Just so, it's not your Father in heaven's will that any of my little ones be lost.

¹⁵ "If your fellow believer sins against you, go and face them with it just between the two of you alone. If they listen to you, then you have regained your colleague. ¹⁶ But if they don't listen, take one or two people along with you, so that every matter can be testified to by two or three witnesses. ¹⁷ And if they refuse to listen, then tell the congregation; and if they won't even listen to the congregation, let them be treated like a gentile and tax collector. ¹⁸ I'm telling you, whatever you bind on earth will be bound in heaven and whatever you forgive on earth will be forgiven in heaven. ¹⁹ And again I tell you, if two of you agree on earth about any matter about which you are asking, it will be granted them by my Father in heaven. ²⁰ For where two or three have come together in my name. I will be there among them."

²¹ Then Peter approached him, saying, "Lord, how often when fellow believers sin against me should I forgive them, as many as seven times?" ²² Jesus told him, "I tell you, not seven times but seventy times seven. ²³ For the kingdom of heaven is like a certain king who wanted to settle accounts with his slaves. ²⁴ When he started settling accounts, one person was brought to him who was indebted to him for ten thousand talents. ²⁵ Because he did not have the wherewithal to repay, the master commanded that he, along with his wife and children and all he had, be sold and the repayment be met that way. ²⁶ So the slave fell down before him, begging him, 'Please be patient with me and I'll pay it all back to you.' ²⁷ The master had compassion on that slave and let him off, canceling the debt he owed him.

²⁸ "That slave then went out and found one of his fellow slaves who owed him a hundred denarii and, grabbing him by the throat, said, 'Repay what you owe me!' ²⁹ The fellow slave then fell down

before him urging him, 'Be patient with me and I'll repay you.' [30] He refused and went off and had him put in prison till he'd paid what he owed. [31] His fellow slaves, when they saw what had happened, were greatly distressed and came and reported to their master all that had taken place. [32] Then his master summoned him and told him, 'You wicked slave! I let you off all that debt when you appealed to me. [33] Shouldn't you then have had pity on your fellow slave, as I had for you?' [34] Then in anger the master handed him over to the torturers till he'd paid all that he owed. [35] Just so my Father in heaven will do to you if any of you do not forgive your fellow believers from your heart."

Thinking About Matthew

Matthew adapts what in Mark had been an account of the disciples arguing among themselves about who among them was the greatest (Mark 9:33–35), in stark contrast to Jesus just having said that his would be a path of lowliness (Mark 9:30–32). It portrayed the disciples in a very poor light. Instead, Matthew has them asking in general about who might be greatest in the kingdom of heaven. The question can still be symptomatic of an unhealthy preoccupation with position and power that finds itself as much inside the church as outside it.

Jesus' response is to confront them with a child, probably a little child. Children, too, can learn at a very early age to embark on a life agenda of competing for attention with others and wanting to be the center and then keep up that behavior all their life till they die. The image here is of a child not yet taken over by such ambition, and we may imagine therefore a child feeling enough love to be secure. Feeling and taking on board enough love can also help adults be secure and give up all the compensatory behaviors that arise from insecurity. Ultimately, the message of divine love sets people free and so is a core element of the gospel. Matthew has Jesus declare that this is what it means to enter God's kingdom, to embrace God's love.

While this may be true of all and is how love works, Matthew's concern is to apply it to what it means to live the life of faith in community. Accordingly, he has Jesus turn his attention to believers as those embracing that child-like trust that characterizes sharing God's life and affirming God's love in the faith community. People become ambassadors or agents and bearers of God's love, and so Jesus declares that accepting them means also accepting the one who sent them, himself, and ultimately God.

There follows a series of warnings that used variations of the word that appears in English as "scandal," *skandalon*. It literally means "stumbling block," something that causes people to fall, an image of sin and wrongdoing. The focus of the warning is on the one who causes others to fall rather than just the one who falls. The target is the perpetrators, and so I could have used the word "abuse" for translating the word. They initiate, and so carry responsibility. The warning against the abuse of causing one of these little ones to sin is about causing believers to go astray. Perhaps originally the saying addressed abuse of children and targeted child sexual abuse.

The word *skandalon* was used sometimes also of sexual wrongdoing. A warning against pederasty may explain the extreme formulation of getting drowned in the sea with a millstone around your neck! When Matthew moves to bring similarly graphic warnings about cutting off limbs and plucking out eyes, not meant literally, sexual wrongdoing may well have occurred to listeners to his Gospel since it was in addressing sexual wrongdoing in the Sermon on the Mount that these sayings were first used (Matt 5:29–30).

Matthew continues the focus on living responsibly in community by addressing various other aspects of wrongdoing, including when someone has gone off the rails, as it were. When he has Jesus speak of little ones, he probably means believers in general, but the saying may originally have meant children. The notion of people having guardian angels derives from this saying. It is another way of saying: God cares, so you, care, too!

Older translations include a verse 11, but most now see this as a later addition inserted from Luke 19:10, to help smooth the transition to the parable about sheep. Church members who become like straying sheep are not to be written off and abandoned but are to be sought out and found. Jesus had originally used the parable of the ninety-nine sheep to defend his reaching out to tax collectors and sinners, as we see in the earlier form of the parable in Luke 15, where it sits alongside other parables with the same theme, the parable of the lost coin and the parable of the prodigal son. Matthew's innovation is to apply the parable of the lost sheep to the church and church members who might go astray.

Next, we find a first-century version of conflict resolution, which retains its wisdom through to our own world. Deal with conflict where possible by a one-to-one encounter. By implication, don't go gossiping to others, or at least talk to others only if you need help for your one-to-one encounter. The next steps, taking others along, and then dealing with it in the congregation, point to the wisdom of thinking carefully about how you handle conflict.

Congregations would have had to deal with issues of church discipline, and these are signs that they sought to take it seriously. The fact that Matthew is addressing a predominantly Jewish believing community explains the somewhat off-putting prejudice that those who refuse to acknowledge their wrong be treated like gentiles or tax collectors. By implication, have nothing to do with them! This stands in contrast to Jesus, who was famous for engaging with tax collectors and sinners and to the wide church that had learned to embrace gentiles. Matthew is portraying Jesus as speaking what was the wisdom and advice of the time as he saw it, even if it may need revision.

Authority to adjudicate and reach decisions on matters of discipline would not have been easy, and so Matthew has Jesus give congregations the same authority given to Peter in Matt 16:19, with the daring suggestion that what they decide on earth would be ratified in heaven, a conviction fraught with difficulty as history has taught us when fallible people have sometimes made very fallible decisions. The promise of Jesus' presence with two or three is not a general statement about his presence with believers, but a very specific promise that he would be with them when they dealt with issues of discipline. Rabbinic tradition similarly promised that where leaders were faced with applying the Law they could be assured of God's holy presence with them.

Compassion pushes to the fore in Jesus' exchange with Peter, where forgiveness is emphasized and by implication is never to be given up. In this way Matthew surrounds the statements about conflict resolution with exhortations that people be compassionate: on one side the parable of the lost sheep and on the other the exchange with Peter and then the parable about forgiveness and forgiving.

The parable with its absurdities of a king's slave owing him ten thousand talents, a stupendous amount, worth more than many economies of the time, makes the point that forgiveness and grace always matter. The image of slaves owning property at all and incurring debts might seem strange, but slaves could indeed carry major responsibility, and some could even earn money despite being slaves.

Matthew regularly reinforces challenges to moral uprightness and goodness with threats, as had John the Baptist. It is a tendency that easily shifts the focus from enabling love to seeking change by frightening people with consequences and can produce images of God as ceasing to be the God of confronting love and forgiveness and becoming more like the fearful tyrants of their world.

Reflection: How has Matthew couched his account of Jesus' instruction about conflict resolution and church discipline and what might it say to such issues in our world?

Grow Up! (Matthew 19:1–30)

Listening to Matthew

19:1 Now when Jesus had finished saying these things, he left Galilee and came into the territory of Judea beyond the Jordan. **2** Many crowds followed him, and he healed them there.

3 Then some Pharisees approached him to test him out, asking, "Is it lawful for a man to divorce his wife for any reason at all?" **4** In response he said, "Haven't you read that the creator from the beginning 'made them male and female'?" **5** and added, "'This is why a man will leave behind his father and mother and will be joined to his wife, and the two shall become one flesh.' **6** So they are no longer two but one flesh. What God therefore has joined together is not for humans to separate." **7** They said to him, "Why then did Moses give the instruction to give the wife a bill of divorce and send her away?" **8** He answered them, "Moses allowed you to divorce your wives because of your hardheartedness, but from the beginning it wasn't so. **9** I'm telling you, whoever divorces his wife except on grounds of sexual immorality and marries another commits adultery."

10 His disciples then said to him, "If that's the case between a man and his wife, it's better not to marry." **11** He responded to them, "Not everyone can live with that stance but only those given the call to do so. **12** For there are eunuchs who have been so from the time they emerged from their mother's womb; and there are eunuchs made so by people castrating them; and there are eunuchs who have made themselves eunuchs for the sake of the kingdom of heaven. If you can live with it, do so!"

13 Then people brought children to him for him to lay his hands on them and pray for them, but his disciples told them off for doing so. **14** Jesus then said, "Let the children come and don't stop them from coming to me. For the kingdom of heaven belongs to such little ones." [15] And he laid hands on them and sent them on their way.

[16] Then, lo and behold, a man approached him with the request, "Teacher, what good deed do I need to do to obtain eternal life?" [17] He answered, "Why do you ask me about what is good? There is only one who is good. If you want to enter life, keep the commandments." [18] He said, "Which ones?" Jesus replied, "The ones that say, 'You shall not kill, you shall not commit adultery you shall not steal, you shall not lie, [19] honor your father and your mother' and 'You shall love your neighbor as yourself.'" [20] The young man responded, "I've kept all these; what more do I need to do?" [21] Jesus said, "If you want to be perfect, go and sell your possessions and give the proceeds to the poor and you will have treasure in heaven, and come and follow me." [22] When the young man heard this response, he went off disappointed because he had a lot of possessions.

[23] Jesus then said to his disciples, "Truly I tell you, rich people will have a hard time getting into the kingdom of heaven. [24] Again, let me tell you, it is easier for a camel to pass through the eye of a needle than for a rich person to enter the kingdom of God." [25] When the disciples heard this, they were rather nonplussed and said, "Who then can be saved?" [26] Looking at them, Jesus said, "This is impossible at a human level, but everything's possible with God."

[27] Then Peter replied, "Look we've left everything and followed you. How does it stand with us?" [28] Jesus said to them, "Truly I tell you, when it comes to the day of resurrection when the Son of Man will be sitting on his throne, you who have followed me will sit alongside me on twelve thrones conducting judgment over the twelve tribes of Israel. [29] And there's no one who has left their homes, or brothers or sisters or father or mother or children, who will not receive a hundredfold more and inherit eternal life. [30] Many who are first will be last and are last who will be first."

Thinking About Matthew

Matthew 18 was Matthew's fourth major speech of Jesus, and so he transitions from it in the familiar way that follows all five speeches, "Now when Jesus had finished saying these things," and returns to Mark 10, repeating the brief summary there about Jesus moving from Galilee to the

Transjordan area belonging to Judea with a big following. Matthew then follows Mark in bringing three key episodes that belong to the teaching to which faith communities should listen, as the voice from heaven at Jesus' transfiguration instructed, if they are going to live well.

The first is about divorce. It had become a subject of debate especially as people turned away from polygamy, or, strictly speaking, polygyny, that is, having more than one wife. In polygynous marriages conflicts could be resolved by a man taking another wife. There were even stories of men falling in love again with their first wife. Polygyny was forbidden in the influential Greek and Roman culture which came to penetrate Palestine, and so not only fell out of fashion but increasingly was also seen as not what God preferred. The texts from Genesis cited by Jesus helped reinforce this view. God made male and female (Gen 1:27) and a man was to leave home to set up a new household by becoming one flesh through sexual union with his wife (Gen 2:24). These texts came to be read as implying that a man should have only one wife.

Once polygyny was rejected, the alternative in cases of conflict was divorce. We see this reflected indirectly in Deut 24:1–4, to which the Pharisees in this episode appeal. It is about not remarrying your original wife once you had divorced her and she had married another man and then been divorced again. In the process of rejecting such remarriage the passage incidentally allows us to see what divorce entailed. A man (and it usually was a man's prerogative in Israel) gave his wife a certificate of divorce which would free her to remarry, and then sent her away. The basis for divorce according to this text was "something objectionable" in the wife. What did that mean? We know of debates between Jewish leaders before and after the time of Jesus about what it could mean. Was it, as the School of Hillel suggested, something as trivial as bad cooking, or was it, as the stricter School of Shammai suggested, some form of sexual wrongdoing? Earlier tradition had required that people caught in adultery be executed, but, when the Romans withheld from the Jewish state the right of capital punishment, it required that the partners divorce.

We can imagine that divorce, whatever the justification, placed many women in a very vulnerable position. Divorced, they might return to their parents' home or marry again or find some independent form of survival, which in some instances might include prostitution. Jesus' response to the issue is an absolute: no, no divorce! He argued that divorce was never meant to be and appealed to what were then favorite Genesis texts to defend marriage. The assumption is that sexual intercourse, joining, connected people together for life. They became one flesh. Don't unjoin what God has joined! Matthew knows Jesus' prohibition of divorce not just from Mark but also from the source he shared with Luke, when he cites it in the Sermon on the Mount (Matt 5:31–32; Luke 16:18). Paul, too, cites the prohibition when writing to the Corinthians (1 Cor 7:10–11).

Matthew's version of the prohibition in both places, here and in 5:32, has an exception: "except for sexual immorality," and almost certainly means: except where adultery has taken place, the assumption being that this would indeed sever the relationship. In some languages the word for adultery means literally severing the marriage. This exception is very likely to have been assumed from the beginning, not least because it was the law of the land. Indeed, the Roman Empire reinforced it and even prosecuted men who did not divorce wives who had committed adultery.

Subsequent generations had to grapple with how flexible or otherwise this prohibition was. Did it allow for circumstances where a good case could be made for divorce, such as in situations of domestic abuse? The flexibility to make adjustments when faced with new situations was characteristic of the Jesus movement from the beginning, inspired in part by Jesus' insistence that in interpreting the Law people needed to take into account that for God people mattered most, love mattered most. The early church had to take that further and sit loose to some biblical laws, such as circumcision of males and food laws. Paul illustrates such flexibility well when, having cited Jesus' prohibition of divorce in 1 Cor 7:10–11, he offers the suggestion that in the situation of a mixed marriage where a non-believing partner wants it, then divorce (and so remarriage) could be contemplated. We have learned that a commitment to love and health does mean that sometimes divorce may be the more loving and caring option, once all other avenues for healing and reconciliation have been explored.

Only Matthew brings the conversation that follows where the disciples suggest that it may be better to avoid marriage altogether. It's too much trouble! In addition, we know that there were movements within the early Christian communities that pushed the view that all should abandon marriage anyway, especially because of the widespread belief that marriage and marital life would have no place in the life to come, as reflected in Mark 12:27, followed by Matthew in 22:30. Those who believed that the age to come was about to come into reality pressed the argument that celibacy and singleness should henceforth be the norm.

Paul had to combat such views in Corinth where, despite his personal preference to be unmarried, he had to defend marriage as an option that many would take. Matthew's community may well have had such streams of thought, so that Matthew here has Jesus insist that while some may choose to remain unmarried, it was not for everyone, but only for those especially called to it.

The saying of Jesus uses the image of eunuchs. Eunuchs were men who either through castration or from birth were incapable of reproducing. Eunuchs were also seen as useful to have as public servants in royal courts with harems, because they were also not able to bring about unwanted pregnancies among female staff, but also because they were mostly not involved in supporting families, though we know of some who married. In that sense they were a suitable image to use for disciples who would carry ministerial responsibility. Some have suggested that reference to eunuchs may be a way of referring to gay men or reflect an acceptance of some people being gay from birth, but the saying does not imply this. Accepting that some people are gay has more secure grounds than trying to find biblical texts to argue for it.

The next scene has a clear message: children have their place and are not to be shunted aside, true then and just as much today. That is Matthew's message, as he portrays the disciples' concerns, who might well have been saying: "He's too busy!"

Matthew's creativity is to be seen in his retelling of the story of the rich man who approaches Jesus. He changes the initial exchange where Mark reported Jesus as saying, "Why do you call me good? No one is good but God alone" (Mark 10:18). Removing the possible misunderstanding that Jesus was saying he was not good, Matthew changes the conversation so that it focuses on what is good: "Why do you ask me about what is good?" He also reshapes Jesus' answer from referring to commandments as "Do not kill" etc., to the way they are formulated in the Ten Commandments: "You shall not kill," etc. Mark's "Do not defraud" is not in the ten, so Matthew leaves it out, but then adds: "You shall love your neighbor as yourself," which fits the focus of the passage well. Jesus' response is a good, standard, Jewish response and is consistent with Matthew's presentation of Jesus as a faithful and observant Jew.

Another creative innovation is that he turns the man into a young man and so trims the comment, "All these I have kept since my youth" (Mark 10:20) to "All these I have kept." That playfulness continues when Matthew has Jesus say, "If you want to be perfect," because the word "perfect" is also the word for "grown up," "mature." Grow up, young man! Jesus is not asking a higher level of obedience as though this is something beyond keeping the commandments. Rather it is a challenge to see if the young man is really in touch with what the commandments are about. A commitment to do God's will is about more than just keeping commandments; it is also about embracing the spirit that lies behind them and being willing even to sell all and give to the poor, become good news for the poor. Jesus is not now withdrawing from his previous answer as though it was inadequate or no longer applies because now it needs to include following Jesus. On the contrary, to follow Jesus was to follow the way he understood the commandments and what lay behind them. As expounded in the Sermon on the Mount, upholding the Law meant embracing compassion. That is the way to life and the way to share God's life.

The scene illustrates what Jesus asked some to do: follow him literally. Others he told to stay home but equally to be good news for the poor. Like Mark, Matthew goes on to have Jesus emphasize how difficult it is for people wedded to their wealth to let it go. Jesus challenged people to let God and not wealth be God. There must have been pain for those who took the radical option of abandoning everything, and for them Matthew has Jesus offer the comfort of finding what he suggests is more than adequate compensation. The passage is subversive and ends subversively with the first ending up last and the last first.

Reflection: What underlies the clash of values evident in these stories?

God's Priorities (Matthew 20:1–34)

Listening to Matthew

20:1 "The kingdom of heaven is like a certain householder who went out early one morning to hire workers for his vineyard. **2** Having settled with them on paying them a denarius a day, he sent them off into his vineyard. **3** Then around nine in the morning he went out and saw others standing around in the marketplace doing nothing **4** and he told them, 'You, come, too into my vineyard and I'll pay you a fair wage.' **5** So they came. And again, when he went out around midday and around three in the afternoon he did the same. **6** Then late afternoon around five he went out and found others standing around and said to them, 'Why are you hanging around here the whole day doing nothing?' **7** They told him, 'No one's given us a job.' He then said to them, 'You, come, too, into my vineyard.'

8 "That evening the owner of the vineyard told his admin officer, 'Call the workers and pay them their wages, starting with these last workers and ending with those employed first.' **9** So those who came at around five each got a denarius. **10** So those employed first thought that they would get more, but they, too, each received a denarius. **11** When they got it, they complained to the householder, **12** 'These workers worked for just one hour and got a denarius. You've treated them the same as us who have carried the day's tasks and put up with its heat.' **13** He responded to one of them, 'My friend, I'm not doing you an injustice. Didn't you agree on a denarius as your wage? **14** Take it and go! It's my choice to give those last employed the same wage as you. **15** Can't I do what I like with my own money? Or are you with your greedy eye saying I'm not a good man?' **16** Just so, the last will be first and the first last."

¹⁷ On his way up to Jerusalem Jesus took his disciples aside and told them as they went along, ¹⁸ "Look, we're going up to Jerusalem, and the Son of Man is going to be handed over to the chief priests and scribes, and they will impose the death penalty on him ¹⁹ and hand him over to the gentiles for them to mock him and beat him and crucify him, and then on the third day he will be raised."

²⁰ Then the mother of Zebedee's sons approached him along with them and kneeling in front of him asked him for a favor. ²¹ He said to her, "What is it you want?" She replied, "Decree that my two sons are to sit on your right and left-hand side in your kingdom." ²² Jesus answered, "You don't know what you're asking for. Can you drink the cup I'm going to drink?" They replied, "We can." ²³ He said to them, "You'll drink of my cup, but to sit on my right and left-hand side, that's not for me to grant, but that's for those prepared for it by my Father."

²⁴ When the other ten heard this, they were angry with the two brothers. ²⁵ So Jesus called them together and said, "You know that those who rule among the gentiles like to exercise power over them and to boss them around. ²⁶ It's not to be like that with you. Rather whoever wants to be great among you needs to be your servant ²⁷ and whoever wants to be first among you is to be your slave, ²⁸ just as the Son of Man did not come to be served but to serve and give his life as a ransom for many."

²⁹ As they were heading out of Jericho, a big crowd was following him. ³⁰ Then, lo and behold, two blind men who were sitting beside the road, when they heard that Jesus was coming along, shouted out, "Have pity on us, sir, Son of David!" ³¹ The crowd tried to shut them up, but they shouted out all the more, "Have pity on us, sir, Son of David!" ³² Jesus stopped and called them and said, "What do you want me to do for you?" ³³ They said to him, "Please, sir, to help us see!" ³⁴ Moved with compassion, Jesus touched their eyes, and immediately they recovered their sight and they followed him.

Thinking About Matthew

Matthew ended Matt 19 with the statement that "Many who are first will be last and are last who will be first" (Matt 19:30), which he took up from Mark 10:31. He then repeats a variation of it in 20:16, "The last will be first and the first last," a more absolute statement implying it would apply to all. Both statements reflect an overall assumption that the order of society as they saw it was not the way God wanted it. The previous context had related this to those who pursue wealth and, as Matthew continues, he will bring further material from Mark that shows Jesus challenging the wealthy and powerful and contrasting it with the kind of greatness and leadership that Jesus modeled.

By repeating this saying in 19:30 and 20:16 that looks to a reversal of fortunes, Matthew has created a frame around the parable of the workers in the vineyard and thereby interprets it in this sense. The parable itself is making a slightly different point. It has a vineyard owner pay everyone who worked for him a day's wage, as a denarius was reckoned to be. It is not laziness, nor injustice on his part, but rather a concern to give these people what they needed to live on which leads to his giving everyone a denarius. We might compare it to our unemployment benefits. In that sense its focus is human need.

Behind it is Jesus' effort to defend his reaching out to people who ranked very low on the scale of society values at that time: the poor, the sick, the marginalized, but also people who marginalized themselves and people who were blatantly sinful and despised. Offering God's love to them, when they least deserved it according to the values of the time, seemed so inappropriate. The parable of the prodigal son has the older brother express similar sentiments (Luke 15:11–32), and the parable of the rogue servant who wrote off or reduced the debts of his master's debtors only to find his master's approval (Luke 16:1–8) seems similarly to address the criticism that Jesus faced. The offer of a relationship of love and acceptance was being offered to all, including sinners, not just the righteous, and including both the poor and the rich.

Matthew then returns to Mark and brings the third occasion when Jesus speaks of the fate that awaits him in Jerusalem. Surely not, Peter had argued (Matt 16:22). Matthew stays with Mark in going on to contrast Jesus' approach with that of James and John who are bent on being first and having power. Matthew's modification is to have their mother take the initiative, perhaps a rather cruel twist, but then as the story goes on, it is clear that Matthew sees them as equally behind the move. They insist that they will drink the same cup as Jesus, a slight irony because Matthew's readers probably know of their martyrdom, or at least that of James (Acts 12:2).

THE COMMUNITY

The matter comes to a head, as in Mark, when the other ten disciples hear of their move and Jesus addresses the issue of power again. A generalizing observation from his Jewish perspective points to the behavior of gentile rulers who love having power over people. Of course, we know that politicians of Israel are just as human, but the point is not the accuracy of the observation nor the promotion of prejudice about non-Jews. What Jesus points to is the lust for power and control which so often arises when people engage in leadership to meet their own egotistical ends, a phenomenon of every age.

As in the subversive statements about the last being first and the first last, so, here, Jesus juxtaposes the powerful and the powerless, the mighty and the meek. For Jesus, love is greatness, and that may look like being a slave and a servant in contrast to the high and mighty, but it is not about being a doormat and submissive. It is about persisting with love and compassion and taking its journey wherever it leads even when it is costly. Such is also God's greatness in creativity and love. God is not like the power-hungry, namely, obsessed with power and being the center of admiration, as many images of God suggest. People often project their models of greatness onto God, creating God in their own image. Jesus makes it very clear: he came not to be served but to serve, a striking confrontation of what many would see as their priority and ambition. This is how Jesus is and how God is. God is love.

Jesus' statement about himself mentions not just serving but also his death as like an act of ransoming people from bondage, bringing liberation, another aspect of the love he represents. Some move beyond the imagery to postulate that we need to take the statement literally and ask questions like: did Jesus pay a ransom to God, paying for forgiveness? Or to the devil, to release us? This fails to appreciate the long tradition of using the language of ransoming or redeeming to mean simply liberating, such as when they spoke of God liberating Israel from slavery in Egypt. No one imagined a transaction like an actual payment of a ransom to a Pharaoh or such like. Jesus' death, like his life, was an act of liberation, of bringing the love that sets people free, and images abounded that sought to express its impact.

Continuing with Mark, Matthew takes up the story of blind Bartimaeus, but, as he had done already using a version of the story in 9:27–31, he drops the name and instead depicts two blind men calling out to Jesus. According to Jewish law evidence needs to be substantiated by at least two or three witnesses (Deut 17:6). This probably explains the doubling; the two in that sense become valid testimony to who Jesus is. The appeal is to Jesus as Son of David, a title for the Jewish Messiah of the line of David, but it probably also plays on its literal meaning as alluding to David's son, Solomon, who was believed to have been the source of medical wisdom.

In Mark the story echoes the healing at Bethsaida (Mark 8:22–26) and, like that story, forms a framework around the intervening episodes. They function also as a symbol; they show blind people made to see in contrast to the blindness of the disciples who constantly fail to see what mattered for Jesus and what leadership truly means. Matthew may well have had similar thoughts. The disciples were to be confronted with the path of Jesus and its consequences in reality.

Reflection: What do these passages tell us about how Matthew saw God's priorities?

Failure to Bear Fruit (Matthew 21:1–22)

Listening to Matthew

21:1 When they approached Jerusalem and came to Bethphage at the Mount of Olives, Jesus then sent off two of his disciples, **2** telling them, "Go into the village opposite and straightaway you'll find a donkey tied up along with a foal. Untie them and bring them to me. **3** If anyone asks you, 'Why are you doing that?' tell them their master needs them." So he send them off straightaway. **4** This happened so that what was said by the prophet might come true, namely, **5** "Tell the daughter of Zion, 'Look your king is coming to you, humble and mounted on a donkey and on a working donkey's foal.'"

6 So off the disciples went and did what Jesus told them to do. **7** They brought the donkey and its foal and decked them with garments and mounted Jesus on them. **8** The huge crowd spread their garments out on the road and others cut branches from the trees and spread them on the road. **9** The crowds going ahead of him and those following him shouted out, "Hosanna to the Son of David! Blessed is the one who comes in the name of the Lord! Hosanna in the highest!" **10** When they reached Jerusalem, the whole city was in turmoil, saying, "Who is this?" **11** The crowds said, "This is the prophet Jesus from Nazareth in Galilee."

12 Then Jesus entered the temple and drove out all who were selling and buying things in the temple and overturned the tables of the moneychangers and the chairs of those selling doves. **13** And he said to them, "It is written, 'My house shall be called a house of prayer' but you are making it 'a den of crooks.'"

14 Blind and lame people who were in the temple approached him and he healed them. **15** When the chief priests and scribes saw the wonders he performed and the children shouting, "Hosanna to the Son of David!" in the temple, they were annoyed [16] and told him, "Do you hear what these kids are saying?" Jesus replied, "Yes. Haven't you ever read, 'From the mouths of infants and breastfeeding babies I shall elicit praise'?" [17] Then he left them and exited the city for Bethany and stayed there overnight.

[18] Next morning, as he was heading back to the city, he was hungry, [19] and, seeing a single fig tree by the road, he went to it but found nothing on it but just leaves, and so he said to it, "May no fruit come from you ever again!" And immediately the fig tree shriveled up. [20] When the disciples saw this they were amazed and said, "How come the fig tree suddenly shriveled up?" [21] Jesus replied, "Truly I tell you, if you have faith and don't doubt, you'll not just be able to do this to a fig tree but you'll also be able to say to this mountain, 'Up from here and get into the sea,' and it will happen. [22] Everything you ask for in prayer, if you have faith, you'll get."

Thinking About Matthew

As Matthew continues to take up Mark, he tells the story of Jesus' arrival at Jerusalem. So he begins with the fetching of the donkey on which Jesus would ride into Jerusalem. As he usually does, Matthew takes up the allusion to Scripture and turns it into a direct quotation introduced by his standard reference to Scripture being fulfilled. In this instance, therefore, he cites Zech 9:9, with its reference to a donkey and its foal, but leaves out its reference to the king having been "triumphant and victorious" as clearly unsuitable for the story. Donkeys were used for transport, hence the reference to the foal as the foal of a working donkey. The citation could be read to imply that the king was somehow riding on both, if not read as poetic parallelism, and so Matthew rewrites Mark to have Jesus riding on both, however they would have imagined that! The context in Zechariah was about the hope that this victorious king would rule Israel and bring peace that would extend to the nations of the world. It, therefore, fitted the hope for a messiah in David's line and so helps explain why people greeted Jesus as Son of David.

Those who retold Jesus' last days drew upon such texts, even when they knew that Jesus was not the kind of triumphant military messiah those texts envisaged. Going back behind such stories to what might actually have happened when Jesus arrived at Jerusalem is difficult. John's

Gospel tells the story, too (John 12:12-19), but suggests that it was only after Easter that the disciples saw any messianic connection (John 12:16). Greeting pilgrims using the words of Ps 118 was not uncommon. It reads, "Save us, we beseech you, O Lord! O Lord, we beseech you, give us success! Blessed is the one who comes in the name of the Lord. We bless you from the house of the Lord" (Ps 118:25-26). It has been adapted to apply to Jesus, retaining the Hebrew for "Save us," transliterated as "Hosanna," and adding the title "Son of David." Just one verse earlier Ps 118 spoke of the rejected stone whose fate was reversed when it was made the main cornerstone (Ps 118:22-23). It would be employed as something that Mark and so Matthew has Jesus cite after telling the parable of the tenants, which soon follows, with reference to his death and resurrection (Mark 12:10-11; Matt 21:42).

A storyteller may have imagined the scene and colored it with such biblical allusions; or perhaps there was a special welcome historically. It would, however, have had to have been rather low key; otherwise, we can be sure that the Roman authorities would have pounced and nothing that follows suggested that it was taken up in the charges against Jesus. It is, however, a story that invites identification and fantasy, and people have found themselves entering into the story, either as one of those whom Jesus' ministry has touched, or as a person of our own time welcoming this Jesus into our cities or into our individual lives.

In contrast, the story of Jesus' action in the temple, taken up in the charges against him, very likely alludes to an event that actually took place. It coheres with Jesus' challenge to the temple authorities, that is widely attested, in which he called their integrity and behavior into question, such as in Mark 12:38-40; in the parable of the Good Samaritan in Luke 10:25-37; and behind the expanded accusations in Matt 23. Disrupting the commerce, the currency exchange facility, and those selling doves was a prophetic act of judgment against what the temple had become. It is misread if we think its focus was on sellers charging too much, for instance, or corruption in currency exchange. No such abuses receive mention. People needed the exchange because the temple wanted contributions in the coinage of Tyrian shekels. Enabling people to purchase doves for sacrifices was also necessary. Rather the objection is to what the temple had become, a commercial operation that failed to give highest priority to worship and prayer and to caring about people.

The words "'My house shall be called a house of prayer' but you are making it 'a den of crooks'" (Matt 21:13) are not focusing on crooked dealings by those expelled, but on what Jesus and many others of the period saw as a failure of the temple and temple authorities to enable the temple to be what it was meant to be. "Den of crooks" is a phrase taken from Jeremiah's critique of the temple establishment in his day for similar reasons (Jer 7:11). The word I have translated "crooks" has a range of meaning from "robbers/thieves" to "revolutionaries/brigands." The historian Josephus uses it for groups involved in the revolt against Rome in 66–70 CE, who for part of the time made the temple their base. This is also the sense of the word when used of those crucified for subversion along with Jesus, not "robbers/thieves" but rather "revolutionaries/brigands." It is likely that many hearing Matthew's Gospel would have thought of such groups.

In its context, however, the reference is more likely to be to the corruption of the temple in general, which led many to long for a new temple, often associating it with the coming of the Messiah who would have it built or rebuilt. John's Gospel reports that Jesus declared on this occasion: "Destroy this temple, and in three days I will raise it up" (John 2:19), which the author treats symbolically as alluding to Jesus' resurrection. Behind it, however, was probably a prediction on the part of Jesus about a replacement for the actual temple. An accusation based on this appears in Jesus' hearing before the Sanhedrin according to which Jesus had declared, "We heard him say, 'I will destroy this temple that is made with hands, and in three days I will build another, not made with hands'" (Mark 14:58). It is, doubtless correctly, labeled as false: he was not going to do it, but not false in the prediction of what God would do. As it stands, Mark's version also reworks the prediction symbolically by adding the references to "made with hands" and "not made with hands," pointing to the community of faith as the new temple. Matthew appears not to embrace that view and so omits these additions. Very likely he retains the hope for an actual new temple.

Jesus' action in the temple would certainly have attracted attention and is thinkable historically as an occurrence within the outer court of the temple. It was huge, some six football fields in size, and likely on Passover weekend to have been filled with pilgrims, enabling Jesus to perform the act and then disappear into the crowd. Rome guaranteed protection of sacred sites in its realm, including the Jerusalem temple, so that any act against the temple would also count as an act against Rome. He was placing himself in danger.

Already in Mark's version of the story we have an allusion to Scripture in Jesus' statement. It reads: "My house shall be called a house of prayer for all peoples" (Mark 11:17), citing Isa 56:7. The outer court of the temple where Jesus' action took place was called the Court of the Gentiles. Gentiles could enter that part of the temple. Mark, or perhaps his source, was therefore pointing forward to the gentile mission in which Israel's dream of having all nations come to Jerusalem and live at peace with the people of God would be fulfilled (Isa 2:2–4). Matthew, however, decided to omit the words "for all peoples." That is a theme he takes up at the end of his Gospel.

Unique to Matthew is his reference to the blind and lame coming to Jesus in the temple and his healing them and also his reference to children acclaiming him with the same words as the crowds' initial acclamation at his entry, "Hosanna to the Son of David!" (Matt 21:15). There follows Jesus' response to the anger it evoked in the chief priests and scribes, namely another quotation of Scripture (Ps 8:2). Its form, "From the mouths of infants and breastfeeding babies I shall elicit praise," does not correspond to what we find in the original Hebrew text, but to the version found in the Greek translation. It may reflect an alternative Hebrew text, as sometimes happens, or it may reflect that the story comes from the post-Easter period in a context where, like Matthew's Gospel, Greek was the language spoken. It fitted the theme of showing that the children and the ordinary people saw who Jesus was, whereas the authorities did not.

Matthew then returns to Mark with his story of the fig tree but rearranges the material. Mark has Jesus see it, note it had no fruit, and curse it (Mark 11:12–14), then enter the temple and perform his act and on his way back see it had completely withered (Mark 11:20–21). Mark also explains that it was not the time of year when one should expect figs on the tree (Mark 11:13). They would appear in summer. This way Mark is giving us a loud hint that the story is to be taken symbolically. Cursing a tree for not bearing any fruit for you when it is not the fruit bearing season is an irrational act. By putting the fig tree episode on either side of the account of Jesus' action in the temple, Mark is using it to symbolize the meaning of that act: a foreshadowing of the temple's destruction because it, that is, its leaders, failed to bear fruit. Matthew keeps the story together, but will also be using it to foreshadow the temple's destruction as God's judgment.

Like Mark, Matthew, too, then appends to the fig tree episode amazing promises which appear to suggest that such magic to shrivel fig trees will be available to the disciples if only they believe. Mark includes also sayings about community and forgiveness, suggestive of a new community, a temple not made with hands, where love prevails (Mark 11:25). That is not how Matthew saw it, so he does not use that saying here. He had instead used these words about forgiveness earlier, after his presentation of the Lord's Prayer (Matt 6:14–15).

Matthew does, however, stay with the stupendous claims of what believers should now be able to do. Matthew has already had Jesus make such claims after the account of transfiguration when he found his disciples had failed to exorcise a demon from a boy (Matt 17:20). Those who knew the location of the temple on Mount Zion may well have heard the promise to move mountains here in 21:21 and smiled. They could tell Mount Zion to relocate to the ocean depths! Really? Not literally, but a major shift of faith's focus was to take place, and Matthew was part of it. Promises that prayers will be answered are not to be generalized into a strategy for meeting greed. They are rather an assurance of assistance in the challenges of engaging in mission and keeping going despite setbacks.

We need to hear both Mark's and Matthew's story in the light of what had happened to the temple and how they had come to terms with it. Very close to when Mark was writing, around 70 CE, the Romans crushed the revolt and destroyed the temple. For Matthew it was back perhaps a decade and half, but for Jews in his faith communities for whom he was mostly writing, the temple would have been so central and so its destruction such a disaster. However we, for our part, might see it as a consequence of the revolt, Matthew, for his part, seeks to help them come to terms with the disaster by interpreting it as God's action, punishing the temple authorities.

The temple's destruction becomes a major theme as Matthew proceeds through his account of Jesus' last days. Like Mark, he has a further three references to Jesus' prediction of this disastrous event: during the trial before the Sanhedrin (Matt 26:61; Mark 14:58), in the words of those mocking Jesus on the cross (Matt 27:39; Mark 15:29–30), and in the symbolic event of the tearing of the curtain at Jesus' death (Matt 27:51; Mark 15:38), pointing to the fulfillment of the prediction. Bitter pain is reflected in these attempts to come to terms with what had happened and also with the rejection they faced from fellow Jews.

There is little doubt that Jesus himself confronted the religious authorities of his day, so that it was not just something read back on the basis of its destruction, seeing the latter as punishment for their rejecting

Jesus. Jesus, himself, may well have warned of the dangers that faced the temple and the temple leadership.

Failure in leadership of religious bodies is not uncommon, including among Christian churches when the focus on being good news for the poor is lost and they morph into being chaplains for the status quo. Even efforts at expansion can turn into empire building. Matthew's story of Jesus is informed by the values of his hero who declared that he came not to be served but to serve and called on his followers to see leadership in those terms.

Reflection: What does Matthew suggest lies behind the temple's destruction, and what issues do his interpretation of the event raise for us today?

Get Dressed! (Matthew 21:23—22:14)

Listening to Matthew

21:23 When he came into the temple, the chief priests and the elders of the people approached him while he was teaching and said, "By what authority are you doing these things and who gave you this authority?" **24** Jesus replied, "Let me ask you one question and then if you give me an answer, I'll tell you by what authority I'm doing these things: **25** John's baptism, what was it based on? Heaven's authority or just a human initiative?" They discussed the issue among themselves, saying, "If we say authority from heaven, he'll say to us, 'Then why didn't you believe him?' **26** but if we say, 'Just a human initiative,' we're afraid of the crowd's reaction because they all treat John like a prophet." **27** So they replied to Jesus, "We don't know." Then he said to them, "Then neither will I tell you by what authority I'm doing these things.

28 "What do you think? A man had two sons. He approached the first and said, 'My son, go and work in the vineyard today.' **29** He said, 'I don't want to.' But later he changed his mind and went. **30** Then he approached the other son and gave him similar instructions and he replied, 'Sure, my master,' but didn't go. **31** Which of the two did what his father wanted?" They said, "The first." Then Jesus said to them, "Truly I am telling you, tax collectors and prostitutes are going to get into the kingdom of God ahead of you. **32** For John came to you advocating what is right and good and you didn't believe him, but the tax collectors and prostitutes did believe him. You then saw this, but still you didn't later change your mind and believe him.

33 "Listen, too, to this parable: there was a householder who planted a vineyard and erected a fence around it and dug a winepress for it and built a watchtower and leased it to tenants and went away.

³⁴ When the time came for the grape harvest, he sent his slaves to the tenants to collect his harvest of grapes. ³⁵ But the tenants grabbed the slaves, beat up one of them and killed one and stoned one. ³⁶ Again he sent other slaves, more than previously, and they treated them similarly. ³⁷ Finally he sent his son to them thinking, 'They'll surely respect my son.' ³⁸ When, however, the tenants saw the son, they said to each other, 'This is the heir. Come on, let's kill him and we'll get hold of his inheritance.' ³⁹ So they grabbed him and forced him out of the vineyard and killed him. ⁴⁰ When the master of the vineyard came back, what do you reckon he would do to those tenants?" ⁴¹ They said, "He'd send those wicked men to an awful death and give the vineyard to other tenants, who would make sure he got his harvest of grapes when it was due."

⁴² Jesus then said to them, "Haven't you ever read in the Scriptures, 'The stone which the builders rejected has become the head of the corner. This is the Lord's doing, and it is wonderful to behold'? ⁴³ That's why I'm telling you, the kingdom of God will be taken away from you and given to a people prepared to produce fruit. [⁴⁴ And anyone falling over this stone will be smashed to pieces and anyone it falls onto, it will crush them.]"

⁴⁵ When the chief priests and Pharisees heard his parables, they recognized that he was talking about them. ⁴⁶ So they sought an opportunity to arrest him but were anxious about the crowds' response because they considered him to be a prophet.

²²:¹ In response Jesus again addressed them in parables, saying, ² "The kingdom of heaven is like a certain king who put on a wedding banquet for his son. ³ So he sent his slaves to summon those who had been invited to the wedding banquet, but they didn't want to come. ⁴ And again he sent other slaves, telling them, 'Say to those invited, look I've prepared the feast, my beef cattle and my veal calves have been butchered and I've got everything ready, so come to the wedding banquet.' ⁵ But they didn't take it seriously and went off, one to his own farm, another to his business enterprise; ⁶ and the rest grabbed his slaves, abused them, and then killed them.

⁷ "The king was furious and sent his troops to kill those murderers and burned down their city. ⁸ Then he said to his slaves, 'The wedding feast is all prepared and those invited proved not to be worthy. ⁹ So go out to the crossroads and, if you find anyone, invite them to the wedding banquet.' ¹⁰ So those slaves went out on the roads

and gathered everyone they found, bad folk and good folk, and the wedding banquet was full of people sharing the meal. ¹¹ When the king came in to see the guests engaging in the meal, he saw a person not dressed appropriately for a wedding banquet, ¹² and said to him, 'My friend, how come you've got in here not dressed properly for a wedding banquet?' The fellow said nothing. ¹³ Then the king said to his servants, 'Tie this fellow up, hands and feet, and throw him into outer darkness.' There, there'll be weeping and grinding of teeth. ¹⁴ For many are called but few are chosen."

Thinking About Matthew

As Matthew brings us to the climax of Jesus' ministry, he takes us back to where it began: John the Baptist. Like John, Jesus was exercising leadership outside the normal structures of authority. Nothing John was doing was contrary to the Law, but it was very odd. Fancy not just encouraging people to change their ways and immerse themselves for cleansing as people usually did, but actually immersing them yourself! John the dipper, indeed! It would have been tidier if John had operated within the norms of the established order. Jesus also knows that there was nothing contrary to the Law in what he, himself, was doing either, even if he did disagree with his critics about how to interpret the Law. Was there room for a prophet like John and a prophet like Jesus?

The story very much ties Jesus and John together, reflecting not just that both operated outside the usual system but also the doubtless historical reality that they had much in common, that John baptized Jesus and, in a sense, helped to get him underway. Within Israel's tradition there had always been room for extras like prophets, so the authorities were in a sense caught in a bind, not least because Jesus had a strong popular following. We might wonder if the authorities were simply being territorial, wanting to defend their patch, as it were, but much more was at stake, not least Jesus' calling their integrity into question. To do so was ultimately also to call into question the power of Rome that kept them in power.

In Mark the parable of the tenants in the vineyard follows. Instead of just bringing that parable, Matthew has Jesus present three parables, adding one on either side of the parable he drew from Mark. The three parables reflect on three ministries: John the Baptist's, Jesus' own ministry, and the church's ministry. Connecting all three recalls the fact that

Matthew had summarized the message of each in the same way. John and Jesus: "Turn to God, because the kingdom of heaven has come near" (Matt 3:2; 4:17); the disciples: "The kingdom of heaven has come near" (Matt 10:7).

We begin with the simple parable of the two sons with its very simple message, applied to John the Baptist's ministry that was welcomed by tax collectors and prostitutes but rejected by the authorities. It could just as easily have been said of Jesus' own ministry. It confronts the religious leaders.

The second parable, which Matthew took up from Mark, is similarly a confrontation of the authorities. A vineyard was a common image for Israel and had been used to confront Israel for being vines that failed to produce grapes. Here the image is rather that, while the vines do produce grapes, the tenants don't make them available to the owner of the vineyard. The tenants represent those in leadership. The message is clear and follows what we also find in the biblical prophets, the complaint that Israel refused to welcome or respond to the prophets God sent to it.

Here in the parable the focus is not Israel but the leadership. The climax, their rejection of the owner's son, is an obvious reference to Jesus himself. In its present form the parable is shaped by a post-Easter perspective that reflects on Jesus' death. This includes also the implication from the parable that new tenants now carry responsibility for managing the vineyard, namely that Jesus' disciples and their successors are now the true spiritual leaders of Israel. This claim is reflected in the citation from Ps 118:22 according to which Jesus is effectively the foundation of a new structure within Israel that will ensure it produces fruit. Matthew adds to Mark's citation of Ps 118:22 a statement making that clear: "The kingdom of God will be taken away from you and given to a people prepared to produce fruit" (Matt 21:43). Luke's version has the saying about the stone as a rock that will trip people up or will crush them, which some manuscripts bring in Matt 21:44, but may not have been part of Matthew's original text and so is cited in brackets.

Having noted that these parables offended the chief priests and Pharisees, Matthew adds a third parable, which appears to be a reworked version of a parable which Luke also knew, namely the parable of the great banquet, which Luke brings in Luke 14:15-24. Originally, it plays with what was typical when someone planned to put on a banquet. Weddings were a main occasion for such endeavors. You invited people from your village who would then have an approximate idea of when it would take place, but the exact time would be determined by when it was ready. The host would send his slaves or servants to tell them when it was ready and then those who had been invited would come. If the parable goes back to Jesus, he was in all probability confronting his contemporaries over the fact that those who should have responded to his message did not, and so those who did respond and come to him were the poor and down and outs, usually excluded.

However Jesus might have told it and meant it, it invited elaboration and enhancement. We see this in Luke's version, where there are two missions by the slaves to call people to the banquet, which he uses to symbolize the missions to the Jews and then to the gentiles. Matthew's reworking goes a lot further and, in the process, takes the imagery far beyond that of a local village event. It is now an image of a king putting on a wedding banquet for his son, an obvious allusion to Jesus. The king's slaves now appear to symbolize those engaged in mission who have faced persecution and death. The burning of the city is an allusion to the disaster which befell Jerusalem in 70 CE, read by Matthew as God's punishment because of their rejection of Jesus and the disciples. We may imagine that this had been a reading of the parable even before it reached Matthew.

Now, however, there is a twist at the end where one of those invited was not properly dressed for the occasion. Applied to Matthew's context this would refer to a member of the church not exhibiting what should be the right behavior of a disciple of Jesus. Being clothed is often used as an image of behavior. Concern with believers who hail Jesus as "Lord" but fail to show the right behavior of love is a common theme of Matthew throughout his Gospel. The Sermon on the Mount concludes with warnings about such people (Matt 7:21–23) and Matthew's image of the last judgment as Jesus' last public words similarly confronts those who acclaim him "Lord" but fail to deliver love and support to their fellow believers (Matt 25:31–46).

Matthew clearly views the disasters of 70 CE as God's punishment, but also clearly goes beyond that, indeed challenges the complacency of those who might find some satisfaction in seeing such vengeance. He is telling them that they will face the same fate if they don't take their faith seriously and fail to exhibit the goodness and love that Jesus championed and modeled. The parable ends accordingly where Matthew has Jesus leave the frame of reference of the story and take over the statement of the king. Accordingly, instead of having the king expel the badly dressed out into the night, he has Jesus speak as the Son of Man, the judge, banishing this believer to outer darkness and the horrors of hell.

Matthew often has Jesus give such warnings to bring about the change that might be better achieved by less violent persuasion. The closing comment might have read, "Many are called but few respond," but uses, instead, the language of being chosen, by implication, chosen by God. One of the ways of people gaining reassurance among such minorities was to assert that they are the chosen ones. At one level, such claims reflect the language of love. I am chosen. I am loved. The dark side of such claims is when they are turned into dogma and carry the implication that those who do not join our group are not chosen or are people God chose not to accept. This is a divisive and discriminatory notion that runs contrary to the message of Jesus, who offered the invitation of grace to all without discrimination.

We do not see the literal, exclusive view of God predestining some people to hell in Matthew, but we do nevertheless see in his Gospel a tendency to revert to warnings of brutal, violent punishment in hell as a means of persuasion. Such strategies of persuasion are in tension with strands of faith that have Jesus implore people to love enemies and surely do not see God as an exemption from such loving. Gospel traditions thus carry within them strands of violence that claims to righteous anger will often want to emulate, and by contrast also strands of confronting but persistent love that seeks to bring change and forgiveness and hope and values every human being.

Reflection: What according to Matthew did John the Baptist, Jesus, and the church have in common, and what do you think Matthew is wanting to say to church members of his day?

Give to God What Is God's! (Matthew 22:15–46)

Listening to Matthew

22:15 Then the Pharisees went off and held a consultation about how they might trap him through what he was saying. **16** So they sent their disciples to him along with the Herodians and asked him, "Teacher, we know that you tell the truth and teach the way of God truthfully and are not bothered about what people might think, because you don't focus on how people seem outwardly. **17** So, tell us, what do you think? Is it right to pay tax to the emperor or not?" **18** Jesus was aware of their wicked intent and so replied, "Why you are testing me out, you hypocrites? **19** Show me the coin needed to pay the tax." They brought him a denarius. **20** Then he said to them, "Whose image is on this and what does the inscription say?" **21** They answered him, "The emperor's." Then he said to them, "So give the emperor what is the emperor's and to God what is God's." **22** When they heard this they were amazed, and they left him and went away.

23 The same day some Sadducees, who don't believe in resurrection, approached him, and they said, **24** "Teacher, Moses instructed that if a man dies without producing children, his brother should marry his wife and raise up children for his brother. **25** Now there were seven brothers and the first married but then died, and, not having produced offspring, left his wife to his brother. **26** The same happened also to the second brother and the third and then all seven. **27** Then finally after they'd all died the woman died. **28** So at the resurrection who's going to be the woman's husband, because they all had her?" **29** Jesus answered, "You're off track and know neither the Scriptures nor the power of God, **30** because at the resurrection they won't marry and or be given in marriage but will be like the angels in heaven. **31** And as for resurrection of the dead, haven't you read what was said to you by God, ³² 'I am the God of Abraham and the God of Isaac and the God of Jacob'? God is not God of the dead but God of the living." ³³ And when the crowds heard his response, they were really amazed at his teaching.

³⁴ When the Pharisees heard that he had silenced the Sadducees, they came together to the same location ³⁵ and one of them put a question to him wanting to test him out, saying, ³⁶ "Teacher, which commandment is the most important in the Law?" ³⁷ He said, "'You shall love the Lord your God with all your heart and with all your existence and with all your intelligence.' ³⁸ This is the most important and the first commandment. ³⁹ The second is similar: 'You shall love your neighbor as yourself.' ⁴⁰ On these two commandments the whole of the Law and the Prophets are based."

⁴¹ While the Pharisees were all gathered together, Jesus asked them, ⁴² "What do you reckon about the Messiah? Whose son is he?" They said to him, "David's." ⁴³ Then he said to them, "How come then that David, inspired by the Spirit, called him 'Lord,' saying, ⁴⁴ 'The Lord said to my lord, "Sit at my right hand till I make your enemies the footstool for your feet"'? ⁴⁵ If David then called him 'Lord,' how can he be his son?" ⁴⁶ No one could answer him a word nor did anyone dare to question him anymore from that point on.

Thinking About Matthew

After the parable of the wedding feast Matthew now returns to Mark 12. In the first scene the attempt is being made to have Jesus exposed as subversive. That is in part why the Pharisees come with the Herodians. The latter will be people loyal to Herod Antipas, so belonging to officialdom as part of the apparatus of the Roman Empire. Mark had mentioned Pharisees and Herodians conspiring together to have Jesus killed after Jesus healed the man with the shriveled hand in the synagogue (Mark 3:6). When Matthew reports that initiative, he omits mention of the Herodians (Matt 12:14) but keeps the reference here. Refusing to pay tax or teaching others not to pay tax would have been seen as subversive. It is therefore not an innocent question on the part of these Pharisees. Their intent, according to the story, is to have Jesus executed.

Jesus' response is on all accounts clever, but potentially ambiguous, perhaps intentionally so and typical of the two-liner responses we know that feature in many anecdotes about his engagement with his critics. Some have misread it as an indication from Jesus that there are two separate realms: the secular and the religious. This has led people sometimes to make claims like, religion should have nothing to do with politics, and worse, to affirm actions by a state that run contrary to what Jesus taught. Then faith is about a person's individual religious devotion and has no wider social or political implications. Accordingly, a person of faith is never to question civil authorities.

This is surely not so. It misses the subtlety in Jesus' answer, in what it says about God. What is God's? Surely all things, not just a religious or private realm. Jesus' response, therefore, both affirms paying tax and affirms that ultimately God is God of all and so God's will is to be obeyed in all things, including, therefore, not just the private devotional life of the believers, or the life of the church, but the world of all humanity and human community and its social structures. We would today want to add, as never before, also the world of creation.

The Sadducees were an influential elite at the time of Jesus and filled many of the senior positions in Jewish leadership. They were the dominant power in the temple establishment but, as a consequence of their involvement in resisting the Roman crushing of the revolt in 66–70 and the temple's destruction in 70, they ceased to be a force to be reckoned with among the movements that survived. Instead, Pharisaic influence became dominant.

The Sadducees were conservative and so resisted some of the newer ideas which had come to be popular among Jews, such as belief in resurrection from the dead and the development of oral law traditions beside the written Law. They would have shared the ancient belief in Hades as the place of the dead after death, but resisted the notion of resurrection, which does not occur in the Hebrew Scriptures, with just one exception, namely the book of Daniel, written in the 160s BCE. It speaks of a future time when many of the dead would be raised, "some to everlasting life, and some to shame and everlasting contempt" (Dan 12:2). By Jesus' time many had come to believe that hope could never be realized in this age. It would only be possible through divine intervention, beginning all over again with a new age. That would finally mean that Israel would be liberated from its oppressors, and God would bring back the dead either to participate in the new order or to be brought to judgment for their wickedness.

The Sadducees' question seeks to ridicule such thought, and one can imagine it was accompanied by a male snigger—a woman having slept with so many brothers! Jesus' response asserts the common view that resurrection was not resuscitation, but transformation of corpses into a different order of reality, to be more like angelic beings, and that in such a state marrying and being married would play no role. Paul wrote to the Corinthians defending resurrection and making a similar point: people will have not physical but spiritual bodies (1 Cor 15:44). This is why the Easter stories can speak of Jesus appearing and disappearing, materializing and dematerializing.

The notion that in the age to come marriage and by implication sexual relations will have no part inspired some to argue that all should live now as they will then. They argued that one should, therefore, refrain from sexual relations and so marriage. Paul had to counter this view in 1 Cor 7, and, as we have seen, Matthew also has Jesus counter it (Matt 19:12). Despite his own preference and general advice about not marrying in view of his belief that the new age would soon dawn, Paul emphasizes that sexual desire is not sin and marriage in this age is not to be seen as failure (1 Cor 7:7–9, 28, 36). The age to come will be of a different order of reality where physical things like sex and marriage will no longer apply.

The second counterargument to the Sadducees is rather less cogent. It cites the reference to God speaking of being the God of Abraham, Isaac, and Jacob, as though that referred to their still being alive and so going to be raised from the dead. In its original context that statement referred to the God whom Abraham, Isaac, and Jacob worshiped, but those telling this story assumed otherwise and cited it accordingly.

Matthew trims the next scene he found in Mark where one of Jesus' critics asks him about the most important commandment. Thus he leaves out the initial part of the citation from Deut 6:4, "Hear, O Israel, the Lord our God is one" (Mark 12:29) and brings only Deut 6:5 as enjoining love for God "with all your heart and with all your existence and with all your intelligence" trimmed from Mark's longer "with all your heart, and with all your existence, and with all your intelligence and with all your strength" (Mark 12:30). I have chosen to translate the words usually translated "soul" and "mind" by "existence" and "intelligence" to stay closer to what I believe was meant.

Matthew also omits the conversation with which the scene concludes in Mark, where the scribe wins Jesus' approval when he not only repeats the citation but adds the comment that such commitment to compassion was more important than sacrifices (Mark 12:32–34). Instead, Matthew has Jesus cite Deut 6:5 about loving God and Lev 19:18 about loving neighbors and conclude by adding the comment that the Law and the Prophets are based on these, literally, hang on these.

This final statement echoes what Matthew has Jesus state in the Sermon on the Mount: "Everything you want people to do for you, do likewise for them, for this is what the Law and the Prophets are about" (Matt 7:12). Throughout his Gospel Matthew has made it clear that Jesus upholds the biblical law, the Law and the Prophets, and does so on the basis of interpreting Scripture by using love for God and neighbor as the primary criterion. While he omits Mark's reference to sacrifice here, he twice inserted Hos 6:6 into his story: "I desire compassion not sacrifice," as words spoken by Jesus (Matt 9:13; 12:7). As Matthew portrays him, Jesus is the authorized exponent of the Law and of Jewish faith. He is, after all, the judge to come.

The final scene taken from Mark in all likelihood reflects later discussion about how best to talk about Jesus and his authority. It assumes that David wrote the Psalms, a common view at the time, and that the Spirit inspired him to do so. That did create a problem when people spoke of Jesus as Son of David, as indeed Matthew has done in his opening chapter. For on those assumptions, why would David address him as Lord? Historically, we now understand that Ps 110 is a coronation psalm that speaks of the enthronement of a king and is spoken by a member of the royal court giving voice to what people imagined would have been the words of God addressed to a king at his coronation: "The Lord said to my lord, 'Sit at my right hand till I make your enemies the footstool for your feet'" (Ps 110:1). Later generations who embraced the hope for a messiah of David's line came to read these words as spoken about that messiah. Psalm 110:1 then became a favorite citation to use in explaining Jesus' resurrection as God enthroning him to be the Messiah, and we hear it echoed in the creed that speaks of his sitting down at God's right hand.

Our story reflects some assumptions we do not share, such as the authorship of the Psalm by David, but we can see that its point is to say that Jesus must be seen as more than the Son of David, the Messiah. Matthew clearly affirms Son of David as a title for Jesus as Messiah and uses it positively through his Gospel, but his inclusion of this story from Mark indicates that he, too, understands that seeing Jesus as Son of David, Messiah, is not enough if we are to understand who Jesus is. Perhaps the concern was also to avoid limiting Jesus to being Israel's Messiah. He is going to be so much more than that, as Matthew will show. He will bring hope for all nations.

Reflection: What issues then are still issues now, and what responses then do you see as still alive today?

Confronting Abuses (Matthew 23:1–39)

Listening to Matthew

23:1 Then Jesus spoke to the crowds and his disciples, **2** saying, "The scribes and the Pharisees sit on Moses' seat. **3** So do and keep to all they tell you, but don't do what they do. For they say things but don't themselves do them. **4** They bind together heavy burdens [hard to bear] and land them on people's shoulders but themselves won't lift a finger to help them carry them. **5** They do all their deeds so as to be seen by people, making their phylacteries wide and their fringes long. **6** They love to get the most honored positions at banquets and the best seats in the synagogues **7** and to be hailed in the marketplace and be called 'Rabbi' by people. **8** But don't you get yourself called 'Rabbi,' for there's one person who's your teacher, and you are all brothers. **9** And don't call anyone father on earth, because there is only one person who is, namely, your Father in heaven. **10** And don't be called instructors, because there's only one who is your instructor, the Messiah. **11** The greatest among you will be your servant. **12** And those who exalt themselves will be humbled and those who humble themselves will be exalted.

13 "Woe betide you scribes and Pharisees, hypocrites, because you shut people out from the kingdom of heaven. For you yourselves don't enter it and you don't let anyone else enter either.

15 "Woe betide you scribes and Pharisees, hypocrites, because you travel across sea and land to make one convert, and, when you do, you make them twice worse a candidate for hell than what you yourselves are.

16 "Woe betide you blind guides, who say, 'Whoever swears by the temple it's nothing, but whoever swears by the gold of the temple is bound by their oath.' **17** You're foolish and blind. What is greater, the gold or the temple which renders the gold sacred? [18] And 'Whoever swears by the altar, it's nothing, but whoever swears by the gift placed on it is bound by their oath.' [19] Are you blind? What is greater, the gift or the altar which renders the gift sacred? [20] For whoever swears by the altar swears by all that's on it and above it; [21] and whoever swears by the temple swears by the one who dwells in it, [22] and whoever swears by heaven swears by the throne of God and by the one seated on it.

[23] "Woe betide you scribes and Pharisees, hypocrites, because you tithe mint and dill and cumin and neglect the weightier matters of the Law: justice and compassion and faithfulness. These are what you ought to be doing without neglecting those requirements. [24] Blind guides, straining for a gnat but swallowing a camel!

[25] "Woe betide you scribes and Pharisees, hypocrites, because you clean the outside of the cup and the plate but inside, they are full of greed and self-indulgence. [26] Blind Pharisee, first clean up the inside of the cup so that its outside may also become clean.

[27] "Woe betide you scribes and Pharisees, hypocrites, because you're like whitewashed tombs which look beautiful on the outside but inside are full of the bones of the dead and all kinds of impurity. [28] Just so, you like to appear to people as good, when inside you're full of hypocrisy and lawlessness.

[29] "Woe betide you scribes and Pharisees, hypocrites, because you build the tombs of the prophets and decorate the memorials to the upright, [30] and say, 'If we'd been there in the days of our forebears, we wouldn't have had any part in shedding the blood of the prophets,' [31] so that you in fact testify to the fact that you are the children of those who slew the prophets. [32] So, now, you lot, bring the stance of your forebears to its inevitable conclusion! [33] You snakes, you nest of pythons, how are you going to escape being condemned to hell?

[34] "Therefore, look, I send you prophets and sages and scribes and some of them you'll kill and crucify and some of them you'll beat up in your synagogues and chase from city to city; [35] so the blood of the upright which has spilt out onto the earth from the blood of Abel the upright to the blood of Zechariah son of Barachiah, whom you murdered between the sanctuary and the altar, will be laid as a charge at your feet. [36] Truly I'm telling you, all this is going to come upon this generation.

> ³⁷ "Jerusalem, Jerusalem, killing the prophets and stoning those sent to it, how often have I wanted to gather your children together as a hen gathers its chicks, but you weren't willing to come. ³⁸ Look, your house is left desolate. ³⁹ For I'm telling you, you're not going to see me from now on until you say, 'Blessed is the one who comes in the name of the Lord!'"

Thinking About Matthew

Matthew has assembled sayings of Jesus which confront religious leaders. His starting point was Mark's brief account of Jesus' warning against scribes who flaunted themselves and engaged in extortion (Mark 12:38–40). Matthew goes far further and, drawing in part on material he shared with Luke, presents us with a major confrontation which will have had relevance particularly for his own day. In the 80s, following the disaster of 70 CE when the Romans destroyed the temple, Jewish movements were beginning to be resurgent. Sadducees, dominant among the temple authorities, ceased to be central. Instead, Pharisaism, in particular, emerged as the dominant movement alongside other Jewish movements, including the Jesus movement.

Quite often Matthew has Jesus speak as if to the contemporary setting in which Matthew found himself. We see it as this chapter ends where Matthew has Jesus refer to the temple now lying desolate, as it had been for perhaps some fifteen years by Matthew's time. Matthew has Jesus begin his confrontation here by acknowledging that the scribes and the Pharisees exercised the leadership in the synagogues in his time, as was the case in the 80s. It is also typical of Matthew that he has Jesus affirm the Law of Moses, just as he had Jesus affirm the Law and the Prophets in the Sermon on the Mount and underline that he in no way intended to set them aside or replace them, as was alleged that some in the Jesus movement were doing.

The conflict was not over whether to uphold the Law but how to do so. On the one hand, Matthew is addressing the situation of his own day, but, on the other, is also seeing the abuses of the scribes and Pharisees as going back a long time and warranting already what Matthew saw as God's punishment through the disaster of 70 CE. By implication Matthew is making the claim that the Jesus movement which he represents are the ones who truly know how to interpret the Law, something Jesus had taught them.

The problem with the scribes and Pharisees was that they were not practicing what they preached, as Matthew will go on to show in the allegations that later follow. In addition, their interpretations were imposing unnecessary burdens on people, and here Matthew will be targeting the imposition of the oral law, which could be overly restrictive.

The list of accusations that follow might apply in any age and apply just as much to church preachers as to scribes and Pharisees. They should also not, therefore, be generalized as though there is an assumption that all scribes and Pharisees were guilty of the abuses listed, anymore than we would want to generalize that abuse by some Christian preachers must mean that all do the same things.

Traditional orthodox Jewish dress included elements that carried religious significance. Phylacteries were small leather boxes containing a fragment of the Law worn on the arm and on the forehead especially during morning prayers, serving to remind the wearer of the need to keep the Law. They have their origin in the instruction in Deut 6:8. Blue fringes or tassels were to be attached to the corner of garments and had a similar function (Num 15:37–41). Matthew does not have Jesus question such practices. Matthew mentions Jesus wearing such tassels (Matt 9:20; 14:36). The issue was using them to impress other people. The neediness that seeks compensation by trying to win the admiration of others is sad and leads to manipulative behavior. Telling people off for doing so is one approach. Helping them face up to the need that drives it is another, and a more effective way of addressing it.

The sad specter of insecure men seeking status meets us also in the sayings that Matthew took from Mark about their wanting the best places at banquets and in synagogues. The norm at special meals was that people reclined and did so in an order in which the most important reclined closest to the host. Jesus appears to poke fun at it according to Luke when he suggests that people start at the bottom end and hope to be shifted up (Luke 14:7–11). Status seeking also plays itself out as people seek titles, and little has changed. Titles or at least descriptors can fulfill an informative function (tell me who is the teacher, the minister, the manager, etc.) but serve vanity when used for status.

There follows a series of seven accusations introduced with the words "Woe betide you scribes and Pharisees, hypocrites," with the exception of the third, which reads, "Woe betide you blind guides." They derive mainly from the source which Luke and Matthew have in common and so are found also in Luke 11:39–52, though in less developed form. Older translations include a verse 14, but most now see this as a later addition inserted from Mark 12:40 or Luke 20:47. Each accusation describes an abuse that can arise when insecurity drives people, and none is unique to those addressed. By not embracing the promise of the kingdom of God and God's love, such people also block others from doing so. When making converts drives an evangelism to build numbers, the same blockage occurs.

The third accusation about use of oaths exposes an obsession with rules that make no real sense and which have lost connection with what matters. They seem rather to be designed to avoid upholding truthfulness and integrity. Meticulous tithing, as in the fourth accusation, can also be a distraction from what really matters, "justice and compassion and faithfulness." It is important to note that Matthew does not have Jesus therefore set such tithing aside, for no part of the Law is to be set aside, including even the rather finicky application of the Law of tithing to herbs, which went beyond the written Law. Similarly, putting the focus on external washing, as in the fifth accusation, and neglecting inner cleansing makes no sense, as does seeking to make a good impression outwardly while not attending to inner purity. These are religious distractions which have a way of repeating themselves in ever new forms when people do not take love seriously for themselves and for others.

The final accusation turns sharply toward something even more serious: killing off God's messengers. Matthew uses it then to have Jesus speak with the voice of God's Wisdom, who over history has sent agents who brought God's message of love and change and faced death and harassment. In Luke's version, these words are expressly identified as spoken by Wisdom (Luke 11:49–51). Here in Matthew, as already in 11:27–30, Jesus speaks Wisdom's words, covering history from well before his time up to the present. Second Chronicles refers to the killing of Zechariah, son of the priest Jehoiada, in the temple (2 Chr 24:21), whereas we know nothing about the death of Nehemiah of the book of the same name, who was the son of Barachiah. The two appear to have been confused by whoever created the saying.

The words "all this is going to come upon this generation" (Matt 23:36) are ominous and point forward to the disaster of 70 CE, which Matthew sees as God's punishment for the sins outlined above and for rejecting Jesus. It is a theme Matthew inserts into his account of Jesus' death. Such generalizing conclusions do not sit well with the realization of the immense suffering inflicted on the people of Jerusalem, men, women, and children, most of whom would have been innocent of the allegations listed above.

The final words, also to be understood as Jesus' voicing Wisdom's message, present us with the sympathetic image of the hen caring for its chicks, but ends by again pointing to the disaster of 70 CE. Hope returns when Matthew has Jesus point forward to his return to Jerusalem, where again he would be greeted as pilgrims to the temple were greeted, with the words of the psalm, "Blessed is the one who comes in the name of the Lord!" (Ps 118:26). This hope remained alive for Matthew, who in the next chapter promises that it would be fulfilled in his generation (Matt 24:34). That hope was not realized, but hope imagines because its foundation is God and God's goodness, and that is something no image can define.

Reflection: What abuses are being confronted in this chapter and how and why are they not unique to those times?

— 5 —

The End

Coming, Ready or Not! (Matthew 24:1–51)

Listening to Matthew

24:1 Leaving the temple, Jesus went on his way and his disciples approached him to draw his attention to the temple buildings. **2** In response he said to them, "You see all these? I'm telling you, not one stone will be left on another here which will not be pulled down."

3 And while he was sitting on the Mount of Olives, his disciples asked him privately, "Tell us, when will this happen and what will be the indication pointing to your coming again and to the end of the age?"

4 In response Jesus said, "Beware no one leads you astray; **5** because many will come in my name saying, 'I'm the Messiah' and will lead many astray. **6** You're going to hear of wars and reports of wars. See you're not thrown by that, because that all needs to happen, but that won't yet be the end. **7** For nation will rise up against nation and kingdom against kingdom and there'll be famines and earthquakes in many places. **8** All these are the start of the contraction pains. **9** Then they'll hand you over to face abuse and they'll put you to death and you'll be hated by all peoples because of my name.

10 "And then many will fall by the wayside and betray one another and hate one another; **11** and many false prophets will arise and lead many astray; ¹² and because lawlessness will be on the rise, the love of many will grow cold. ¹³ Yet anyone holding out to the end will be saved. ¹⁴ And this gospel of the kingdom will be proclaimed in all the world as a testimony to all peoples and then the end will come.

¹⁵ "When you see 'the abomination which produces desolation' spoken of by Daniel the prophet set up in the holy place—let the reader understand!—¹⁶ then let those in Judea flee to the mountains, ¹⁷ and let anyone on the roof top not go down to fetch things from his house, ¹⁸ and let those working on their farm not turn round to get their coat. ¹⁹ Pity those who are pregnant and breastfeeding in those days. ²⁰ Pray that when you have to flee it won't be in wintertime or on a Sabbath. ²¹ For at that time there's going to be awful suffering such as there's never been since the world began right up to now and never will be again. ²² And were those days not shortened, no human being would survive, but because of the chosen ones those days will be shortened.

²³ "Then if anyone tells you, 'Look, here is the Messiah or there!' don't believe them. ²⁴ For false messiahs and false prophets will arise and produce fantastic signs and wonders to lead astray even the chosen ones, if it were possible. ²⁵ Look, I've told you about this in advance. ²⁶ If they say to you, 'Look, he's in the outback,' don't go out there, or 'Look, he's among the tombs,' don't believe them. ²⁷ For as lightning flashes across the sky from east to west, that's how the coming of the Son of Man will be. ²⁸ Where the corpse is, there the vultures will be gathered.

²⁹ "And immediately after the suffering of those days, the sun will be darkened and the moon won't shed its light, and the stars will fall from the sky, and the forces of the heavens will be shaken. ³⁰ Then the sign of the Son of Man will appear in the sky and then all the tribes of earth will mourn and they'll see 'the Son of Man coming on the clouds of heaven' with power and great glory; ³¹ and he will send out his angels with the sound of a loud trumpet call and gather his chosen ones from the four winds from one end of heaven to the other.

³² "Learn from the fig tree as a parable: when its branch is still at an early stage of growth and sprouts leaves, you know there's a harvest coming. ³³ So you, too, when you see all these things, know that the end is right at your doorstep. ³⁴ Truly I'm telling you, this

generation will not pass away until all these things have happened. [35] Heaven and earth will pass away, but my words will never pass away. [36] But with regard to when that day will come and at what hour no one knows, neither the angels of heaven nor the Son, but the Father only.

[37] "For as it was in the days of Noah, that's how it will be with the coming of the Son of Man. [38] For as in those days before the flood they were eating and drinking, marrying and being given in marriage, right up to the day when Noah embarked on the ark, [39] and they had no inkling of what was to come until the flood hit them and swept them all away, that's how it will be with the coming of the Son of Man. [40] Then two will be out on the farm and one will be taken and the other will be left; [41] and two women will be grinding at the mill and one will be taken and the other left.

[42] "So stay awake, because you've no idea at what hour your Lord will come. [43] And know this, that if the householder had known at what watch of the night the burglar would come, he would have stayed awake and not allowed him to break into his house. [44] So you, too, be ready, because you've no idea when the Son of Man is coming.

[45] "Who's a trustworthy and sensible slave whom his master would put in charge of his household to make provision for food at the right time? [46] Happy is that slave, who when his master comes he finds him having done just that. [47] Truly, I'm telling you, he'll put him in charge of all his property. [48] But if that slave is bad and thinks in his mind, 'My master is delayed,' [49] and starts to beat his fellow slaves and to eat and drink with drunkards, [50] then that slave's master will come on a day when he wasn't expecting him and at a time he didn't know about [51] and will cut him to pieces and assign him a place with the hypocrites, and there will be weeping and grinding of teeth."

Thinking About Matthew

Matthew now brings his fifth major speech of Jesus. It is based on Mark 13, but he revises it and doubles its length, so that it now covers two chapters, Matt 24–25. In their world it was common when writing the biography of great people of the past to create a final speech in which they offered advice to future generations. Sometimes people produced such farewell speeches as separate documents. They were often called "testaments." Among those surviving from Matthew's era are the testaments of Abraham, Job, and Solomon, for instance. *The Testaments of the Twelve Patriarchs* was produced in this period, for instance, which has each of Jacob's sons offer advice to their descendants. Deuteronomy functions in a similar way in offering Moses' parting advice. In John's Gospel, Jesus' farewell speech covers five chapters and concludes with a prayer for his future followers (John 13–17).

As in Mark, Matthew has Jesus talk to his disciples on the hillside of the Mount of Olives from which, looking over the Kidron valley, they could see the temple buildings. Matthew has the disciples point to the temple's impressive structures. They were indeed impressive and widely known throughout the empire. Jesus' response as in Mark is to point to their destruction.

Mark was probably writing shortly after the debacle of 70 CE when the Romans, in crushing the revolt which had begun in 66 CE, destroyed the temple. Only its massive foundation survives to today and is the focus of prayer and devotion, the so-called Wailing Wall. For Matthew, that event lay probably some decade and a half in the past but remained of major significance, not least because of his Jewish context. He, or someone before him, had adapted the parable of the great feast to become the wedding feast of a king's son. In response to the refusal of those invited to come the king then destroyed their city (Matt 22:1–14), an allusion to what was seen as God's punishment of Jerusalem and its people for rejecting the gospel. Also in the verses immediately before our passage, Matthew had Jesus speak of the temple's devastation (Matt 23:38).

If Matt 23 was primarily about the scribes and Pharisees, representing the opponents of Matthew's day, Jesus' final speech addresses the disciples and their future. Imaginative traditions fed into Mark 13 and reappear in Matthew. There are subtle changes. In Mark the disciples ask when this destruction will occur and what will be the indication that it is going to happen (Mark 13:4). Matthew reshapes the question so that it continues to refer to the temple's demise but then separately asks about the return of the Son of Man and the end of the age, when they will occur (Matt 24:3). Mark may have seen it very much as a single event beginning to happen, starting with the temple's demise, but Matthew puts some distance between the destruction of the temple and the end.

As Matthew puts it more clearly, there would be people claiming to be the messiah, as indeed there were among leaders of the various factions involved in the 66–70 CE revolt. Mark already knew that this did not yet mean the end, and Matthew repeats this and also Mark's image of such suffering being like the beginning of contractions before childbirth, a common image in fantasies about the future that envisaged suffering before the final birth of relief and hope. Matthew follows Mark in fleshing out that suffering as related to wars between nations and such phenomena as famines and earthquakes.

Mark next has Jesus speak of the suffering that would await disciples (Mark 13:9–13). Matthew had already taken up some of this into Jesus' second speech in Matt 10, where he sent out his disciples on mission, including how the Spirit would help them when facing interrogation (Matt 10:17–22). Instead, here Matthew keeps some predictions about suffering and martyrdom, but then adds reference to people failing under such pressure and to false prophets (Matt 24:10–12). This must be something that had happened. We may wonder who might have been false prophets, presumably teachers within the church and, given the allusion to lawlessness, probably those teaching that the Law be set aside. The outcome, love growing cold, may well indicate not only loss of faith but also loss of love between members.

Matthew then concludes this somber prediction with the assurance that those holding out to the end would be saved (from all this suffering) and here places the prediction that the gospel was to be proclaimed throughout the world and that then the end would come (Matt 24:14). That gives a clearer answer to the disciples' question as Matthew portrayed it.

Mark continues with some specific references to the 70 CE debacle and Matthew follows him (Mark 13:14–20; Matt 24:15–22). Antiochus IV Epiphanes of the Seleucid dynasty of Syria, whose father wrested Palestine from the Ptolemies of Egypt around 200 CE, caused outrage in 167 BCE by setting up an image of a god on the altar of the Jerusalem temple, thus polluting it. Daniel refers to it as "the abomination which produces desolation" (Dan 9:27; 11:31; 12:11). Later generations took Daniel's reference as a predictor also of future actions which might pollute the temple. In 40 CE the emperor Caligula decreed that a statue of himself as Zeus be set up in the temple but was thwarted. Something like this must have happened or been seen as likely to happen during the siege of Jerusalem. The advice to drop everything and flee is as in Mark except that Matthew adds that they should pray that they not have to do so on the Sabbath (Matt 24:20), reflecting his concern with Law observance. Like

Mark, Matthew would also know that the siege brought terrible suffering on all, but relief came.

Following Mark, Matthew brings another reference to false messiahs and false prophets, probably reflecting the desperate fantasies among the revolutionaries of those times (Mark 13:21-23), which Matthew supplements (Matt 24:23-25). Then Matthew turns the focus to Jesus' sudden return as the Son of Man, using sayings from the source he shared with Luke (Matt 24:27; Luke 17:24). The somewhat enigmatic comment about vultures assembling over a corpse may be meant positively: in the midst of all this suffering the Son of Man will appear with his angels (Matt 24:28; Luke 17:37), but probably it just means it will be a very visible event.

Matthew follows Mark in using the dramatic imagery of Isaiah to depict major cosmic events affecting the sun, moon, and stars (Isa 13:10) before finally the Son of Man is to come on the clouds. Coming on the clouds is an image drawn from Dan 7:13, which depicts God's agent as a human rather than an animal as previous rulers of empires had been depicted, and coming to God riding on clouds to be installed to rule instead of them. By Matthew's time, that imagery had given rise to the expectation that God's messiah would be that Son of Man and as Son of Man would be God's agent in executing judgment. Matthew had already given us a picture of the Son of Man sending his angels out to gather his chosen ones in his interpretation of the parable of the wheat and the weeds (Matt 13:37-43).

Matthew continues with Mark in having Jesus use the image of leaves appearing on a fig tree as a promise of a harvest to come (Matt 24:32-36; Mark 13:28-32). Matthew, too, wants those listening to his Gospel to read the signs of the times that he takes to indicate that the end would indeed occur during their lifetime, an extraordinary claim when seen from our vantage point, even with the caveat that neither angels nor Jesus himself knew exactly when. We find ourselves transported back into a world where Matthew and his community saw themselves under enormous stress and were convinced that they would soon find relief with the return of Jesus.

Matthew now departs from Mark and, as he often does in constructing his five speeches, draws on other sources, in particular the source he shared with Luke (Matt 24:37-44; Luke 17:26-36). People were simply carrying on oblivious to what was going to happen in Noah's time. That should not be how disciples behave in the light of Jesus' return. People will suddenly be taken away to be with Jesus and the rest abandoned. The message of remaining ready receives reinforcement with the image of a householder being prepared for a burglar (Matt 24:43-44; Luke 12:39-40). The same point is made then with the illustration of the slave who remains alert and well prepared for his master's return (Matt 24:45-51; Luke 12:41-45). If you are not prepared, you will be treated like the hypocrites, Matthew's cross reference back to his account of Jesus' judgments against the scribes and Pharisees in Matt 23. As commonly in Matthew, their fate is described as hell, a place of weeping and grinding of teeth. The warnings to believers continue through into Matt 25.

When faced with this first half of Matthew's final speech of Jesus we cannot avoid sensing distance. The Son of Man did not come in their generation, as they expected. We are, however, not left without connections. History has brought more suffering and more catastrophes, and we are still here. More specifically, people have been persecuted and sometimes killed for their faith. False teaching has found ways to undermine Jesus' teaching, reducing it to otherworldly concerns, rendering it safe from criticism by having it not offend rulers in high places but rather serving their interests, and by being their chaplains. Readiness may be a response to fear of being caught unprepared but is best embodied within a mind and attitude of love, which will show compassion whatever the consequences. Hope generates fantasies ultimately because it is real in the sense that its reality is based on the being of God. Anything more than this is necessarily fantasy, as here, with all its fallibilities as it seeks to put flesh and blood on hope.

Reflection: What does Matthew understand by readiness, and what significance can we give to his reading of the signs of the times and future hope?

Don't Run Out of Lamp Oil! (Matthew 25:1–46)

Listening to Matthew

25:1 "Then the kingdom of heaven will be like ten girls who took their lamps and went out to meet the bridegroom. **2** Five of them were foolish and five were sensible, **3** because the five foolish girls took their lamps but didn't take along any oil, **4** whereas the five sensible girls took oil in flasks along with their lamps. **5** When the bridegroom was delayed, they all became drowsy and were sleeping. **6** Then in the middle of the night the cry went up, 'Look, the bridegroom's arriving, come out to meet him!' **7** Then those girls all got up and trimmed their lamps. **8** The foolish ones said to the sensible ones. 'Give us some of your oil, because our lamps are going out.' **9** The sensible ones replied, 'No, because there won't be enough for us and you, so go to those who sell oil and buy some for yourselves.' **10** While they were on their way to buy some, the bridegroom arrived and the girls who were prepared went in with him to the wedding party and the door was shut. **11** Later the rest of the girls came and said, 'Sir, sir, open the door for us, please!' **12** In response he said, 'I'm telling you the truth; I don't recognize you.' **13** Watch therefore because you don't know the day nor the hour.

14 "For it's like a man going abroad who called his slaves and handed his property over to them. **15** To one he gave five talents and to another two and to another one, depending on the capacity of each, and straightaway off he went. **16** The one receiving five talents put them to work and made another five talents; **17** and similarly the one with two made another two. **18** But the one receiving one talent went off and dug a hole in the ground and hid his master's money.

19 "After some time the master of those slaves came back and was settling accounts with them. **20** And the one who received five talents brought him another five talents and said, 'Master, you entrusted me with five talents. Look, I've made five more.' **21** His master said to him, 'Well done, good and reliable slave; you've been reliable with a few things; I'll put you in charge of many. Join in your master's happiness.' **22** Then the one with two talents said, 'Master, you entrusted me with two talents; look, I have another two talents.' **23** The master said to him, 'Well done, good and reliable slave; you were reliable with two talents; I'll put you in charge of many. Join in your master's happiness.'

24 "Then the one having received one talent also came and said, 'Master, I know you, that you're a hard man, reaping where you didn't sow and gathering where you haven't scattered seed, **25** so I was scared and went off and hid your talent in the ground. Here's your talent.' **26** In response his master said to him, 'You wicked and lazy slave. You knew, did you, that I reap where I haven't sown and gather where I haven't scattered? **27** Then you ought to have put my money with the bankers and coming back I would at least have got it back with interest. **28** So take the talent from him and give it to the one who has ten talents. **29** To all those who have, more will be given, much more, but as for those who don't have anything, even what they have will be taken away from them. **30** And throw this useless slave into outer darkness and there will be weeping and grinding of teeth.'

31 "When the Son of Man comes in his glory and all the angels with him, then he will sit on his glorious throne **32** and all the nations will be brought together before him and he will separate them from one another, like a shepherd separates the sheep from the goats. **33** And he'll place the sheep on his right-hand side and the goats on his left. **34** Then the king will say to those on his right, 'Come, you who are blessed by my Father, inherit the kingdom prepared for you since before the foundation of the world, **35** because I was hungry and you gave me something to eat and was thirsty and you gave me something to drink, a stranger and you welcomed me in, **36** naked and you gave me clothes, sick and you took care of me, and in prison and you came to see me.' **37** Then the upright will answer him, saying, 'Lord, when did we see you hungry and feed you or thirsty and give you something to drink? **38** And when did we see you as a stranger and welcome you or naked and give you clothes? **39** And when did we see you sick or in prison and go to see you?' **40** Then the king will tell them, 'Truly I tell you, as much as you did so for one of the least of these members of my family, you did so to me.'

⁴¹ "Then he will say to those on his left, 'Get away from me you cursed lot, and off you go into the everlasting fire prepared for the devil and his angels. ⁴² For I was hungry, and you didn't give me anything to eat; I was thirsty, and you gave me nothing to drink. ⁴³ I was a stranger and you didn't welcome me in, naked and you gave me no clothes, sick and in prison and you didn't come to see me.' ⁴⁴ Then they will answer, 'Lord, when did we see you hungry or thirsty or as a stranger or naked or sick or in prison and didn't come to your aid?' ⁴⁵ Then he will respond to them, 'Truly I tell you, as much as you didn't do so for one of the least of these, it was like you didn't do so for me.' ⁴⁶ And these will go off to eternal punishment, but the upright to eternal life."

Thinking About Matthew

Matthew 25 brings us the second half of the fifth major address that Matthew has Jesus bring. As with the other four speeches, he assembles the material for the speech from various sources. Matthew 24 takes up most of Mark 13, and in Matt 25, Matthew brings three parables. It was common in biographies of famous people of the past to have the hero offer advice for future generations. Accordingly, Matthew has this final speech of Jesus address disciples and those who would be disciples after them. For this purpose, he takes up a parable about ten girls which may well be a creative elaboration of existing imagery, the parable of the talents from the source he shared with Luke (Luke 19:12–27), and concludes with a scene unique to his Gospel, the judgment of the sheep and the goats.

At one level, all three parables use fear to motivate behavior and in that sense continue the theme with which Matt 24 ended, namely, about being ready for when Jesus returns. Stay ready or you'll go to hell is the message. There are much more profound reasons than fear for remaining engaged in a faithful relationship with God, sharing God's love. Beyond the appeal to fear, however, these parables offer much more.

The parable of the ten girls takes us back into another world and its norms surrounding marriage and weddings. The pattern appears to have been that the husband to be goes to his bride's house and brings her back to his house or that of his family where there are celebrations. We can imagine a scene where girls, teenage girls, also viewed as ready for marriage, were given the role to welcome the bridal party. They were to meet the bridegroom as he approached his home with his bride and accompany him as he entered the house. For that purpose, they had to wait around for his arrival, but remain ready for when he came. In the parable, some were not, because their lamps were running out of oil.

The message is clear: be ready or else you will be shut out of the kingdom of God. It is a message directed to church members. It is in that sense similar to the way Matthew has Jesus in the Sermon on the Mount warn about those who would claim to be his and to do wondrous things in his name but are then to be disowned at the end because they failed to live by the Law as Jesus taught it (Matt 7:21–23).

The point of the parable is obvious—be ready or miss out! It also has rich allusions. Matthew has already used a wedding feast as an image of future hope in 22:1–14, and this continued what we know was a favorite way that the Jesus of history spoke of hope, namely as a feast to which all were invited. There, in 22:1–14, Matthew supplements the parable to have it address those who had embraced the gospel but were no longer showing the fruits of goodness, symbolized in not being appropriately clothed for the wedding celebration.

It is natural also to see the bridegroom as an image for Jesus, himself, a usage reflected elsewhere, for instance in Jesus' response to the question why his disciples did not fast (Matt 9:15; Mark 2:19-20)—the bridegroom is with them! Might the oil refer to the Spirit? The readiness implies attitude and behavior, and these are then spelled out in the final parable of the sheep and the goats but here only implied.

The parable of the talents, which follows, is one of the best known of Jesus' parables and has made its way into our language where "talents" have come to refer to people's natural abilities. Parables invite creative elaboration like that, even if it was not Matthew's meaning. The story comes from the world of slavery and the master seems a rather doubtful character, so matching the master to God and the slaves to believers does not really work.

Talents refer to amounts of money, not to natural abilities. A talent was worth around six thousand denarii, in other words, six thousand days' wages. We are dealing with huge sums, such as one might find in such made up stories. The talents, the money, refer in the parable to what the master entrusted the slaves with. We might hear it saying that, like using the power of money to make more, we should engage in active partnership with the Spirit, but even that perhaps goes beyond Matthew's parable. He is having Jesus warn believers to be active in sharing God's goodness, spelled out with specific examples in the final parable of the sheep and the goats.

The parable of the sheep and the goats is not really a parable but an extended simile. Matthew is having Jesus describe what will happen on the day of judgment and is likening the separation that will occur then to the way a shepherd separates sheep and goats. Matthew has Jesus begin by referring to himself, namely his enthronement when he comes as Son of Man, using language that echoes Jewish expectations of the time. This coming has been the focus of the warnings expressed in the preceding parables. Now Matthew has Jesus spell out what being ready in those parables actually means.

It is a regular theme in Matthew to have Jesus address disciples, and especially disciples of Matthew's time and beyond, with the warning that what matters is an ongoing life of love and generosity and that without that, any appeal to status on the basis of conversion or any grand acts of acclamation count for nothing. A wedding does not make a marriage; ongoing commitment of love makes a marriage. The life of compassion and generosity as outlined in the Sermon on the Mount is what matters.

Matthew has something specific in mind, namely acts of love and generosity to fellow believers, and this will doubtless have had relevance in his setting where he must have seen it as lacking. We might embrace this insight on a broader scale than Matthew does and apply it generally, which would certainly cohere with the teaching of Jesus, namely love and compassion for all people, not just believers. Matthew is not saying we should do good deeds in order to earn a place for ourselves in God's kingdom. Nor is he saying we should pretend we are helping Jesus when we see people in need and therefore help them. To feel treated kindly not for your own sake but because someone imagines you as Jesus and sees it as a way to get ahead spiritually is not to be loved at all. Those in the story who loved, when told it was like they were showing love to Jesus, had no such idea in their heads. They just loved, not for reward, not for themselves, but because they saw need and responded by caring about the person they were helping.

This depiction of the judgment forms the climax of Jesus' public ministry in Matthew and is typical of his portrayal of Jesus as John the Baptist had announced him, namely as the judge to come who came to help people understand what it truly meant to uphold the Law. That has two sides to it. The one is that Matthew has Jesus expound the Law in terms of love and compassion, indeed in such a way that it calls all else into question that does not make love central, including even Matthew's own theology.

The other side is the persistent tendency of Matthew, nevertheless, to portray Jesus as seeking to turn people to the way of love by threatening them with hellfire. The latter as we have seen often seems in stark contrast to the message of love and threatens to make the ultimate model of God one of unforgiving vengeance, more typical of angry men. The motif of weeping and grinding of teeth is a favorite formulation of Matthew that he brings six times (Matt 8:12; 13:42; 13:50; 22:13; 24:51; 25:30) against only once elsewhere (Luke 13:28).

Engaging with Matthew means listening to what he says and seeking to understand why. His is a challenge to believers to understand what it truly means to follow Jesus and what it means to miss what he was about, even while hailing him as Lord.

Reflection: What message do you hear Matthew addressing to members of the church, and why and what tensions do you detect in his portrait of Jesus' message?

"Take this and eat it! This is my body." (Matthew 26:1–35)

Listening to Matthew

26:1 Now when Jesus had finished saying all these things, he told his disciples, **2** "You know that Passover festival is taking place in two days' time and that the Son of Man will be handed over to be crucified." **3** Then the chief priests and the elders of the people came together at the palace of the high priest, called Caiaphas, **4** and consulted about how they might use stealth to get hold of Jesus and kill him, **5** but they were saying, "Let's not do so during the festival, so we don't cause an uproar among the people."

6 While Jesus was in Bethany in the house of Simon the leper, **7** a woman approached him with an alabaster flask of expensive myrrh and poured it out onto his head as he was reclining there. **8** When the disciples saw this, they were angry, saying, "Why this waste? **9** Because this could have been sold for a high price and the proceeds given to the poor." **10** Realizing this, Jesus told them, "Why are you hassling this woman? She's done me a good deed. **11** You'll always have the poor with you, but you won't always have me. **12** You see, in putting myrrh on my body she's done something to prepare it for my burial. **13** Truly I tell you, wherever this gospel is proclaimed in all the world, what she's done will be talked about in her memory."

14 Then one of the twelve called Judas Iscariot went to the chief priests **15** and said, "What are you willing to give me if I hand him over to you?" They offered him thirty silver coins. **16** Then from that point on he looked for an opportunity to betray him.

17 On the first day of the Feast of Unleavened Bread Jesus' disciples approached him saying, "Where do you want us to prepare a place for you to eat the Passover meal?" **18** He told them, "Go into the city to a certain man there and tell him, 'The teacher says, "My time has come. I'm going to celebrate Passover with my disciples at your place."'" ¹⁹ The disciples did as Jesus had instructed them and prepared the Passover meal.

²⁰ When evening came, he reclined for the meal together with the twelve. ²¹ Then, while they were eating, he said, "I tell you the truth: one of you is going to betray me." ²² They were distraught and each of them started saying to him, "Surely you don't think it's me, Lord, do you?" ²³ In response he said, "One of you who has dipped his hand in the bowl with me, he's the one going to betray me. ²⁴ The Son of Man is going as has been written about him, but woe betide that man who's instrumental in having the Son of Man handed over. It would be better for that man never to have been born." ²⁵ Judas, the one about to betray him, replied, "Surely you don't think it's me, rabbi, do you?" He told him, "You said it!"

²⁶ Then while they were eating, Jesus took a loaf of bread, blessed it, and broke it up and gave it to his disciples, saying, "Take this and eat it! This is my body." ²⁷ Then he took a cup and giving thanks gave it to them, saying, "Drink from this all of you. ²⁸ For this is my blood of the covenant poured out for many for the forgiveness of sins. ²⁹ I tell you, I won't be drinking of this fruit of the vine from now on until that day when I drink it with you anew in the kingdom of my Father." ³⁰ And after singing a hymn they left for the Mount of Olives.

³¹ Then Jesus said to them, "You're all going to be offended because of me tonight, for it is written, 'I shall strike the shepherd, and the flock of sheep will be scattered in all directions.' ³² But after I'm raised from the dead, I'll go ahead of you to Galilee." ³³ In response Peter said to him, "Even if everyone else is offended because of you, I won't be. I'll never be so offended." ³⁴ Jesus said to him, "I tell you the truth, tonight before the cock crows, you'll deny me three times." ³⁵ Peter responded, "If need be, I'll die with you, no way will I betray you!" The other disciples responded similarly.

Thinking About Matthew

Matthew concludes his fifth major speech in the same way as he had concluded the other four speeches, but now adding the word "all," having completed all five blocks of teaching: "Now when Jesus had finished saying *all* these things" (Matt 26:1). He then returns to the account in Mark, but adds another reference on the part of Jesus to his impending fate as Son of Man. Apart from that, like Mark, he indicates the approach of the Passover festival and the plotting of the temple authorities to exterminate Jesus but without causing an uproar among the crowds who would have come as pilgrims to the festival.

Matthew's version of the woman who anoints Jesus' head follows Mark closely, though with the usual trimming of what he would have seen as unnecessary detail. Apart from Mark and Matthew, we have two further versions of the story. Luke places it earlier in Jesus' ministry (Luke 7:36–50) and locates it in the house of a Pharisee who had invited Jesus for a meal, but he, too, is called, Simon, as in their version. Similarly, Luke has the woman come with an alabaster flask of myrrh, but he portrays her as a woman recognized as a sinner in that town, perhaps, as often, implying she engaged in prostitution, though that is not said. Massage oils were used in such contexts. She then pours the myrrh not on Jesus' head but comes up behind him as he was reclining and pours it on his feet, wiping and kissing them while at the same time shedding tears. Luke then has an exchange not with the disciples about the waste, but with Simon the Pharisee in which he has Jesus defend the woman's behavior as expressing gratitude for having had her sins forgiven.

The version in John's Gospel looks in part like a merging and revision of these two versions, Mark and Matthew's, on the one hand, and Luke's, on the other, because it has most of the exchange with the disciples drawn from Mark's account, but has her anoint not Jesus' head but his feet and then wipe them with her hair, but not weeping, for John's version identifies her as Jesus' friend Mary, sister of Martha and Lazarus (John 12:1–8). She is certainly not a sinner in John. John has the occasion take place before Jesus' entry into Jerusalem, not in the days after his initial entry as in Mark and Matthew.

We are left to speculate about what might lie behind these developments of the story. For people of those days, it would have raised eyebrows that Jesus permitted a woman, presumably a stranger, to do this to him. The men would have been uncomfortable. She was probably seen as an outsider and perhaps even as a person of doubtful moral status, which might have occurred to some seeing her with what could be used as massage oil. The story is best understood as another example of where Jesus was prepared to engage with someone whom others spurned or treated with suspicion and with a woman in a relatively public setting.

The awkwardness for men of the time of the story probably accounts for the many different justifications which appear in the exchange with the disciples. Beyond that, we cannot be sure.

Perhaps it did take place much earlier in Jesus' ministry, as Luke has it. Was it the suggestion that it pointed to what would be done to his corpse when he died that persuaded Mark to locate it in Jesus' last days? Was identifying her as a friend, in John, an attempt to render the story inoffensive? And was Luke's portraying her as a repentant sinner also about rendering the event inoffensive? She does, in any case, become a symbol of Jesus' refusal to embrace the kind of discrimination against women that was common among many at the time. Women matter, too!

As in Mark, Matthew follows the pattern in the narrative of contrasting positive and negative responses to Jesus and so returns to Judas and his initiative to betray Jesus for a sum. Only Matthew identified the request for money, reflecting on Judas as mercenary, and the sum as thirty pieces of silver or silver coins. It recalls statements in the book of the prophet Zechariah, which speak of a shepherd of sheep destined for slaughter being paid thirty silver shekels and then being told by God to throw them into the temple treasury (Zech 11:12–13). Matthew will later draw on that source again when he has Judas, too, throw his thirty coins into the treasury (Matt 27:6). Zechariah was a source for some of the imagery we see reflected in the story of Jesus' last days already in Mark, including that of Jesus entering Jerusalem on a donkey (Zech 9:9; Matt 21:5; Mark 11:2; John 12:15), reference to the blood of the covenant (Zech 9:11; Matt 26:28; Mark 14:24), and the citation which Matthew is about to bring where he has Jesus predict the failure of his disciples to stand by him (Zech 13:7; Matt 26:31; Mark 14:27;).

While some have speculated that Judas was simply wanting to prompt Jesus into more aggressive action, nothing in our sources suggests this. Instead, he will doubtless have been seen as a forerunner of those who would later betray fellow believers to the authorities, and his story will have served therefore as part of their process of coming to terms with the pain and hurt of such treachery.

The next scene, as in Mark, depicts arrangements for celebrating the Passover meal, perhaps by prearrangement, but more likely being depicted by the storytellers as something Jesus arranged by supernatural knowledge, like the provision of the donkey for his entry. Mark, followed by Matthew and Luke, has Jesus die on Passover Day, understood as running from sunset Thursday to sunset Friday. John's Gospel differs. While it, too, depicts Jesus' crucifixion as occurring on the Friday, that Friday was not Passover Day, but the day before, the day of preparation. According to John, therefore, Passover Day ran from Friday evening and to Saturday evening and so was deemed a special Sabbath (John 19:31).

We many never know whose tradition preserves what happened historically and whose symbolic sensitivity caused the changes. Was it John's tradition that therefore depicted Jesus by implication as dying when the lambs were slaughtered for the Passover meal that evening or was it Mark's, trying to portray Jesus' last meal as a Passover meal? Such discrepancies were probably inevitable as the movement spread and as people sought to retell the story of Jesus in ways that went beyond mere history.

We return to the negative in the pattern of the narrative with the prediction that one of the disciples would betray Jesus. Neither Mark nor Matthew indicates that Jesus openly identifies Judas as the perpetrator before his disciples. At most, Matthew adds that Jesus indicates to Judas that he knows he is the one. John's Gospel has Jesus share that information with the figure portrayed as Jesus' best friend and through him with Peter (John 18:23–26). Such betrayal was abhorrent and served as a warning to all who might contemplate it.

Matthew's version of Jesus' special initiative during the meal closely follows Mark (Mark 14:22–25; Matt 26:26–29). Matthew changes how the story reports Jesus' words about the bread and the cup so that they are closer in structure, "Take this and eat it. This is my body" and "Drink from this all of you," rather than Mark's "Take, this is my body" and no instruction to drink of the cup. The bread will have been unleavened bread, so rather flat, and the breaking will have been more like tearing into smaller pieces. Already this might have symbolized what his body was to endure, but that is not intimated or alluded to. Instead, in inviting them to share the bread he is sharing himself, saying in effect, "This is me." He had given his life for them and was about to do so even in death.

Paul's tradition has "This is my body for you" and Luke's, "This is my body given for you." With or without express indication that it was "for" them, the underlying meaning reflects a key understanding of Jesus' death, namely that it produced benefit for them, particularly in the sense of bringing forgiveness, a consistent theme in Jesus' life and now associated with his death. It then easily evoked the notion of his death as a sacrifice. Sacrifices were believed to produce benefit. A whole range of imagery developed from there, applying various forms of sacrifice to explain Jesus' death. These traditions feature large in Paul's theology: Christ died for our sins. His death especially brought reconciliation with God and a sacrifice effected restoration to a right relationship with God. This was now for all.

The strength of this reflection on Jesus' death and its significance also informs the way Jesus' words about the cup have been understood and shaped. Body and blood are not two separate things but two ways of speaking about Jesus in his death. Matthew follows Mark in reporting Jesus as saying, "This is my blood of the covenant poured out for many" but adds "for the forgiveness of sins." Some have noted that Mark had used the same phrase to describe John's baptism (Mark 1:4) and that Matthew did not take it over as such from Mark and have suggested that Matthew must be wanting to say that now there is forgiveness only through the death of Jesus. However, so much in Matthew contradicts that, including Jesus' offer of God's forgiveness during his ministry, and he also clearly assumes that forgiveness must follow submission to baptism by John accompanied by confessing one's sins. There is no need to try to tidy early Christian thought in this way. For they were able to hail Jesus' death as a sacrifice for sins and at the same time declare that forgiveness was something that was offered already by John and Jesus in his ministry and, indeed, as the Psalms attest, already before that in history.

Covenant sacrifices were primarily for sharing in meals to celebrate agreement between two parties which needed to be reconciled or had come to a special agreement, a covenant. They play a role in imagery that saw Israel's relationship with God as a covenant. We see this in Exod 24 where Moses helps the people celebrate their relationship with God, a story cited in the letter to the Hebrews, which depicts the sprinkling of blood from the sacrifice as purifying the people and their resources for worship, including the scroll, the vessels for worship, and the tent (Heb 9:19–22). Zechariah has God point to the covenant sacrifice as evidence that he would help Israel (Zech 9:11).

The tradition that Paul uses, and Luke also follows, speaks of a new covenant, alluding to what we find in the prophet Jeremiah, the promise of a renewed covenant that would result in hearts and minds being attuned to the Law (Jer 31:31–34). Clearly a range of imagery has come together to give meaning to this event, and it defies attempts to reduce it all to one single meaning. It represents all Jesus was and stood for.

Much is misunderstood about Jesus' meal with his disciples. This has at times been the result of profound spiritual experience, which people have then taken and tried to explain. For instance, some claimed that such an experience of Jesus' presence meant that somehow the bread and wine must at some point somehow turn into Jesus, himself, his actual body and blood, enabling him to be really present. We can affirm the experience without affirming such human explanations.

As in Mark, Matthew has Jesus depict this meal as a foretaste of what is central to his message, namely the vision of a great feast to which all are invited. To engage in that feast in the present is both to reaffirm one's commitment to that vision and to be nourished for making it your agenda for action in the present. The meal then is one of thankful memory of the past, something emphasized in Luke and Paul's version with the words "Do this in remembrance of me" in thanksgiving, the meaning of the word "eucharist." It is also nourishment in the present with a sense of oneness, "communion," and it is also future focused: a foretaste of hope as expressed in the image of the great feast, the vision of change that then inspires engagement with Christ in the world.

From the positive, we return again to the negative as we hear Jesus' stark prediction that all his disciples would fail him that very night when faced with the authorities coming to arrest him. We may imagine that it might have also brought to mind for Matthew's hearers similar experiences and failures of their own when faced with such danger. As in Mark, Matthew has Jesus immediately speak not of his abandoning them as a result, but of his promise to go ahead of them to Galilee following his resurrection. This reflects the very early tradition about Jesus appearing to his disciples, especially to Peter in Galilee, the foundation of their continuing faith, and an indication of grace and forgiveness for their failure.

As the story of Jesus continues, both Matthew and Mark retell it in a way that speaks to the challenges which faced disciples in their day and the need to remain faithful, even in face of persecution and danger. Peter, the hero, is also an example of failure but then rehabilitation. Matthew makes a small change that renders his story more credible when he has Jesus predict that Peter would betray Jesus three times before the cock crowed once, not twice as in Mark (Mark 14:30), which would make one wonder why Peter did not hear it the first time. Jesus' story is unique, but it is also a story that would repeat itself in the lives of disciples such that its retelling would have been at times doubtless close to the bone.

Reflection: In what ways does Matthew address the dangers and needs facing believers of his day, and what hope does he offer for them and for us?

Facing Testing Times (Matthew 26:36–75)

Listening to Matthew

26:36 Then Jesus went with them to a place called Gethsemane and told his disciples, "Sit here while I go off elsewhere and pray." **37** And taking Peter and the two sons of Zebedee with him he began to be sad and distressed. **38** Then he told them, "My soul feels so sad as to want to die. Stay here and keep watch with me." **39** And going on a bit further he bowed down with his face to the ground and prayed, "My Father, if possible let this cup pass me by, but may what you want happen, not what I want." **40** Then he came to his disciples and found them sleeping and said to Peter, "So you don't even have the strength to watch with me for an hour? **41** Watch and pray that you don't enter a time of testing; the spirit is willing, but the flesh is weak."

42 Then he went off a second time and prayed, "My Father, if it's not possible for it to pass me by without my having to drink from it, may your will be done!" **43** And, returning again, he found them sleeping, for their eyes were heavy with sleep. **44** So leaving them, he went off again and prayed a third time, saying the same prayer again. **45** Then when he returned to his disciples, he said, "Still asleep and resting? Look, the hour has arrived, and the Son of Man is going to be betrayed into the hands of sinners. **46** Wake up, let's go. See, the one betraying me has arrived."

47 Then, lo and behold, while he was still speaking, Judas, one of the twelve, arrived and with him a large crowd from the chief priests and elders of the people with swords and clubs. **48** The one to betray him had given them a sign saying, "Whoever I kiss, that's the man; arrest him." **49** And straightaway he went to Jesus and said, "Greetings, rabbi!" and kissed him. **50** Jesus responded to him, "My friend, do what you need to do!" Then they came and laid hands on Jesus and arrested him.

⁵¹ And one of those with Jesus reached out and drew his sword and struck the high priest's slave and cut off his ear. ⁵² Then Jesus told him, "Put your sword back in its sheath, because all who take up a sword will die by the sword. ⁵³ Do you think I couldn't ask my Father and he could put more than twelve legions of angels at my disposal? ⁵⁴ But how then would the Scriptures be fulfilled which indicated it must happen like this?" ⁵⁵ At that moment Jesus addressed the crowds, saying, "Have you come out with swords and clubs to arrest me like I'm a brigand? I sat every day in the temple teaching, and you didn't arrest me. ⁵⁶ But all this has taken place that the writings of the prophets might be fulfilled." Then his disciples all abandoned him and fled for their lives.

⁵⁷ Those who had arrested Jesus brought him to Caiaphas the high priest, where the scribes and elders had gathered together. ⁵⁸ Peter followed him at a distance into the high priest's courtyard and, entering, sat down inside along with his assistants to see the outcome.

⁵⁹ The chief priests and the whole council tried to find false evidence against Jesus to be able to execute him, ⁶⁰ but found none despite many false witnesses coming forward. Then later two approached ⁶¹ and said, "This man said, 'I can destroy the temple of God and rebuild it in three days.'" ⁶² So the high priest got up and said to him, "Have you no response to the accusation these men are bringing against you?" ⁶³ Jesus stayed silent. Then the high priest said, "In the name of the living God I am asking under oath that you tell us whether you are the Messiah, the Son of God." ⁶⁴ Jesus answered him, "You said it, but I'm telling you, in days to come you will see the Son of Man sitting on the right side of power and coming on the clouds of heaven." ⁶⁵ Then the high priest tore his clothes and said, "He has blasphemed. ⁶⁶ What do you think?" They all said in response, "He deserves to die." ⁶⁷ Then they spat on his face and clobbered him, and some slapped him, ⁶⁸ saying, "Prophesy to us, Messiah! Who just hit you?"

⁶⁹ Peter was sitting outside in the courtyard when one of the female servants approached him and said, "You, too, were with Jesus the Galilean." ⁷⁰ He denied it in front of them all, saying, "I don't know what you're talking about." ⁷¹ When he went out to the

entrance, another woman saw him and said to those there, "This fellow was with Jesus of Nazareth." [72] And again he denied it with an oath, saying, "I don't know the fellow." [73] A short time later some who were standing there approached Peter and said, "You really are one of them, because your accent gives you away." [74] Then Peter started to curse and swear, saying, "I don't know the fellow." And immediately the rooster crowed. [75] And Peter remembered the prediction Jesus had made, "Before the rooster crows you will deny me three times." And heading outside he broke down and cried his eyes out.

Thinking About Matthew

Matthew continues his use of Mark in telling how Jesus went with his disciples to Gethsemane. Only John's Gospel, which does not mention the name Gethsemane, suggests it was a garden, hence the traditional name, the garden of Gethsemane. The scene reflects the fondness of Mark, or perhaps Mark's sources, of the use of sets of three in telling the story. Jesus prays three times. Peter is to deny Jesus three times. Jesus will be mocked three times. Beyond the storytellers' art is the concern both to depict Jesus facing distress but not turning aside from his commitment and to challenge disciples to do the same.

Mark mentions what Jesus prays the first time, but then simply says he repeats the prayer in the same words the second and third time (Mark 14:32–42). Matthew adds the words he envisaged Jesus would have prayed the second time, and they are slightly different. For he has Jesus echo the Lord's Prayer as he prays: "Your will be done" (Matt 26:42; 6:10). There was already an echo of the Lord's Prayer in Jesus' comments when he returned the first time to his disciples and found them sleeping and challenged them to pray that they not "enter a testing time," just as in the Lord's Prayer they were told to pray, "And don't lead us into testing times" (Matt 6:13). The concern is the prospect that they might find themselves faced with the prospect of suffering and might in the light of it be tempted to give up their faith.

Jesus is the model of remaining faithful, reinforced by his echoing the Lord's Prayer. Matthew's account, following Mark, gives an image of a very human Jesus distressed at the prospect which awaits him, depicted using traditional imagery as drinking from a cup of suffering. He used the image previously in the exchange with James and John (Matt 20:22).

Despite the distress, Jesus was not willing to abandon his commitment. Hebrews cites Jesus' distress (Heb 5:7), probably based on the Gethsemane story, when it underlines that Jesus would therefore understand what believers would be going through when they faced suffering and would pray for them with empathy (Heb 7:25). John's Gospel similarly depicts Jesus as facing distress but has revised Jesus' words to read, "For now, I'm feeling troubled. And what can I say? 'Father, save me from this hour?' But it's for this purpose that I've come to this hour. Father, glorify your name!" (John 12:27–28).

The message for the disciples is clear and follows the concern that runs through the story of Jesus' final days in Mark and Matthew. They are not to fail when similarly faced with the prospect of suffering and not to deny their faith, let alone to betray fellow believers. The call to "watch" means more than staying awake literally. It means being alert to what is going on, as Matthew and Mark emphasized in Jesus' final instructions to his disciples (Matt 24:44; 25:13; Mark 13:33, 35).

In Mark, and so Matthew, Judas then comes with a crowd armed with swords and clubs. John's Gospel includes soldiers, implying that Roman authorities were already involved (John 18:3). A kiss was a usual form of greeting but here has a sinister function. Matthew's version enhances the drama by adding the Greek word *chaire*, meaning "Hi!" or "Greetings!" to Judas's words and then adding the Greek word *hetaire*, meaning "Friend" or "My friend" to Jesus' response, both sounding similar and so heightening the contrast and conflict. Matthew also omits from Mark's version Judas's request that they lead Jesus away safely (Mark 14:44). All four Gospels mention that one of the disciples lashed out. Luke's version and John's add that it was the slave's right ear that was cut off, all the more serious by their values, which saw the right side as superior (Luke 22:50; John 18:10). John's Gospel in addition identifies the assailant as Peter and names the slave, Malchus (John 18:10).

Matthew's major addition is to have Jesus not only rebuke the assailant but also declare that those who take the sword will die by it and claim that he could summon more than twelve legions of angels to come to his aid, which Matthew must have deemed possible. This would have relevance in helping people of his day answer suspicions that the church was somehow a danger to the empire. He then typically returns to his theme of Scripture fulfillment, which he does again after Jesus confronts the crowd (Matt 26:54, 56).

The detail that the disciples fled for their lives (Matt 26:56) is as in Mark, but Matthew does not take up the reference to the young man who fled naked (Mark 14:50–52), perhaps realizing that it was an element of Mark's artistry that he could leave aside. The message for future disciples is clear: don't do as the disciples did! This focus continues as Matthew brings Mark's account of Peter denying Jesus. Like Mark, he has it frame the account of Jesus before the high priest and the council, thus highlighting the contrast between Jesus' unwavering faithfulness and Peter's failure (Mark 14:54, 66–71).

Matthew makes minor changes to the interrogation. Instead of reporting the false allegation that Jesus declared he would destroy the temple and rebuild it in three days (Mark 14:57), he has the allegation brought after the false charges were dismissed and brought by two witnesses, giving it legal weight, based on the rule of requiring at least two witnesses if evidence is to be counted (Matt 26:60–61; Deut 17:6). Accordingly, their witness is not false, but to make that work in the story Matthew has to change it so that in Matthew Jesus now declares, "I can destroy the temple of God and rebuild it in three days" (Matt 26:61), which Matthew depicts as true. Gone from Mark, too, are the comments about the temple being made with hands and the one he would build not being made with human hands. That reflected Mark's view that now the community of faith is the temple. This is not how Matthew sees it.

Matthew then has the high priest not just ask, as in Mark, but ask under oath, and so put Jesus under oath to answer the question whether he is, as Matthew puts it, "the Messiah, the Son of God." This gives weight not only to the question but, more significantly, also to the answer. In Mark, the question uses a more conservative formulation, asking if Jesus is "the Messiah, the Son of the Blessed One." Mark's tradition would have put it this way, reflecting the custom among some of not naming God directly but using an equivalent (Mark 14:61). The royal messiah was to be a king of David's line, and, as Ps 2:8 illustrates, kings were adopted as God's sons to rule on God's behalf. Normally, that would not therefore count as blasphemy, but in Mark's day, and later in Matthew's day, such a claim to be "Son of God" carried much more meaning and was seen as a claim to be divine. This accounts for the high priest's charge of blasphemy. Mark has Jesus answer "I am," whereas Matthew answers: "You say so," but clearly a positive answer is assumed, hence the accusation.

It looks very much like the scene has been created in the light of the charge that believers were facing in later times. John's Gospel, which may at this point be drawing on better informed historical tradition, has no such trial, but instead just a hearing before Annas, father-in-law of Caiaphas (John 18:13). Luke, realizing that such a trial could not plausibly have happened at night, given Jewish law, let alone on Passover Day, relocates it to the morning (Luke 22:66–71). Much imagination was required to reconstruct what must have happened, given that there would have been few if any witnesses of what went on behind closed doors, hence the variation in the accounts.

Matthew follows Mark in depicting Jesus as the victim of abuse, but with the variation that he omits the blindfolding of Jesus, that for Mark made sense of the mocking challenge to identify who hit him, and instead leaves it simply as a question about who slapped him, presumably to name the person.

Matthew now tells the contrasting story of Peter's failure, as in Mark, but more concisely. Slight variations are that it is a different female slave who raises the issue of his belonging with Jesus the second time, but, more significantly, Matthew enhances Peter's guilt by having him swear on oath that he did not know Jesus. This recalled Jesus' affirmation when put under oath that he was the Messiah (Matt 26:63). He changes the wording of the final challenge to Peter from referring to his being a Galilean to his accent betraying him. As previously (Matt 26:34), he renders Jesus' prediction more credible by having it refer not to the rooster crowing a second time (Mark 14:72), but to its crowing just once. Peter's remorse is a warning to all who might in future deny that they belong to Jesus.

Jesus remained faithful when confronted by the dire situation of his arrest and trial. The disciples, urged to watch and be faithful, did not, and Peter as exemplar denied Jesus. Those first hearing these stories would sense the connections to their own settings when charged with blasphemy for what they claimed about Jesus. Jesus was the model to follow.

Reflection: In what ways does Matthew contrast Jesus with his disciples, and how might this have related to experience in Matthew's day?

Killing Subversives and Keeping the Peace (Matthew 27:1–32)

Listening to Matthew

²⁷:¹ When morning came all the chief priests and elders of the people worked out their plan against Jesus, how they would have him killed, ² and so they bound him and led him off to Pilate the governor.

³ Then Judas, who betrayed him, saw that he had been convicted, regretted what he had done, and brought the thirty silver coins back to the chief priests and elders, ⁴ saying, "I've done wrong. I've betrayed innocent blood." They replied, "What do we care! It's for you to deal with." ⁵ He threw the money into the temple, left, and went off and hanged himself. ⁶ The chief priests took the money but said, "It's illegal to put it into the treasury because it's blood money." ⁷ Then they came to the decision to buy the potter's field with it for burial of foreigners. ⁸ That's why that field is called the "Field of Blood" to this day. ⁹ So in this way what was spoken by the prophet Jeremiah was fulfilled when he said, "And they took the thirty silver coins, as the price that was paid for the one on whom a price had been set by some Israelites, ¹⁰ and they put it toward purchase of the potter's field, as the Lord instructed me."

¹¹ Jesus stood before the governor and the governor questioned him, saying, "Are you the king of the Jews?" And Jesus responded, "You say so." ¹² And when he was confronted with the accusations of the chief priest and elders, he gave no answer. ¹³ Then Pilate said to him, "They're accusing you of a lot. Aren't you listening?" ¹⁴ And to not one charge did he respond with a single comment, so that the governor was quite astonished.

¹⁵ Now at the festival the governor had the custom of releasing one of the prisoners to the crowd, whomever they chose. ¹⁶ They had at that time a notorious prisoner called [Jesus] Barabbas. ¹⁷ So when

THE END

they were assembled, Pilate said to them, "Who do you want me to free for you, [Jesus] Barabbas or Jesus called the Messiah?" [18] For he knew that they had handed Jesus over out of envy.

[19] While he was seated on his judging seat, his wife sent him a message saying, "Don't have anything to do with that upright man, because I've had a really bad dream because of him." [20] The chief priests and the elders persuaded the crowds to ask for Barabbas and to have Jesus executed. [21] The governor then responded to them, saying, "Which of the two do you want me to free?" And they said, "Barabbas." [22] Pilate then said to them, "What am I to do then with Jesus called the Messiah?" They all said, "Let him be crucified!" [23] He said, "Why, what crime has he committed?" They shouted out all the more, "Let him be crucified!"

[24] Realizing that it was no use continuing but that there could be an uproar, he took some water and washed his hands in front of them and said, "I am innocent of the blood of this man. You see to it!" [25] Then all the people replied, "His blood be upon us and on our children!" [26] Then he freed Barabbas for them and had Jesus flogged and handed over to be crucified.

[27] Then the governor's soldiers took Jesus into the headquarters and brought together the whole troop, [28] and, stripping him, they put a scarlet robe on him, [29] and twisting thorny twigs together to make a crown they put it on his head and put a reed in his right hand and bowed their knee before him, making fun of him, saying, "Hail, king of the Jews!" [30] And they spat on him and took the reed and hit him on the head with it. [31] And when they'd finished holding him up to ridicule, they removed the cloak and put his own clothes back on him and led him away to crucify him. [32] As they were on their way, they found a man called Simon from Cyrene and they commandeered him to carry his cross.

Thinking About Matthew

As in Mark, Matthew has the religious authorities deliver Jesus to Pilate. While Matthew then continues to follow Mark, he also supplements and reedits Mark's story. We see this first in his first major addition, the account of the fate of Judas Iscariot (Matt 27:3–10). Already back at the beginning of the previous chapter Matthew had supplemented Mark's account of Judas's decision to betray Jesus by using imagery from Zechariah, which speaks of a shepherd of sheep destined for slaughter being paid thirty silver shekels and then being told by God to throw them into the temple treasury (Zech 11:12–13; Matt 26:14–16). It is the origin of the reference to thirty silver coins there.

Here in chapter 27, it is the origin of the story of Judas returning the money by throwing it into the temple. There were, however, some ambiguities in the text of Zechariah, which in one variant mentions a potter. Matthew or his source has played with these options to introduce the reference to the potter and then relate it to parts of Jeremiah who was asked to visit a potter and to buy a field (Jer 18:2–3; 19:1–2; 32:6–8). This then accounts for Matthew mistakenly attributing the citation from Zechariah in Matt 27:9–10 not to Zechariah but to Jeremiah. Such confusion of sources sometimes happened when citations were merged or authors alluded to two different sources.

Apparently, there was a field used for burial of strangers, which would therefore have been considered ritually unclean, called a Field of Blood, and this story in Matthew speculates that its name derives from its purchase by the temple authorities with Judas's blood money. Luke also knows such speculation and gives the Aramaic name, Hakeldama, but in his version it was Judas who bought the field and then did not commit suicide, as in Matthew, but, having had a headlong fall, "burst open in the middle and all his bowels gushed out" (Acts 1:18), a gory story. The story of Judas's fate, which developed with imagination, is told not with the empathy we might expect, but as a warning to those who in future might betray fellow believers.

The story of Jesus before Pilate also has application for disciples of Matthew's time and beyond. Pilate's technical designation was "prefect," sometimes later called "procurator," but not "governor," as in Matthew. He was, however, in any case, appointed by Rome to govern on its behalf. Rome's historical concerns are likely to be accurately reflected in the question that Pilate asked, as Matthew puts it, following Mark: "Are you the king of the Jews?" That was asking whether Jesus was claiming to be the leader of his people against Rome's rule, namely a would-be Jewish messiah. From the perspective of the state, such would-be messiahs had to be exterminated if Rome's rule was to remain and peace to be maintained. "King of the Jews" became the charge attached to the cross to serve as a deterrent to all such would-be revolutionaries and was why he was crucified along with other rebels. As Pilate saw it, he belonged in the same category as Barabbas and the two rebels, namely as someone causing instability and unrest. Historically, Jesus was one of a number of such figures whom Rome saw it had to get rid of.

Matthew's retelling reflects a new set of circumstances where believers had to be very careful as good citizens not to give the impression that they were subversive of Rome's rule. The danger for them would be exacerbated by fellow Jews making the case that these believers belonged to a sect of Judaism that was indeed a danger to the state. There had been plenty of evidence in recent decades, as they could easily argue, that such groups could be a danger. Matthew has, accordingly, taken the liberty to rewrite the story to depict the Jerusalem crowd and its leaders as the real problem, and so as forerunners of the enemies of Matthew's time.

As for Pilate, he is drawn as someone who saw no problems in Jesus. Matthew enhances this claim by the legendary addition of Pilate's wife being aided from the world of the supernatural, as dreams were understood. She concludes that Jesus was innocent and tells Pilate. Matthew then goes further in having Pilate wash his hands to affirm that Jesus was indeed innocent and that he, too, was innocent of what might happen to Jesus.

Even more striking and disturbing is that Matthew adds into his story a terrible declaration by the crowd, effectively that vengeance for Jesus' death if he is innocent was to be visited on their heads and the heads of their poor children: "His blood be upon us and on our children!" (Matt 27:25). This is indeed how Matthew saw it. He interpreted the terrible disaster of 70 CE as divine vengeance, as illustrated in the parable of the wedding feast (Matt 22:1–14). Starvation, slaughter of men, women, and children, and the destruction of the temple, all laid at the feet of the crowd for pushing for Jesus to be crucified. Later generations, alas, would make this a theme of anti-Semitic hate against all Jews, as "Christ-killers," which found its most horrific form of expression in the gassing of six million Jews by the Nazi regime. Matthew was not to know how his redrawn scene would be read. It is a very sad chapter.

Matthew's rewriting of Mark's account also reframes the Barabbas scene to bring out the choice more starkly (Matt 27:15–23; Mark 15:6–14). Only Matthew has Barabbas called Jesus, preserved in many of the best manuscripts, but enclosed in brackets in my translation because not all have it. Surprisingly, neither Mark nor Matthew points out that the name Barabbas means "son of the father." Earlier storytellers were surely playing with the names and may indeed have invented the story. If they did, they did at least preserve the historical frame of reference, namely Rome's concern with subversion. In Mark, it is the crowd egged on by the authorities who propose that Barabbas and not Jesus be freed (Mark 15:9). In Matthew, Pilate directly offers them a choice between Barabbas and Jesus. His version also has the crowd shout, "Let him be crucified!" instead of the direct address to Pilate: "Crucify him!"

Pilate's accession to their wishes reflects, however, very badly on him as a governor. All respectable Roman leaders would insist that their leaders should never respond to popular demands like that but always remain faithful to what is just. Matthew cannot therefore whitewash Pilate, but what he does imply is that a true Roman official would never act like Pilate, not then, not in Matthew's time, and not in the future.

Abuse of prisoners and convicted felons was a norm in such regimes and still is, and Matthew follows Mark in showing Jesus abused psychologically and physically. Again, the charge is clearly that he was a would-be leader challenging Rome's rule, hence dressing him up as a king with a royal robe, a scepter, and a crown, a shaming, humiliating mockery. We might want to sit down with the authorities and explain that he should not have been categorized as a rebel and treated this way and that his message of the reign of God was not an invitation to rise up against Rome, let alone by force of arms, as most of the other such leaders advocated whom they crucified. That would probably, however, have been asking too much of those authorities. He's a subversive with a following. That was enough. They couldn't give attention to fine distinctions. Maintaining peace and stability mattered most.

It would have been a difficult conversation anyway because there was an element of subversion in one regular theme of Jesus' preaching, the kingdom of God, especially if you heard it as the empire of God; and clearly, he was raising people's hopes for change even though not espousing a military option. It would have been much less controversial and dangerous if he made going to heaven the heart of his message and depicted hope in those terms, as to do with a spiritual world, not this world. However, like John the Baptist before him, he did no such thing and would now suffer the consequences, however unjust the process.

Reflection: Why would Rome want to execute Jesus, and what problems did that create for Matthew's day, and what issues does Matthew's account raise for our day?

The Cross and the Climax of History (Matthew 27:33–66)

Listening to Matthew

27:33 So they came to the place called Golgotha, which means the place of a skull, *34* and they gave him wine laced with poison to drink, and having tasted it he didn't want to drink it. *35* Having crucified him, they divided up his clothes, casting lots, *36* and sitting down, they kept watch over him there. *37* And above his head they placed the charge laid against him, which read: "This is Jesus, the King of the Jews."

38 Then two rebels were crucified along with him, one on his right, the other on his left. *39* People passing by shouted abuse at him, shaking their heads *40* and saying, "You're the one who was going to destroy the temple and rebuild it in three days. Rescue yourself, if you're the Son of God, and come down from the cross!" *41* Similarly, the chief priests along with the scribes and elders also made fun of him, saying, *42* "He saved others, but he can't save himself! The king of Israel, is he? Then let him come down from the cross and then we'll believe in him. *43* He put his faith in God, so let him rescue him if it's his will. After all, he said, 'I'm the Son of God.'" *44* In the same way the rebels crucified along with him were also ridiculing him.

45 Now from the sixth hour darkness came over all the land until the ninth hour. *46* And around the ninth hour Jesus cried out loud, "*Eli, Eli, lema sabachthani!*" which means in translation, "My God, my God, why have you abandoned me?" *47* Some of those standing there heard it and said, "He's calling Elijah." *48* So immediately one of them ran and fetched a sponge filled with sour wine and put it on a reed and offered him a drink. *49* Others said, "Leave it. Let's see if Elijah comes to rescue him." *50* Then Jesus cried out loud again and gave up his spirit.

⁵¹ And, lo and behold, the temple curtain split in two from top to bottom and there was an earthquake and rocks were split, ⁵² and tombs were opened and many bodies of holy people who had been in death's sleep rose up, ⁵³ and they left their tombs after his resurrection and went into the holy city and appeared to many. ⁵⁴ The centurion and those with him who were keeping watch over Jesus, when they saw the earthquake and what had happened, were scared stiff, saying, "This really was God's Son!"

⁵⁵ Now there were many women watching on from a distance who had followed Jesus from Galilee to provide support for him, ⁵⁶ including Mary Magdalene, Mary the mother of James, the mother of Joseph, and the mother of the sons of Zebedee.

⁵⁷ That evening a rich man from Arimathea called Joseph, who had become a disciple of Jesus, ⁵⁸ went to Pilate to ask for the body of Jesus. Pilate ordered that it be given to him. ⁵⁹ So, taking the body, Joseph wrapped it in clean linen cloth ⁶⁰ and placed it in his new tomb, which had been carved out of a rock, and rolled a big boulder across the entrance to the tomb and then left. ⁶¹ Mary Magdalene and the other Mary were sitting opposite the tomb. ⁶² The next day, which was the day after the Day of Preparation, the chief priests and the Pharisees went together to Pilate, ⁶³ saying, "Sir, we remember that that fraudster said while he was still alive that he would rise again after three days. ⁶⁴ Give a command that the tomb be kept secure until the third day, so that his disciples won't come and steal him and tell people, 'He's risen from the dead,' because that will make the final swindle worse than the first." ⁶⁵ Pilate told them, "Here's a set of guards; go and make it as secure as you can." ⁶⁶ They went off with the guards and secured the tomb by sealing the boulder tight.

Thinking About Matthew

Matthew follows Mark's account of Jesus' crucifixion closely. This includes the allusions to Scripture with which the account was constructed. The first is an allusion to Ps 69 where the psalmist speaks of the abuse he suffered: "They gave me poison for food, and for my thirst they gave me vinegar to drink" (Ps 69:21). Mark speaks of wine mixed with myrrh, which Matthew changes to wine mixed with poison, a word traditionally translated as "gall," that is, bile from the gall bladder, but which can also be translated generally as poison. The poison would have given Jesus the ability to die more quickly and so not endure so much suffering.

The next allusion includes a partial quotation from Ps 22. This psalm is indeed cited three times in depicting the scene of Jesus on the cross. Its first verse is cited as Jesus' final cry: "My God, my God, why have you abandoned me?" (Ps 22:1; Matt 27:45; Mark 15:34). The first element to be cited from the psalm is about the soldiers casting lots over Jesus' clothes: "They divide my clothes among themselves, and for my clothing they cast lots" (Ps 22:18; Matt 27:35; Mark 15:24). The next is more an allusion than a citation: "All who see me mock at me; they make mouths at me, they shake their heads; 'Commit your cause to the Lord; let him deliver—let him rescue the one in whom he delights!'" (Ps 22:7–8), though Matthew cites part of it directly.

Those who first developed this portrait of Jesus' suffering on the cross drew in this way on the accounts of the suffering righteous as expressed in the psalms and, in particular, Ps 22. They may have been needing to fill a gap, given that in reality there would have been few able to witness the event and none close at hand, the nearest according to Mark and Matthew being some distance away (Matt 27:55; Mark 15:40). Matthew adds that the soldiers who performed the execution sat down to keep watch over events. This will be because he will later have them all, and not just the centurion as in Mark, respond to what happened, and so prepares for that by mentioning their presence.

Both Jesus' charge and his being accompanied by two rebels reflect likely bedrock information reflecting how the Roman authorities saw Jesus, namely as a subversive, at least by word even though not by sword. The Psalmist's reference to mockery inspired Mark or his source to portray the abusive ridicule hurled at Jesus. Mark, who as a storyteller showed a fondness for sets of three, mentions three acts of abuse, and in this Matthew follows Mark. The first picks up the charge laid against Jesus before the chief priests, namely about destroying the temple and rebuilding it in three days (Matt 26:61; Mark 14:58), and the second, the charge about being the Messiah, Son of God (Matt 26:63; Mark 14:61). The third of the set of insults comes from Jesus' co-crucified but is not spelled out (Matt 27:44; Mark 15:32). The words "If you're the Son of God" (Matt 27:41) echo Satan's words in the temptation scene (Matt 4:3, 6) and so by implication portray the abusers as in league with Satan.

The first two of these insults are also part of a series of three. Thus with regard to the temple there is first the charge before the council (Matt

26:61; Mark 14:58), then the insult here (Matt 27:41; Mark 14:59), and finally the splitting of the temple curtain (Matt 27:51; Mark 15:38), a foretaste of the temple's destruction in 70 CE. Similarly, the insult about his being the Son of God belongs to a set of three, beginning with the charge before the council (Matt 26:63; Mark 14:61), then the insult here (Matt 27:41–43; Mark 15:31–32), and finally the acclamation by the centurion that truly he was the Son of God (Matt 27:54; Mark 15:39).

The predilection for sets of three meets us again when Matthew and Mark refer to timing: the sixth hour (noon) and the ninth hour (3:00 p.m.). Mark had depicted the crucifixion as having taken place at the third hour (9:00 a.m.) (Mark 15:25). Three lots of threes! The artistry of horror has the sky turn black for three hours. That made sense, at least of the awfulness of the event. A citation of Ps 22 serves to picture Jesus' last words, words of devastating suffering, "My God, my God, why have you abandoned me?" (Matt 27:46). They are not a doctrinal statement to be carefully unpacked with speculation about whether Jesus died confused or bewildered, let alone as a crisis in trinitarian relations. They simply express pain and use the pain of the psalmist to bring it to expression.

Matthew follows Mark in bringing what for their Jewish world would have been a reasonable misunderstanding of Jesus' crying out in the words of Ps 22:1, made clear by the authors giving us variants of the Aramaic text, especially in the variation that Matthew brings us, which reads "Eli, Eli," instead of Mark's "Eloi, Eloi," both of which meant "My God, my God." Especially Matthew's variant could have sounded like the beginning of the name of Elijah. Elijah was an expected figure of the end time as already the transfiguration story and, before that, ponderings about Jesus' identity had indicated (Matt 16:14; Mark 6:15; 8:28).

Mark has the person who brought Jesus some cheap wine soaked in a sponge, another allusion to Ps 69:22, also urge they wait to see if Elijah would come to rescue him. Matthew has others do that urging. Both, however, speak of Jesus again crying out loud and expiring. Mark simply has the word for "expire," whereas Matthew has "gave up his spirit," meaning the same, though some have read into it the idea that he gave the Holy Spirit as his dying gift, especially as some read a similar expression in John's Gospel this way (John 19:30). However, nothing in the context in Matthew or John suggests this was so. Here and there it means simply that he died.

At this point Matthew adds additional color to Mark's picture. Mark tells of the curtain splitting and the centurion acclaiming him Son of God

(Mark 15:38-39). As noted above, both complete a set of three: the fulfillment of the prediction of the temple's destruction thus now foreshadowed and the affirmation of Jesus as Son of God, which had been used as a charge and abuse now confirmed by a gentile centurion. Matthew then adds to the symbol of the temple's demise an earthquake, as he does also in his account of the empty tomb. At his death the earthquake split rocks and opened closed tombs as a result of which those in the tombs arose after Jesus' resurrection and appeared to many. In this way Matthew portrays the event of Jesus' death as a foretaste of the general resurrection to come. It is slightly awkward because, while they rise from dead at that point, they have to wait till Jesus rises before they appear to others, reflecting the understanding that Jesus was "the firstborn from the dead," as Colossians puts it (Col 1:18). Thus, Matthew's additional coloring depicts the death of Jesus as a major divine event, literally earth shattering. His adding a big earthquake in describing Jesus' resurrection makes the same point (Matt 28:2).

In addition, Matthew has not only the centurion, but also the other soldiers along with him acclaim Jesus as Son of God. For Matthew, multiple witnesses count more. Their response is also not so much on the basis of how Jesus died as in Mark, which may have been a reflection on his noble death. Rather they are responding on the basis of being terrified by these extraordinary events. It has been a theme in Matthew to portray Jesus as in effect bringing into the present what people expected would occur at the end of time.

Like Mark, Matthew mentions the women who helped provide support for Jesus and presumably his male disciples, a traditional female role in those days (Matt 27:55-56; Mark 15:40-41). They are also, however, to be understood as disciples, despite the fact that the stories told by males typically focused more on the males. The list of names differs slightly between Matthew and Mark. In common are Mary Magdalene, Mary the mother of James, and Joseph's mother. Mark also has Salome and Matthew also has the mother of the sons of Zebedee. The next mention of women is in relation to the burial (Matt 27:61; Mark 15:47), and here, too, the names of the two women mentioned vary. In common is Mary Magdalene. In Mark the second is Mary mother of Joseph, whereas in Matthew it is simply "the other Mary." Then finally the women appear at the opened tomb and Mark tells us they were Mary Magdalene, Mary the mother of James, and Salome (Mark 16:1), whereas Matthew has Mary

Magdalene and the other Mary (Matt 28:1). Presumably, Matthew means the mother of James when he refers simply to the other Mary.

Where were the men? The husbands of those women who would usually have been around fifteen years older than them were probably dead, as we may assume also for Joseph, since men usually married around thirty and rarely reached sixty years of age. As for the other men who had been there, both Mark and Matthew tell us they had fled for their lives (Matt 27:56; Mark 14:50). As male associates of Jesus they would have been in great danger from the authorities. Women were not seen as such a danger, but they, too, would have been taking a risk, even though keeping at a distance. Despite all the pressures to the contrary, women mattered.

Mark describes Joseph of Arimathea as someone who was looking forward expectantly to the coming of the kingdom of God (Mark 15:43), which Matthew recognizes as another way of saying that he was a disciple of Jesus (Matt 27:57). Matthew's account trims the detail but gives what is essential to the story: he acquires access to Jesus' corpse and places it in his newly hewn tomb, closing it up with a big boulder across the entrance. He is also an observant Jew and so gets this done before Sabbath begins while it is still light. Significantly also, the two women see this and, Matthew adds, sat down opposite the tomb. Placing bodies in tombs was common, especially among those who could afford them like Joseph, and many such tombs have survived.

The next scene is unique to Matthew and, like his defense of the story of Mary's virginity, appears to be designed to counter later anti-Christian propaganda which suggested the disciples stole Jesus' body and made up the story of his resurrection. No other source mentions a special initiative of having soldiers guard the tomb and having the entrance somehow sealed, so it is likely to derive from what Matthew imagined or believed would have happened. It will have a significant sequel in his story (Matt 28:11–15).

The peripheral details should not distract from the main event. Jesus goes to his death, a humiliating defeat, shameful, cast off by his fellow human beings, abandoned. Not the victorious king, Messiah and Son of God, he was acclaimed to be, but a failure, the very opposite of the empire's ideal of the triumphant male. Matthew paints up the scene to bring out even more dramatically that where human beings said no, God answered, yes, with an earthquake and a sign that not Jesus but the temple authorities had failed, and their temple would crumble. For the

THE END

eyes of faith, here before them is the judgment day, the day of resurrection about subverting the triumph of hate.

Reflection: In what sense was Jesus' death an earth-shattering event, and how might it speak to today?

New and Bigger! (Matthew 28:1–20)

Listening to Matthew

28:1 With the Sabbath behind them, at dawn on the first day of the week Mary Magdalene and the other Mary went to look at the tomb. **2** And, lo and behold, there was a big earthquake because an angel of the Lord had come down from heaven and had reached the tomb before them, and rolled away the boulder, and then sat down on it. **3** His appearance was like lightning and his clothes as white as snow. **4** And those guarding the tomb shook for fear because of him and became like dead men. **5** The angel's response to the women was to say, "Don't you be scared, because I know you're looking for Jesus who was crucified. **6** He's not here, because he's been raised as he said he would be. Come and look at the place where he was lying. **7** So now quickly go and tell his disciples, 'He's been raised from the dead and he's going ahead of you to Galilee, and you'll see him there.' See, I've told you!"

8 So they quickly left the tomb with both fear and great jubilation and ran to tell his disciples. **9** Then, lo and behold, Jesus met them and said, "Hello!" They ran to him, grasped hold of his feet, and worshiped him. **10** Then Jesus told them, "Don't be scared! Go and tell my brothers that they are to go to Galilee and there they'll see me."

11 While they were on their way, some of the guard went into the city and reported to the chief priests everything that had happened. **12** Getting together with the elders for a consultation they took what they decided was enough money and gave it to the soldiers, **13** telling them, "Say that his disciples came during the night and stole him away while we were sleeping. **14** And if this comes to the ears of the governor, we'll convince him and make sure you'll be okay." [15] They then took the money and did as they had been instructed, and this version of events coming from the Jews has been around to this day.

[16] The eleven disciples traveled to Galilee to the mountain where Jesus had told them to go. [17] And when they saw him, they fell down before him, but some doubted. [18] Then Jesus came to them and said, "All authority in heaven and earth has been put into my hands. [19] So go and make disciples of all peoples, baptizing them in the name of the Father and of the Son and of the Holy Spirit, [20] teaching them to observe everything I've told you, and look, I'm with you for all time to the end of the age."

Thinking About Matthew

As with the account of Jesus' death, so with the account of Jesus' resurrection, Matthew has enhanced the scene to bring out its meaning. Again, as at Jesus' death, he introduces an earthquake. He links it to an angel coming down from heaven who rolls away the big boulder which closed off the tomb and then has him sit on it. This is almost playful, but consistent with the freedom with which Gospel writers sketched such scenes, especially where information was scarce. Mark, for instance, has a young man, understood as an angel, sitting in the tomb, who gives the women the instructions (Mark 16:5). Luke has two such figures engage with the women when they entered the tomb (Luke 24:4). John has none.

The central message was that God had raised Jesus from the dead. Beyond that, much was left to the imagination about how this all played out. Some even see the story of an empty tomb as part of that, because for a resurrection to happen there would have had to have been an empty tomb because their understanding of resurrection was that the corpse underwent a change and became a spiritual body with no remainder. Others assume it was historically so, but the circumstances and detail had to be left to the imagination, hence the variations.

Mark's account is the basis for Matthew's account. Both reflect respect for Sabbath law in having the women come, presumably to give further attention to embalming the body as Mark suggests, not on the Sabbath but only after the Sabbath was over. Matthew trims Mark's story, omitting why they came and their pondering how they would get the tomb open (Mark 16:3). Instead, he has the angel descend and trigger a big earthquake and roll the boulder off to the side of the entrance to the tomb and then adds that the angel's appearance made the guards scared stiff, as if dead.

Matthew had introduced the guards in the previous chapter as part of an elaboration designed to deal with anti-Christian propaganda of his day. According to that propaganda, as Matthew soon goes on to explain (Matt 28:11–15), the tomb was empty only because Jesus' disciples secretly removed his corpse so they could fabricate their message about his resurrection. This account of how the temple authorities paid the guards to spread the lie about the disciples' removal of the body comes only after Matthew has first reported the angel's instructions and then uniquely inserted an encounter already with the risen Jesus.

The angels' instructions match those in Mark, except that Mark names Peter in particular (Mark 16:7), reflecting the early tradition he was the first to whom Jesus appeared (Luke 24:34; 1 Cor 15:5). Strangely, Mark reports that the women did not follow the angel's instruction but kept the information to themselves (Mark 16:8), the implication being that they talked about it only later. This may also reflect the fact that the initial appearance was to Peter and that that was the beginning of resurrection faith, only secondarily reinforced later by the story of the empty tomb.

This is not how Matthew saw it, so he changes Mark. The women do indeed do what they were told. The disciples do go to Galilee following their instruction, whereas Mark implies they went of their own accord but probably also because Jesus had intimated earlier that he would go there (Matt 27:32; Mark 14:28). In addition, Matthew has the women actually encounter the risen Jesus, themselves. John's Gospel, which has only Mary Magdalene encounter Jesus, dramatizes it by having her think he was the gardener, but he also tells her to go and speak to the disciples, called his brothers as here (John 20:11–17). Its author may have known of Matthew's story.

What Jesus tells them to do in Matthew's story is the same as what the angels had told them, so the encounter itself, rather than any message from Jesus, is the main point for Matthew. The variations among the Gospel writers reflect that they saw the need to help their hearers imagine what is likely to have happened, but it leaves us with their artistry where it is not always clear what is reporting and what is artistic elaboration. The core, however, is that where humans said no, God said yes, and so raised

THE END

Jesus to life in a new order of being, which also explains how they could envisage that Jesus would appear and disappear.

Matthew concludes his Gospel with a scene in Galilee where, as promised, Jesus appears to his disciples, depicting it as occurring on a mountain, a regular feature of Matthew's imagery when he wants to symbolize closeness to God. It is not the individual appearance to Peter, which is nowhere described in the Gospels, but an appearance to all eleven disciples. In this scene Matthew brings what in Acts is described as a longer process, resulting in part from gentiles attending synagogues also being enthused by the message preached there about Jesus and ultimately leading in Acts 15 to decisions about the basis on which gentiles could belong. Luke depicts Jesus as intimating to his disciples before his ascension in Acts 1:8 that they would be witnesses in all the world, but only over time would that be shown to be a witness not only to Jews but also to gentiles.

Again, we are dealing with various imaginative elaborations of a key event, namely the decision to take the gospel not just to Jews but also beyond them. Matthew had Jesus tell his disciples to limit themselves to Israel (Matt 10:5–6) and indicated that he saw his own mission as only to the lost sheep of the house of Israel (Matt 15:24), reflecting what was in all likelihood the historical sequence of events. For it appears that Jesus' mission was confined, but probably within the broader framework of the prophetic vision that then one day the nations would also come and worship, beating their swords into ploughs and their spears into pruning hooks (Isa 2:4). Perhaps the parable of the mustard seed alludes to this broader hope with its image of birds, an image sometimes used of gentiles, nesting under its shade (Mark 4:30–32).

Matthew then has the limitation of the mission only to Jews lifted in 28:18 and connects it to Jesus' resurrection or more importantly to what his resurrection initiated. This is something new and bigger. For from the beginning, the message of Jesus' resurrection was not just about Jesus being alive in a new form, but more importantly about the fact that it indicated his appointment to be the Messiah to come. It was understood as God's affirmation of Jesus and his message of the coming kingdom in which Jesus himself would be God's anointed Messiah. Psalm 110 played an important role, as people applied to Jesus what was reported as God's declaration to kings at royal coronations: "Sit at my right hand till I make your enemies into a footstool for your feet" (Ps 110:1). They also cited the coronation words from Ps 2 and applied them to Jesus: "You are my

Son; today I have begotten you" (Ps 2:7). Paul cites an early tradition in Romans that sees Jesus appointed as Son of God/Messiah at his resurrection (Rom 1:4).

That hope will initially have had an earthly kingdom based on Jerusalem as its focus, a vision retained by Luke, but it then broadened to the view that Jesus was already appointed to his role and authorized for it, and that it now encompassed more than just Israel. Hence, when Matthew concertinas a historical process that Luke tells of over at least ten chapters of Acts into a single scene, he has Jesus declare that he had already been installed in his new role. In effect, that meant that he would from now on operate on God's behalf across all of reality, or, at least, all peoples. What in the temptation scene Satan offered him as an enticement to glory and self-indulgence (Matt 4:8–9), he now receives as a commission (Matt 28:18).

That commission is not to embark on a rule of self-indulgence, as many rulers were wont to do, but to engage in love and outreach. Hence, the commissioning of the disciples (and, by implication, us their successors) was to go out to make disciples, make learners, of all peoples. It was to do what John the Baptist did: call people to turn to God and let themselves be immersed in God's goodness for forgiveness and renewal. Now it was to be done in God's name and informed by the message of Jesus and to be energized through God's Spirit, as had been the case of Jesus himself at his baptism. Hence the neat formulation of doing so "in the name of the Father and of the Son and of the Holy Spirit." This was not to be about recruiting as though Jesus was short on admirers or sought adulation or to be concerned with numbers. It was to engage them with the teaching of Jesus, to have them embrace and live by the love and hope that his message and his life conveyed. Seeing discipleship as an ongoing relationship of engagement in love has been a key theme of Matthew and a challenge to some who clearly saw their conversion as all that mattered.

The final promise that he would stay with them might sound like a contradiction of the expectation that one day he would return to establish his kingdom, but that is to impose on such language a strictness that denies its flexibility. They were happy to say both: that Jesus was coming and so was absent and that he was, in fact, also present, and not see in that a problem. Flexibility of language meant that they could sometimes speak of God's Spirit being with them and sometimes of the Spirit of Jesus or just Jesus. We see such flexibility in Paul's writings when he can switch from speaking of the Spirit of Christ to the Holy Spirit and mean the

THE END

same, when he writes, "But you are not in the flesh; you are in the Spirit, since the Spirit of God dwells in you. Anyone who does not have the Spirit of Christ does not belong to him" (Rom 8:9). Similarly, according to John's Gospel Jesus tells his disciples that he was going away and would one day come again (John 14:3) and in the same chapter speaks of coming already by the Spirit to dwell in them (John 14:23).

The same flexibility is assumed here in Matthew. Matthew is probably also aware of Jewish tradition that promised that where people gathered to ponder the meaning of the Law, God's presence would be particularly present with them, echoed in Jesus' words in Matthew's depiction of the church needing to decide on matters of discipline in the congregation: "Where two or three have come together in my name, I will be there among them" (Matt 18:20). Jesus' presence, embodying God's presence, is the promise and has ever since been a rich source of spiritual awareness. It is the presence of authority not to be self-seeking and glorious, but to inspire and empower the commission to love.

Reflection: How does Matthew's story imply that resurrection is not just about Jesus being alive?

Open to the World!

OPEN TO THE WORLD! Not to win converts but to win learners. One of Matthew's themes throughout has been that what matters is not ethnicity, but an ongoing commitment to do God's will, not conversion, but living according to God's Law as expounded by Jesus—a little like saying: not a wedding but a marriage. In this sense Matthew portrays Jesus as continuing the emphasis of John the Baptist, who challenged those who rested on their being descendants of Abraham and declared that God could raise up children to Abraham from stones.

In Matthew's account, John the Baptist identified Jesus as the judge to come who would share the same message as John about the kingdom's coming. Matthew then has Jesus expand that role to portray Jesus as the one who truly expounds God's will, as set forth in the Law and the Prophets, and who engages already in bringing liberation to his fellow Jews. Jesus, the judge to come, is the advocate for God's Law, and spells out its meaning with a particular focus on love and liberation. The criterion on the day of judgment which he as judge, the Son of Man, would conduct would be evidence of a life demonstrating such love and compassion.

Matthew, at one level, has Jesus confront his fellow Jews in these terms, rejecting people's appeals to status, including their being descendants of Abraham, rejecting pretense and hypocrisy and rejecting unreasonable imposition of elaborate rules. At another level, Matthew also portrays an image of Jesus as contemporary with church members of Matthew's own time and confronting them with exactly the same criterion: evidence of a life of love and compassion.

When he has Jesus send disciples out to make disciples, make learners, of all peoples, this is what they are to learn, because this is what the disciples have learned from Jesus and what people who listen to Matthew's Gospel learn. It is not about strict following of rules, but about openness to receive the compassion which Jesus embodied and becoming a tree which can bear good fruit, a theme already central to John the Baptist's message.

Matthew was not written in a vacuum. There are many indications that it was written in a Jewish context and that the author sees himself and his fellow followers of Jesus as not only belonging to Israel, but also as being its most authentic representatives, who, themselves, should have their own scribes sitting on Moses' seat in the synagogues, rather than those of the rival Pharisee movement.

Matthew's Jewish context is also to be seen in his consistent efforts to show connections and fulfillment between Israel's traditions and Jesus' life, whether through direct citations or through typology. His inclusion of disparaging generalizations about gentiles also suggests a conservative Jewish setting. Matthew emphasizes that Jesus' ministry was only to Jews and that his commissioning of the disciples was also directed initially only to Jews. The final opening up to the wider world also still belonged to Jewish hope and remained an opening up on the basis of continuing to uphold what was written in the Law and the Prophets.

Matthew's portrait also reflects tensions, especially over the rejection of the gospel by so many fellow Jews. That hurt and anger is reflected in the way Matthew has Jesus point to the debacle of 70 CE, the destruction of the temple, a trauma for fellow Jews, as something God did to punish the negative response. At the same time, Matthew challenges any hints of self-righteousness among gentiles reflecting on that event, by making very clear that God would equally punish them if they failed to embrace the life of faith.

That challenge to fellow Christ believers may simply be a general warning, fitting for all time, but could well reflect tensions within the Jesus movement, especially between those upholding the Law and those not doing so or allegedly not doing so. The very confronting statements about charismatic, miracle working believers hailing Jesus as "Lord," whom Jesus will disown, may well reflect real situations and faith claims, which Matthew believes Jesus would disown.

Matthew's efforts to challenge complacent believers of his own time often appeal to fear, threatening hell, where, as he often repeats, there will be weeping and grinding of teeth. While threats of judgment characterized John the Baptist's message, it is also evident that Matthew sometimes directly shapes his tradition of Jesus sayings to give prominence to such threats, whether directed to fellow Jews in general or fellow Christians, whether Jews or gentiles. He uses the disaster that befell Jerusalem in 70 CE as an example to reinforce his point.

Such strategies are not easily reconciled with traditions he also brings about forgiveness and compassion and especially difficult when generalized, for instance, in citing the slaughter of 70 CE, which would have cost many innocent lives, as God's initiative. Matthew's highlighting the threat of everlasting torment has sometimes had appalling outcomes when men claiming to be righteous have also embraced vengeance and violence. It has also called into question the nature of God when depicting God as sanctioning and exercising such violence.

While some of Matthew's attempts to reinforce the message of the gospel need therefore to be questioned, the gospel which he seeks to promote leads along paths which are very different and of abiding relevance. These include not least the teachings of Jesus in the Sermon on the Mount about loving enemies and those who reject you and Matthew's tapping into Jesus' parables about not abandoning lost sheep and making sure all have what they need to survive. Matthew envisages community that cares and where acts of compassion come in response to need, not out of obligation to obey rules, let alone to gain rewards.

Now Matthew embraces openness to the world. This assumes that already gentiles have joined the communities of faith whom Matthew has in view. Throughout his Gospel he has hinted at this opening up, from the women outsiders in the genealogy, to the eastern astrologers, to the centurion and the Canaanite woman, to the centurion and his colleagues at the cross. They were embraced and foreshadowed the wider expansion.

All were within the Roman Empire, probably in northern Israel or southern Syria. All were also in potential danger, seen as a new eastern religious sect by Rome and probably reported as untrustworthy and wayward by rival Jewish movements who denied their belonging to the ancient faith that had Rome's respect. Matthew indirectly addresses such dangers by depicting Pilate as officially seeing no problem, but then has him failing to act with integrity as a Roman official should and as Matthew would hope officials of his time would. Matthew shapes much of his story of Jesus' last days to portray such dangers and to show up betrayal and denial that continued to bring pain and to hold up Jesus as a model of faithfulness. Grace and forgiveness, such as found Peter, the foundation of the new community, were a promise of hope. Love came through in the end for the men who fled and also for the women. And reassurance remained in the paradoxical promise that the one who had left them to sit at God's right hand would also sit with them as they contemplated the Scriptures and sought to build a caring community—always!

www.ingramcontent.com/pod-product-compliance
Lightning Source LLC
Chambersburg PA
CBHW031400230426
43670CB00006B/600